LANGUAGE AND SOCIAL CHANGE
IN JAVA

J. Joseph Errington is a professor in the Department of Anthropology at Yale University, P.O. Box 2114, Yale Station, New Haven, Connecticut 06520.

LANGUAGE AND SOCIAL CHANGE IN JAVA

Linguistic Reflexes of Modernization
in a Traditional Royal Polity

by

J. Joseph Errington

Ohio University Center for International Studies
Monographs in International Studies

Southeast Asia Series Number 65
Athens, Ohio 1985

© Copyright 1985 by the
Center for International Studies
Ohio University

Printed in the United States of America
All rights reserved

Second printing 1991

The books in the Center for International Studies
Monograph Series are printed on acid-free paper ∞

Library of Congress Cataloging-in-Publication Data

Errington, James Joseph, 1951–
    Language and social change in Java.
    Monographs in international studies. Southeast Asia series ; no. 65
    Bibliography: p.
        Includes indexes.
        ISBN : 0-89680-120-9
        1. Javanese language–Social aspects.   I. Title II. Series.
PL5161.E77   1984   499'.222   84–19033

FOR MY PARENTS

KATUR TIYANG SEPUH KULA

CONTENTS

PREFACE ix
ON NOTATION AND TRANSCRIPTION xiii

Chapter   page

1. Basic Concepts and Questions 1
2. Priyayi Society and Language
   in Transition 34
3. Structures and Functions of
   Speech Styles 69
4. On the Users and Uses of Madya 118
5. Conclusion 177

APPENDIX 185
REFERENCES CITED 195
AUTHOR INDEX 205
INDEX OF JAVANESE WORDS 207

LIST OF TABLES

Table		page
2.1	Residences of an Extended Priyayi Family	63
3.1	Informants' Classifications of Examples	90
4.1	Obligatory Madya Vocabulary	138
4.2	Discrepancies Between Sources	142
4.3	Some Formal/Informal Alternants in Ngoko and Krama	156
4.4	Variable Acceptability of Krama-Madya Mixture	165
4.5	Observed Occasions of Use of Krama-Madya Mixture	168

LIST OF FIGURES

Figure		page
3.1	Contrasts Between Classifications and Repertoires	99
3.2	Sastrawirya's Conception of Etiquette	107
3.3	Conservative Level Use and Etiquette	107

PREFACE

Presented here is an analysis of material dealt with previously in my dissertation (1981) which has been revised and (I hope) refined to make the social implications of the issues discussed more accessible to readers who are less interested in language change than in social change. The first chapter presents the basic conceptual and expository framework for the study. Chapter 2 provides historical and linguistic background which is then related in chapters three and four to the structures and functions of linguistic etiquette in Surakartan social contexts.

I hope that sociolinguists will also find this material interesting, even in the absence of full discussion of all the relevant theoretical issues and broader implications. I have adapted well-known terms to particular descriptive ends, putting them to uses which differ in some respects from those found in the literature. But I believe that the meanings attached to them and the distinctions drawn with them are clear enough to prevent confusion, and permit me to describe the Surakartan situation (as I see it) simply and straightforwardly.

The benefits of added comments from interested and knowledgeable readers and the opportunity to study written Javanese materials which were previously unavailable to me have led me to rethink some aspects of the situation. Whether or not readers from other disciplines find the approach or conclusions persuasive, acceptable, or even interesting, I hope the general argument is readily understandable.

The longer I have worked on this material, the more complex it has come to appear, and the more numerous too are the debts I have accumulated to interested and helpful readers and advisors, both official and unofficial. A small chapter in an already overly long work would be needed to name all who have helped me; only a few can be mentioned.

I was fortunate to be trained in Indonesian by John Wolff in 1976 and 1977, before and during my first trip to Indonesia. First as teacher, later as fellow researcher, he has given me invaluable instruction, aid, and advice. Before doing research in Surakarta, I lived in Yogyakarta during 1978, and studied Javanese at Universitas Gajah Mada. To members of the department of ethnic languages at UGM, also, my sincere thanks for their patience and willingness to help. My tutor in spoken Javanese during this time was Shita Laksmi Prawirohardjo Van Ness, who taught me how to get closer to the ways people speak, and so to people themselves; I owe her a great debt for her insightfulness, helpfulness, and skill.

The research itself was carried out between February of 1979 and August 1980 with the indispensable support of several agencies and persons. Financial support came from the National Science Foundation, and the Social Science Research Council (in the form of a dissertation research fellowship). Institutional support from the Republic of Indonesia was provided by the Indonesian Academy of Sciences (Lembaga Ilmu Pengetahuan Indonesia). I am grateful to all of these organizations; all opinions expressed in this work are, however, my own, and are not to be attributed to any of these agencies. During my stay in Yogyakarta and Surakarta I was fortunate to have Soepomo and Gloria Poedjosoedarmo as advisors and friends; I am grateful to both. To Professor Soepomo, who further aided me as official regional sponsor for research in Surakarta, I owe a double debt.

Throughout this work I refer to persons as "speakers" and "informants" whom I counted not just as speakers and informants, but as friends and teachers. The English terms are as deficient and ring as hollow as would any lengthy acknowledgement I might make of their help. For their willingness to spend time answering peculiar, repetitious, and picayune questions, for their graciousness in the face of all too frequent ineptness and obtuseness, and for their ability to make me feel less like a foreigner and more like a friend, my heartfelt thanks.

I am grateful also to those who have made the time to work through at least portions of some version of their material, whose stimulating comments have led me to rethink various theoretical and empirical issues. I am hardly finished grappling with many of them, but I hope this presentation does not prove a disappointment to them.

To the many others to whom I am obliged, but cannot name here, and to those who do not wish to be named here, my thanks. *Menawi wonten kelepatan salebeting karangan punika, kula nyuwun pangapunten.*

February 10, 1984
New Haven

ON NOTATION AND TRANSCRIPTION

I have tried to achieve a reasonable compromise between convenience, consistency, and accuracy in the transcription of Javanese words and names mentioned in this work. Because Javanese metalinguistic terminology is used throughout, I have elected to forego italicizing the most crucial elements of the technical vocabulary. The word *priyayi* is also unitalicized after its first use in the body of the text. For ease of presentation, I occasionally use abbreviations for the terms *ngoko* (ng), *krama* (k), and *madya* (md).

Single quotation marks ('like these') are used only for glosses. Double quotation marks ("like these") serve a variety of other purposes. They are used as "scare" quotes, to mark quotations from informants placed in the body of the text, and to set off uses of Javanese metalinguistic terms ("ngoko," "krama," etc.) by native speakers to classify examples (especially in chapter 3).

I have adapted the broadly phonemic orthography developed at a workshop on spelling systems for ethnic languages which was sponsored by the Department of Education and Culture of Indonesia in 1973. (For a concise history of the standard orthography of Javanese, see Subalidinoto and Marsono 1975.) The system used here differs only insofar as diacritics are used to distinguish mid-high front /é/ from mid front /è/ and schwa /e/. Such conventions were in common use before 1973, and are still recommended for printed instructional literature.

Javanese has voiced and voiceless postalveolar stops transcribed /dh/ and /th/, respectively; these contrast phonemically with interdental /d/ and /t/. The velar nasal (engma) is transcribed as /ng/. Palatal voiced and voiceless affricates are transcribed as /j/ and /c/, respectively, and contrast with sequences of dental stop and glide (/dy/ and /ty/). The many patterns of allophonic variation in Javanese are not considered here.

Spellings of proper names and titles are particularly difficult to deal with consistently, since many have been romanized in different ways at different times by different people; in the literature one commonly finds *oe* or *u*, *o* rather than *a*, *j* rather than *y*, and so on. I have taken the liberty of transliterating titles of works cited and examples from the literature with the modified system described above. Proper names are transcribed in accordance with precedents in the literature, my knowledge of the preference of the author in question, and other factors.

1

BASIC CONCEPTS AND QUESTIONS

The Javanese number about sixty million, and make up by far the largest ethnic group in Indonesia's population of roughly one hundred and sixty million people. The archipelago's cultural diversity as home to hundreds of ethnic groups is at once a challenge to the development of an Indonesian nation, and a rich indigenous source for the development of a truly Indonesian culture. Underlying the dynamics of modernization is a double project: creating rationalized, western-style public and private bureaucratic institutions on one hand, while incorporating enduring, pervasive, ethnic cultural traditions into a new-yet-old national entity on the other.

Students of the developing cultural politics of Indonesian national development have been aware for some time that some quintessentially Javanese cultural themes—conceptions of power, interpersonal authority relations, the nature of symbolic legitimization of authority, and much else—have powerfully influenced the development of national and "modern" institutions, and are germane to the patterns of social interaction among Javanese and non-Javanese citizens of Indonesia alike. Some observers treat elements of a Javanese world-view not as just a part of, but the major and perhaps dominant influence on emergent Indonesian cultural politics. Students of business and governmental institutions have cogently argued that social change during the last fifty years has resulted not so much in a displacement of traditional beliefs, institutions or social mores, as in a progressive assimilation of foreign institutions into a traditional social framework, a kind of neotraditional accommodation to modernization.[1] Since that traditional framework is seen as Javanese, the foremost representatives of that culture have been accorded a special place among indigenous influences on social change at the national level.

If some sort of "Javanization" is going on in Indonesia, then the most relevant model out of a Javanese past for would-be members of a modern bureaucratic elite is the exemplar of the traditional Javanese state administrator, an ideal image of traits and values of Javanese elitehood. This is the *priyayi*: a person who, by virtue of proximity to a king through descent and/or office, enjoyed special status in traditional Javanese society, and exemplified the ideals of Javanese culturedness.

Most Javanese live in rural, relatively densely populated areas of the central and eastern provinces of Java, but in south-central Java there are two cities, Surakarta and Yogyakarta, which are famous as homes of the last true kings of Java, centers of the most refined, sophisticated instances of traditional Javanese culture, and homes of the royal Javanese priyayi elite. Surakarta is the site of research reported here. Like Yogyakarta, it's population is approximately half a million people, and it stood for almost two hundred years as royal polity and center of a kingly realm ruled by royal descendants and their servants.

It is doubtful that more than one percent of the residents of Surakarta count as priyayi in the strictest sense of the term,[2] but until recently this tiny fraction of the Javanese community, a statistically miniscule social subgroup, enjoyed an extraordinary degree of prestige and authority exercised in the name of their king. As such, they have been inheritors and to a degree are still primary transmitters of traditional ideals of Javanese conduct and

---

[1] See for instance Anderson 1972, Willner 1966, Emmerson 1976, and on the basic elements of a Javanese world view, or "Javanism," Zoetmulder 1967.

[2] The word has many different meanings for Javanese of different places and eras; for overviews and more detailed discussion see Sutherland 1975, Bachtiar 1973, Geertz 1960, and sources cited therein. Its changing meaning among traditional priyayi in modern Surakarta is discussed in chapter 2.

authority, and have found places in a modern yet traditional Indonesian milieu.

Heads of the royal house of Pakubuwana Adhiningrat ruled Surakarta during periods of relative political stability which were unusual in the context of Javanese dynastic history, but this stability was achieved only through thinly veiled foreign domination which progressively diminished the kings' political power. At first the Dutch were only indirectly responsible for changes in the size and nature of the realm, but acted finally as colonialists to end the traditional dynastic cycle. If the old political order and traditional Javanese elite was not so much destroyed as decapitated, as Benda puts it (1965:1065), then one could say that the head which the Dutch replaced was the king, who was thereby isolated from regions of his former domain and progressively deprived of a land to govern. In response to de facto restrictions on political authority, priyayi responded by further elaborating already complex trappings of traditional power in a symbolic, indirect, and increasingly hollow assertion of political primacy.

The end of the kingdom in 1945 rendered the royal house and traditional priyayi social circles largely irrelevant to and anachronistic in a modernizing pan-ethnic Indonesian context. But the resilient, lingering image of traditional priyayi cultivation, breeding, and proper conduct, is not without relevance to the transition from patrimonial to bureaucratic/technocratic administration. The enterprise of transposing traditional ideals out of history into a modern present, undertaken to create legitimizing links with a glorified past, is at least partially responsible for the adaptation of traditional concepts of social status, conduct, and power to the modern situation.

To the extent that Javanese traditions are becoming Indonesian, so are Javanese themselves becoming Indonesian; since the process of assimilation is reciprocal, members of the traditional priyayi class are continuing to adapt to changes in the sociocultural milieu. The priyayi image continues to occupy a special place in modern Indonesia, but the "true" inheritors of that tradition are themselves being assimilated into a substantially different social milieu.

Traditional priyayi have maintained or lost their elite status according to their ability to exchange old skills and social roles for new ones. These are complementary aspects of a multifaceted process; if national institutions are being subjected to a kind of progressive Javanization or enculturation, how are descendants of the prime exemplars of that cultural tradition themselves adapting and being incorporated into Indonesian society? If Indonesian modernity is developing through accommodation to tradition and incorporation of diversity, are traditional elite members obliged, able, and/or willing to accede to its growth? Is an egalitarian ethic espoused in "modern" Indonesia in fact being mitigated by pervasive, enduring beliefs in and expectations of social stratification and stable patron/client relations?

One might expect that traditional attitudes towards social structure and resistance to social change would be deeply rooted in the traditional elite circles, in which traditional forms of social organization prevailed until recently; the ways priyayi have adapted or failed to adapt might then be indirectly revealing of just how modern contemporary Indonesia is. Perhaps one can study Indonesian modernization as traditionalization by studying the ways inheritors of a great cultural tradition in a dominant ethnic group are themselves being assimilated into a different social milieu.

This study speaks to the linguistic side of these issues, a little-studied facet of modernization and social change. Focused on patterns of language use among members of the traditional priyayi elite of Surakarta, it is designed to document and explain some of the linguistic correlates of real, ongoing social assimilation of traditional priyayi into contemporary Surakartan urban society. This is a study of what can be called, to borrow a phrase from Friedrich (1982), one linguistic reflex of modernization in Java.

Even those with a superficial acquaintance with Javanese culture recognize that Javanese linguistic etiquette is an integral part of the traditional Javanese cultural aesthetic paradigmatically exemplified by priyayi. This elaborate set of speech styles allows (or obliges) speakers to mark their evaluations of social relations between persons spoken of and spoken to, and to mediate their relations to a speech partner in the very act of speaking. Since no form of social behavior is more ubiquitous, structurally complex, or susceptible to expressive nuance than language use, it offers a promising entree to changes in social interaction among priyayi in particular, and Javanese in general.

The Javanese speech levels will be described here so as to show how changes and variation in linguistic etiquette reflect the ongoing transition of Surakartan priyayi from a traditional, to a colonialized, to part of a modern educated urban elite; sociolinguistic changes are studied as clues to the priyayi's perceptions of their place in the larger urban community and, of relations to other Javanese in face-to-face interaction.

The general significance of the Javanese speech levels can be conveniently phrased in Javanese terms: to determine relative status or worth of two people is a process of weighing and comparison, what is often referred to as the *unggah-ungguh* of a relation. As one priyayi said to me:

> Whenever two Javanese meet, they must always ask themselves: "Who is this person? Who am I? What is he to me?" [Here he held out his hands, palms up, as if they were pans of a scale.] That's *unggah-ungguh*.

Since linguistic usage is one obvious and very complex correlate of this reciprocal process of evaluation, the patterns of style choice can be thought of as a way of negotiating or ratifying relations with a speech partner. The specifics of how priyayi figuratively ask and answer the questions verbalized by this gentleman are marked in their speech, and so it is no coincidence that the speech levels themselves are often called *unggah-ungguh ing basa*, i.e., '*unggah-ungguh* of language.' (The meanings of the word *basa*, glossed here as 'language,' are discussed in more detail in chapter 3.)

Proper behavior depends first on control of the proper forms of linguistic expression, and second on the ability to choose the appropriate etiquette pattern by properly gauging social relations. Several persons pointed out to me that it is not as hard to learn the speech levels—different words for things and how they combine in sentences—as it is to learn how to implement them properly in a given situation. This is especially true when the aspects of relationships which are relevant to a choice of speech level are in flux or insufficiently understood. Changes in the system of linguistic etiquette and norms which govern its use among priyayi speakers are the foci of this work.

DESCRIPTIVE ISSUES

Among the "imponderibilia of actual life" (Malinowski 1961:20) nothing is so ponderous to study as particularities of language use like those to be dealt with here. But for that same reason no other aspect of social behavior offers a more promising source of insight into the dynamics of social interaction and change in cultural norms which govern interaction. Readers less interested in linguistic particulars than in broader aspects of social conduct may nonetheless find something of interest in this study if they are willing to consider some basic descriptive distinctions and concepts, the expository strategy adopted, and the social significances of the basic linguistic questions to be considered.

Even a moment's reflection on one's experience as a speaker of a language in a community gives a sense of the individualistic nature of speech as social conduct on one hand, and the strong communal bond created among those who share a language on the other. Members of what can be called a "speech community" (see Gumperz 1968 and Hymes 1972) share language as a conventional instrument of individual expression used to speak of (refer to) something while speaking to (addressing) a speech partner.

The initial problem is not simply to identify phenomena of language use which might correlate with or indicate the nature of nonlinguistic social relations; the Javanese speech levels exhibit an obvious structural complexity which has been described in many different sources over the last century or so. There is rather a need for terms to deal with specific issues and develop broad conclusions. To outline the strategy for isolating socially significant linguistic variation and change, we have to analyze particulars with general terms.

It is useful to dissociate the form or structure of the speech levels from their various social functions, and examine their rule-governed nature first with respect to social contexts of use, and then with respect to larger social issues. The question "What does change in the speech levels indicate about changing traditional elite status in modern Java?" can be simultaneously rephrased, specified, and finally readdressed in other terms. The most basic distinction to be drawn is between "language" as a stratified system of abstract, mutually defining vehicles of conventionally determined meaning, and "language" as concrete, objectively observable, individual occasions of speech in particular social contexts. This simple description of the distinction which linguists make between what Saussure (1966) called *langue* and *parole* is now perhaps more generally known as the distinction between "code" and "message," respectively. *Langue* (or code)—the shared system of rules—is traditionally the object of structural linguistic decription: acquired during childhood, shared with members of a community, and used to make known individual communicative intentions in occasions of use which are themselves evaluated in terms of cultural norms for conduct.

To speak *of* something *to* somebody is to engage in social action which communicates information and simultaneously mediates the social relation with a speech partner (an addressee). A language code is the means for speaking *of* things in referentially meaningful utterances, made up of minimal referentially meaningful units (morphemes), each in turn composed of combinations of sound types (phonemes) which are conventionally associated with concepts. Morphemes combine in rule-governed grammatical patterns to make up words, phrases, and sentences.

The distinction between message and code frames the basic goal and strategy of traditional linguistic description: to determine the structure of a code, or linguistic system, by studying a corpus of messages encodable and decodable with it. The much-envied rigor of the linguistic method depends on the assumption that a stable, homogeneous, abstract system can be postulated to underly the diverse and potentially infinite numbers of actual communicative acts in which speakers engage. Aspects of language use which are invariant vis-a-vis the spoken *of*, or referential meaningfulness, manifest the structure of the code, even though this is only one part of the "meaning" of speech in social context.

But there is much more to human communication. Messages which differ in structure may share referential meaning, and variation in the linguistic structure of speech may covary with particular aspects of contexts of communicative use in socially significant ways. Such variation makes for contrasting styles of speaking which can be said to "meaningfully" contrast with each other when considered with respect to a context of speaking to someone.

This sort of nonreferential or social meaning distinguishes the significances of use of the different Javanese speech levels; they are styles of speaking distinguished by alternations between different words with identical referential meanings. As Geertz has put it:

> [A] number of words (and some affixes) are made to carry in addition to their normal linguistic meaning what might be called a 'status meaning,' i.e., when used in actual conversation they convey not only their fixed detonative [sic] meaning ("house," "body," "eat," "walk," "you," "passive voice") but also a connotative meaning concerning the status of (and/or degree of familiarity between) the speaker and the listener. (Geertz 1960:248)

Such phenomena elude analysis conducted with the simplifying, heuristic assumptions just outlined, and for this reason practitioners of the newer discipline of sociolinguistics criticize traditional approaches to language study, rejecting or at least qualifying traditional assumptions about objects and methods of linguistic research. They have developed models for pursuit of allied but distinct and usually broader goals. As the notion of "style" suggests, linguistic codes may offer more than one way of doing the same referential work (speaking of something) and choice between these means—whether distinguished by pronunciation, intonation, choice of words, or syntactic pattern—can be significant vis-a-vis context in which an act of speaking to someone is carried out.

We can preliminarily distinguish three general kinds of problems implicit in this general range of issues, and in the case at hand. First, to understand the "referential" and "social" meanings of the speech levels, we must understand the structure of the code used by speakers: the range of possible choices between ways of saying the "same thing" which make up speakers' repertoires. Given a knowledge of the structure of the code, the system it forms, we can consider the relation of variants to *contexts of use*, specifically, covariation between recurring features of language and context: place, time, topic, and most important at least for the Javanese, the social relation between partners to the exchange of speech. Finally, there are *norms of use* which guide speakers' choices of styles of social/linguistic conduct, and implicitly link contexts of use with formally defined speech styles in a repertoire. These can be thought of as classifications of language varieties on one hand, and of contexts of social conduct on the other.

THE STRUCTURE OF THE LINGUISTIC CODE

Critical though sociolinguists may be of traditional goals and approaches to linguistic analysis, they nonetheless make crucial use of some traditional descriptive tools in their own work. By focusing on social significances of language variation, they have perhaps revised the notion of "meaning" but have hardly dispensed with a notion of "code." To describe priyayi speech level repertoires, two basic linguistic-structural notions are so crucial as to require explanation here. These are the interrelated notions of paradigmatic and syntagmatic relations which define the code's structure.

Linguists have always laid great stress on the inherently systematic nature of codes, made up of parts which define each other oppositively and correlatively. (See Saussure 1966, Hjelmslev 1944, Benveniste 1971.) A code is stratified in the sense that it consists of several different strata which each form a distinct subsystem. Relations between linguistic elements are then treated as being of two basic sorts. Some are relations of *alternation*, that is, *paradigmatic* relations, while others are relations of *combination*, or *syntagmatic* relations.

So, for instance, the sound-types (or phonemes) /l/ and /r/ in English are uniquely paired as consonantal paradigmatic alternants in a particular syntagmatic environment, namely, in combination with /sp__/. The environment of alternation (represented as __) can be thought of as a slot in which paradigmatically related elements alternate. In other syntagmatic environments, /l/ and /r/ alternate with many other consonants (e.g., at the beginning of a morpheme followed immediately by a vowel: lend, rend, mend, etc.), but the structure of the English morpheme is such that in the environment /sp__/ only those two consonants can appear and contrast. The code of a language specifies what possible elements (here, sound-types) alternate in what environments, and what possible syntagmatic combinations create those environments.

Ngoko, krama, madya

The structure of speech level repertoires can be analyzed in analogous fashion: speech styles are distinct patterned combinations of alternate words or morphemes which share a referential meaning, that is, an aspect of "meaning" which can be fairly readily glossed into English. We can introduce here by way of example the most basic speech level distinction: that between *ngoko*, familiar or "ordinary" speech, and *krama*, which is "polite" speech. These two speech styles are distinguished by paradigmatic alternants, pairs of differing sound-shapes which are associated with the same linguistic-referential meanings, and combine with members of other such alternations in patterned ways. (In fact, relations between alternants in paradigmatic sets are not always one-to-one, but for present purposes these exceptions can be ignored.) So for instance the ngoko word which can be glossed into English as 'red,' *abang*, has for a paradigmatic krama alternant *abrit*, with just the same referential meaning. *Abang* and *abrit* can be treated as synonymous paradigmatic alternants which differ in terms of their combinatory possibilities with members of other pairs of synonymous alternants. Syntagmatic combinations, composed of words and morphemes of krama (which have distinct ngoko alternants) can also be called krama; the same holds for the use of the term "ngoko." As Uhlenbeck has noted:

> One may say that one speaks in or uses *krama, madya,* or *ngoko*, or that a sentence is in *krama, madya*, or *ngoko*. In that case the terms refer to the speech style chosen by the speaker. But one may also say of a word or a grammatical element that it is *krama, madya,* or *ngoko* . . . The ambiguity of the Javanese terminology reflects the important fact that a complete description of the Javanese forms of respect requires attention not only to their paradigmatic aspect, that is to the lexical-morphological relations between the various items involved, but also to their syntagmatic aspect, that is to their co-occurrence in the sentence. This need has not always been recognized in the existing literature. (1978:301)

Every Javanese would agree that the basis of the *unggah-ungguh ing basa* is the distinction betweeen ngoko and krama. Ngoko is the "basic" language, the language one thinks in, speaks to intimates and inferiors in, loses one's temper in, the language of most natural and spontaneous expression. Its intonation, pitch, and stress pattern can change rapidly and strikingly within even a single utterance; morphophonemic processes create many glottal stops and consequently an overall staccato effect which is largely absent from krama.

Krama is polite language. Its words are generally longer than their ngoko equivalents, with a preponderance of closed final syllables; normatively it is smoothly uttered with modulated pitch and stress change; it is permissive of frequent and lengthy pauses when speaking. As is the sensible feeling of the latter speech style, so is the kind of interaction in which it is normatively presupposed: with nonintimates and superiors, and when one wishes to act with maximal care in a social context.

Syntagmatic rules of combination specify which encoded combinations of ngoko and krama elements are acceptable, and which are not. So it is possible to use the elliptical ngoko sentence *Sing abang waé*, or its krama variant *Ingkang abrit kémawon* to say or "mean" (i.e., speak of) the same thing, translatable as 'Just the red one.' *Sing* and *ingkang* are ngoko and krama alternants respectively, which function as topic and relative clause markers in their respective styles; *waé* and *kémawon* are ngoko and krama words which both mean roughly 'only, just.' Because the code specifies possible combinations like those just given, it disallows others which are ill-formed, regardless of any potential occasion of use. *Ingkang abang kémawon* and *Sing abrit waé*, for instance, are combinations which can be understood insofar as they are referentially meaningful—they have the same "meaning" in this respect as the two combinations given above—but are "wrong" because they are can be assigned no social significance; they violate syntagmatic rules for combining elements of the different levels, and cannot fit in any context. Such rules, sometimes called cooccurrence restrictions, can be said to determine or govern combinations of elements, and are a major topic of chapters 3 and 4.

Style depends on variation and therefore on alternation, but it is important to note that the place of some word in a set of forms which share referential meaning and alternate with each other is also determined by cooccurrence restrictions it obeys, its combinatory possibilities with other elements. This can be illustrated with the vocabulary set which distinguishes a third sort of speech style, noted by Uhlenbeck in the passage quoted above: *madya*. Madya speech is set off from ngoko speech by a few particular forms, some of which are identical with or resemble their krama alternants. But it is set off from krama speech as an alternate non-ngoko speech style by other of its members, which are identical with their ngoko equivalents.

For instance, some "mixtures" of the ngoko and krama words discussed above—for instance, *Sing abang mawon* and *Sing abrit mawon*—are structurally allowable and count as sentences of madya, whereas the substitution of krama *ingkang* for *sing* in either would be impossible. Unlike other ngoko words, *sing* and other elements which may be combined in this way can also be classified on structural grounds as madya forms too, and treated as standing in different paradigmatic relations to their alternants.

Madya is structurally interstitial in that some alternants which must be used in madya are identical with their ngoko or krama alternants. Madya speech is also interstitial in the sense that when speaking madya, one can only refer to a wide range of things by choosing between a ngoko and a krama lexeme, like *abang* and *abrit* in the examples above. These choices can be thought of as "raising" or "lowering" the politeness of one's speech, insofar as it is made to resemble krama or ngoko speech.

To understand the social significance of a particular occasion of speech level use, one must know the range of possibilities from which a speaker chooses: all the oppositively related stylistic alternants which make up the repertoire from which a speaker selects. Even a partial description of the structure of the speech levels is thus a prerequisite for further analysis; the first step in describing priyayi use of the speech levels in chapters 3 and 4 is to consider the structure of various subcodes within their repertoires of speech styles. In this way changes and variation in the structure of Javanese linguistic etiquette—that is, in paradigmatic and syntagmatic relations between leveled elements in speakers' repertoires—can be interpreted as the result of and evidence for changing functional significances of their use in social interaction.

Krama inggil: deference and reference

There is another set of words, which share a distinct range of combinatory possibilities, a particular referential range, and a special type of social significance. Ignoring here some of the terminological and structural complications attending the study of it[3] this class of vocabulary and its members will be called *krama inggil* (lit. 'high krama'). The most basic functional commonality of all krama inggil words is that they are used to mark deference for a person spoken *of* (a referent), who may or may not be the person spoken *to* (an addressee). This is why the semantic range of krama inggil words is limited precisely to persons—possessions, relations, body parts, actions, and states—and why they have a combinatory freedom which contrasts with that of ngoko, madya, and krama forms.

Because the deferential krama inggil vocabulary serves a distinct social function in the system of linguistic etiquette and is governed by different combinatory rules, relations between elements of a paradigmatic set containing ngoko, krama, and krama inggil[4] are not homogeneous. The oppositions between krama inggil and non-krama inggil words on one hand, and ngoko and krama words on the other, are skewed formally and functionally, as will be shown in chapter 3.

LANGUAGE IN SOCIAL CONTEXT

To describe the social significances of these variants in social context is to relate patterns of language use—formal encoded features of utterances—to socially significant aspects of contexts of

---

[3]It is itself actually tripartite, and members of subsets of the deferential vocabulary can mark evaluations of different types of social relations. For present purposes it suffices to lump them together. In chapter 3 the uses of this and other terms will be considered again from native speakers' points of view. See Errington 1988.

[4]Since madya alternants exist almost exclusively for grammatical and indexical elements of ngoko and krama, it hardly overlaps with the range of deferentials. The only exception seems to be personal pronouns.

speech exchange. One can thus draw or abstract from facts of covariation between speech and diverse social contexts relatively crucial or salient features which are important for speaking properly and appropriately, that is, in accordance with standards or norms of use shared in a speech community. These standards or norms may differ not only from speech community to speech community, but within a speech community or subcommunity, as is the case (I will argue) in the priyayi class of contemporary Surakarta.

We must distinguish first between two basic types of social, nonreferential significances of language use. On one hand, an occasion of language can be construed to mark something about the context of use: the way the speaker evaluates the setting for speech, and relations between himself/herself and persons somehow connected with the act of speaking. On the other hand, the same occasion of use can be taken to be significant vis-a-vis its user alone, since the simple fact that a person speaks in a given way can be taken as a sign that the speaker at least ostensibly controls the code needed to produce that utterance. If that code or subcode is typical of some social group, so does its use mark its user as allied to or part of that group.

The uses of this dichotomy are less obvious than might be apparent at first; a choice of a speech style can be interpreted by participants and/or observers in two ways, sometimes simultaneously, as marking a speaker's evaluation of an aspect of a social relation, or a speaker's membership or nonmembership in some group. This distinction between varieties of language which are significant vis-a-vis a *situation of use*, and varieties which are significant vis-a-vis the *status of the user* is drawn by Halliday, McIntosh, and Strevens (1972:149) with the terms *register* and *social dialect*, respectively.

The priyayi gentleman who explained the use of the speech levels as involving the questions "Who are you to me?" and "Who am I to you?" thus focused naturally on their use as registers to mark aspects of a situation of use, specifically, the relation between speech partners. But we will see that use of some styles are evaluated by speakers primarily as markers of the status of their users, and so, as social dialects. The interplay between the two, I will argue, underlies the changing forms and uses of the speech levels, and provides evidence of basic changes in social relations among priyayi and non-priyayi in modern Surakarta.

Stylistic registers

Variation which is significant vis-a-vis a situation of use may mark different aspects of social relations. A simple example is the type of patterned clustering of variants which make for the difference between "formal" and "informal" speech in English: choice of vocabulary, forms of address, rate and cadence of speech, carefulness of pronunciation, and so on. These varieties of language are called "formal" and "informal," but these terms can be taken to refer likewise to the contexts in which they are relatively appropriate or inappropriate, what they can be said to presuppose. This type of significance can be attributed to the speech levels—ngoko being relatively informal, krama relatively formal—but only with some qualification and explanation.[5]

First, there exist "formal" and "informal" variants within the subcodes of ngoko and krama, styles marked by contrasts between "full" or "formal," and "short" or "colloquial" variants of lexical elements which contrast within ngoko or krama speech styles, aside from contrasts between leveled alternants. This will be discussed in chapter 4 in relation to forms and functions of krama and madya styles.

Second, it is an oversimplification to say that ngoko/krama styles mark only formality or lack thereof in a social relation between speech partners. Rather, their social significances depend on patterns of exchange of speech styles between speech partners.

---

[5]Sociolinguists have noted that the English words "formal" and "informal" are notoriously imprecise and only of limited use as technical terms (see e.g., Trudgill 1974:107, Lyons 1977:508, Irvine 1979). But they are useful as comparative terms, which conform to what speakers regularly recognize to be differences in speech and social relations. As Halliday et al. have pointed out (1972:154) there is also an unfortunate ambiguity accruing to the use of "formal" in a technical linguistic sense (e.g., "formal" analysis) and its ordinary sense alluded to above. I have tried in this work to avoid using "formal" in the former, technical sense, in favor of less ambiguous terms like "structural."

These patterns are symmetric or asymmetric, and indicate something about relative status and relative formality in context of speech.

In this respect speech level usage resembles other well-known examples of variation found in Western European languages which work in something of the same way. A model devised by Brown and Gilman (1960) to describe personal pronominal variation in French, Spanish, German, Russian, and other languages can be easily extended to the Javanese case.

When speaking of a singular speech partner with a personal pronoun, speakers of these and other languages are obliged to select between two paradigmatic alternants: the second person singular personal pronoun, called by Brown and Gilman the T variety (so, *tu* in French, *du* in German, *ty* in Russian) and the plural personal pronoun, called the V variety (*vous* in French, *Sie* in German, and *vy* in Russian). The T and V forms alternate and covary with aspects of a context of use, and especially with the speaker/addressee relation as evaluated by speaker. In reference to a singular addressee, a speaker's choice will covary with (key to, be made in terms of) aspects of social relations. Part of that context is the personal pronominal form which has been or (the speaker believes) will be returned. The patterns may be symmetric (reciprocal exchange of T or V) or asymmetric (nonreciprocal exchange with one person giving T and getting V in return).

Symmetric exchange marks relative formality or familiarity between speech partners, the T form marking "closeness" (solidarity), the V form "distance" (formality). To use a spatial metaphor, symmetric exchange articulates on a horizontal axis: speech partner A is as "distant from" or "close to" speech partner B as is B from A. Asymmetric exchange marks differences in status, the person who gives the "low" or "familiar" form being the social superior of the person who gives the "high" or "polite" form. This can be visualized as a "vertical" relation between unequals of higher and lower status.

Patterns of use of ngoko and krama are appropriate to, or presuppose, similar types of social relations between speech partners, and stand as metonyms (parts of a whole) of contexts of use. But the model can be revealingly applied only if one understands what counts as "status" in Javanese society among members of different strata and during different eras. In chapter 2 the cultural background for speech level use will be described together with the patterns of use of ngoko and krama in traditional priyayi society. Treated as unitary metonyms of speech situations, patterns of linguistic conduct will be studied as reflections of aspects of the structure of elite society, and as an entree to traditional conceptions of status as defined by distance from a king. This view of social relations, now largely anachronistic, has been supplanted by different conceptions of proper etiquette and forms of speech level use in several ways during the last century.

Krama inggil deferentials may or may not be used to refer to an addressee to mark speaker's deference, and in the former case can complement or augment the choice of a style of address, depending on the pattern of exchange in which it is used. In ngoko address it can mark respect for a nonetheless familiar addressee. In krama speech, it can mark deference for a superior who returns ngoko, or lend formality and gravity to respectful address of someone who is one's equal or of comparable status, not in a familiar relation, and with whom one therefore exchanges krama symmetrically.

Since the significance of any use of a speech style is ultimately determined vis-a-vis a pattern of exchange, it can be seen that such registers truly mediate relations in the reciprocal give-and-take of conversation through which speech partners indicate "who they are" to each other. But rules for use of such patterns vary within the community, and so the social significances of use of registers likewise vary. Comparability of structure of two repertoires may be a prerequisite for but is no guarantee of comparability of repertoire use.

Social dialects

The fact of use of a linguistic variety on a given occasion shows most obviously that a speaker controls that variety, and perhaps by implication does not control another. This can be gauged relatively independently of a relation with a speech partner in the context of use. As a mark or index of speakers' knowledge of a code or subcode, a linguistic variety is a social dialect. In this sense selection of a variety of language "says something" about the speaker independently of any other aspect of the situation of use as an index of membership in a speech community or subcommunity (and by implication not a member of some other community).

As the ordinary sense of the word "dialect" implies, variation in linguistic usage among communities separated by space is a common and obvious phenomenon; regional accents, for instance, are obvious markers of the place of origin of a speaker. But dialectal variation also exists within geographically unitary but socioeconomically diverse communities, among speakers of different socioeconomic strata who move within different subcommunities, are parts of different communication networks, and use different but mutually intelligible varieties of a language or languages. Ability or lack of ability to use some variant of a code, can mark ethnicity, socioeconomic background or other salient aspect of social identity.

A distinction will be drawn here between between "standard" and "nonstandard" dialects of Javanese, and this cross-cuts the social significance of speech level contrast as registers within various repertoires. The term "standard" is understood to refer to a variety of a language accorded special status by members of a speech community as the "best," and such evaluations typically reflect the power of some social institutions and the prestige of speakers of that dialect, usually members of some dominant or prestigious subcommunity. (For a useful introduction see Haugen 1966.) The oral variety associated with literature and a group of literati (like the priyayi), is given allegiance by members of the entire community for whom it is symbolic of the "best" language. To this day, speakers of Javanese from distant parts of the island will name Surakarta, perhaps the best known center of priyayi, as a place where the "best" Javanese is spoken.

Speakers' attitudes to social dialects count as parts of the situations which sociolinguists study; subjective attitudes toward and evaluations of linguistic varieties are treated then as resulting from and manifesting more general types of social stratification. The traits of "inherently bad" and "inherently good" speech which people adduce to justify their evaluations are themselves data, and clues to powerful yet often covert attitudes towards members of a community associated with one dialect or other.[6] Sociolinguists avoid implicit assumptions of inherent comparability of dialects as good or bad by using the term "nonstandard" which, in contrast to "substandard," alludes to the fact of evaluation in a broader social context of the evaluator as well as the evaluated language variety.

The distinction between dialect and register—and under the former rubric, between standard and nonstandard dialect—is important for this description because madya speech styles are judged by some priyayi as "bad," "sloppy," and substandard usage, but by others as informal usage. To draw out the social implications of these views, and understand the varying forms and functions of madya in the repertoires of different priyayi speakers, we must deal with these basic differences in possible multiple significances with which speech is endowed. I will argue that the social meanings of madya use have varied among priyayi speakers of different generations, functioning for some as a register they themselves use, but being evaluated by others as a social dialect used by and associated with an outgroup. Such changes are manifested in differences in structure and functions of speech level repertoires; they are indices of more general changes in the makeup of the new educated class in Surakarta, and in the nature of relations between priyayi and non-priyayi.

Variation in madya usage is particularly revealing of broader social changes in Surakarta precisely because madya styles are functionally ambiguous in speakers' repertoires. Native speakers sometimes evince an awareness of madya's double sociolinguistic significance, even if they express it in experience-near terms which are less objective than those used by analysts. Their attitudes towards varieties of language, discussed in chapter 3, are symptomatic of more general, often covertly held attitudes to members of other social classes. Evaluations of language use can provide important and revealing clues to the nature of social

---

[6]One of the best known cases is Labov's work (see, for instance, Labov 1969) which shows that prejudices among speakers of standard American English concerning Black English—that it is "illogical," "sloppy," "incoherent," etc.—are artifacts of attitudes toward the community of users of the dialect, rather than accurate observations on its "intrinsic nature."

pressures which are being exerted on linguistic codes and the symbolic values of language varieties of different social groups. The ambiguous or dual social functions of madya speech styles make them the most difficult part of the speech level system to describe, but they are central to an understanding of sociolinguistic dynamics in Surakarta during the last century.

The situation is complicated further by the presence of Indonesian (*bahasa Indonesia*), the national language, which is used by most urban Javanese and is appropriate in both formal and informal varieties for use in many kinds of situations. As the language of government, education, and other official institutions, it is the best medium for official and formal interaction, but is also increasingly used as a non-Javanese code which does not necessarily lend great formality to a situation. As the official language of the nation, it is being standardized through governmental, educational, media, and other national institutions; as such it has displaced Javanese as the standardized language in the minds of many Javanese who are also educated Indonesians.[7]

Norms for use

A choice between registers, that is, varieties of language which key to situation of use, can be thought of as relatively appropriate or inappropriate vis-a-vis a situation; dialectal variants on the other hand contrast as "good" or "bad" (standard or nonstandard) speech evaluated according to context-independent social standards. Which aspect of the significance of a choice may be more important on any given occasion for either participant or observer may vary, and such differential significance can itself be highly revealing of how members of a community view language and social relations. Norms for use of language—what might count as polite or impolite, standard or nonstandard—can be described on this basis. Insofar as such norms for use are part of speakers' ability to use language, they are means for classifying social

---

[7]A more detailed description is provided in Wolff and Poedjosoedarmo (1982), and although the place of Indonesian will be considered below in terms of its influence on the changing forms and uses of the speech levels, many important aspects of its place in this complex situation will be largely ignored here as only indirectly relevant.

contexts and social relations, part of social knowledge relevant to far more in interaction than just speaking properly. Nonetheless they may be manifested most clearly and distinctly in specifically linguistic behavior.

Situations are marked or evaluated by choice of speech varieties—ngoko, madya, and krama—in ways which may be said to presuppose aspects of a situation in which they are normatively used. This means that to compare patterns of use one must have some idea not just of what repertoires are available to speakers, but also what norms of use they apply in different situations. Apparently identical parts of formally different repertoires controlled by different (groups of) speakers may thus be endowed with different social significances in use; uneducated or (by traditional standards) undereducated Javanese who do not control "full" krama, for example, use non-ngoko madya speech styles as "polite" language which can be only indirectly compared in social function with usage of formally similar language by those who do control and use "standard" krama.

But even formal identity of repertoires of different speakers does not guarantee that the norms for use of parts of those repertoires will be the same. As Brown and Gilman have shown in the European cases (1960:269), speakers who control the same T and V alternants do not necessarily use them in the same ways; norms for use may differ from subgroup to subgroup, and these group styles, as Brown and Gilman call them, may be typical of speakers of particular social strata within the community at large. Members of the upper classes in Western Europe tend to evaluate social relations in terms of differences between people, what separates rather than draws them together, and use V forms more often to mark status differences and formality in relations. Traditional French nobility, as Brown and Gilman put it, lived in something of a V universe. Lower class speakers more commonly evaluate relations in terms of what speech partners have in common, what draws them together; as the Yugoslavian saying has it, "A peasant will say *tu* to a king"(1960:270).[8] The first part of the task of describing the functions of the levels, then, is to

---

[8]Bax (1975) has made analogous arguments concerning the use of krama and ngoko in rural and urban Java.

determine norms for use which can be attributed to different groups of speakers, and to explicate criteria for classifying situations and relations incorporated in those norms.

Language variation and language change

A study of the structure of speech level codes controlled by members of different speech subcommunities and of the functions of speech levels used in different types of contexts provides the basis for general conclusions about the effects of social change on the traditional priyayi class and their urban social milieu. This focus on variation between functionally distinct repertoires leads naturally to another heuristic assumption at least implicitly made by linguists which is modified or rejected by sociolinguists.

Just as there is no speaker who controls only one variety of a language, so there is no speech community which is entirely linguistically homogeneous, i.e., in which all members share all and only the same linguistic repertoires, and use them in accordance with just the same norms of use. The structural linguists' idealized case is nowhere to be found. Dialectal variation over space and across socioeconomic strata complements variation found over time, the manifestations of change in language codes. The sociolinguistic critique of traditional structural approaches to language change stems naturally from a concern with linguistic variation; a linguist who assumes that an invariant code is shared equally by all members of a homogeneous speech community likewise presupposes that the language is a relatively stable and fixed, rather than mutable object of description. The traditional linguistic approach involves a type of hypostasis from the actuality of ongoing, continuous change, an assumption which excludes from the structural linguistic purview dynamic linguistic interaction between members of a speech community which affects structures of repertoires and norms for use.

Saussure, for instance, postulated "language stages" (1966:81) as the legitimate object of synchronic description, and allotted to historical linguists the task of comparing synchronic descriptions of a language. For Saussure, dynamic analysis of change presupposed static analysis of states. Students of variation—comparative linguists, historical linguists, sociolinguists—have developed more fine-grained, complex views of linguistic variation and change, according to which variation in structure and use of codes in a given community at a given time is really the synchronic correlate of ongoing diachronic change. Any one "state" of a language is drawn from dynamic processes of interaction between speakers which reciprocally affect enduring patterns of usage.

Jakobson (1971) has shown more clearly than anyone, perhaps, how synchronic analysis need not and in fact should not be conceived of as "static." Variation and heterogeneity within a speech community reflects the dynamics of use, and socially salient variation in speech patterns thus provides evidence of the course of linguistic and social change. Such variation is the source of clues to ways the "mechanism of linguistic change," to use Labov's well-known phrase (1972), brings about linguistic change which involves speakers' perspectives on social groups and social relations. A linguistic code does not just "determine" or "constrain" language use; changing patterns of language use in changing social contexts can transform the structure and functions of the code.

What Hockett (1951) calls "age-grading"—systematic variation between dialects and generations of speakers—is particularly important for the study of ongoing language change in Surakarta. The priyayi community has undergone rapid and profound social changes in the last century which are described in chapter 2; erosion and subsequent eradication of traditional class distinctions between nobles and commoners, the introduction of a new set of governmental, educational, and business institutions, and the growth of a new, relatively more heterogeneous educated class, have all affected traditional priyayi society. If priyayi are being progressively assimilated into a new urban society, it is not surprising that there have been changes in the speech levels, which are so intimately tied to contexts of use and speakers' evaluations of social relations.

METHODS AND SOURCES

Although the focus of this work is relatively narrow, and many interesting sociolinguistic problems will be glossed over, it overlaps in several ways with the work of other Javanists and Indonesianists, who have addressed questions, used different methods, and developed conclusions with different types of data.

A problem faced by all who have dealt with this delicately differentiated system of linguistic behavior, so intimately linked to users' social backgrounds and views of situations of use, has been to gather evidence bearing on these various sorts of contextual significance. This obviously requires a great deal of information about and relatively precise descriptions of use. No single source of data is entirely adequate to the task, and one finds that different studies rely primarily but never exclusively on one or another type of information for support; since I too have faced this problem, and make occasional use of other descriptions, the advantages and problems involved with different research methods can be considered together with the literature on the speech levels.

Observed use

There is no substitute for the data of actual spontaneous linguistic usage for sociolinguistic study, but in itself an objective record of an occasion of use of Javanese is incomplete. One needs to know a great deal about the setting of interaction, the range of speakers' repertoires, social backgrounds, and the history of the relation between speech partners (and perhaps bystanders). Some of this information can be gathered and reported by observers, but the lack of other data which may be virtually impossible to obtain, may force one to merely conjecture on reasons a given speaker should choose to speak in a given way on a given occasion. Someone's motivations for speaking in a certain way may involve implicit manipulation of norms of use, for instance, and their speech may be socially significant precisely because of its "wrongness."

A second obvious problem is that the presence of an observer or recorder may be obtrusive, and transform the nature of the situation. Furthermore, if one is concerned with speech variation among speakers of different generations in a given social class, then the sample of observed usage must be obtained not just from speakers of a clearly distinguished and rather small speech subcommunity, but from a sample of persons stratified by age, speaking in a wide range of situations.

Wolff and Poedjosoedarmo (1982) analyze and illustrate use of the speech levels and Indonesian by relying primarily on recordings of Indonesian and Javanese usage. This is a very rich source of data and evidence for their conclusions, and the fact that they were apparently unable to gather all the relevant background information for every occasion of use is not crucial for their goals, which are broader than those adopted here. They are concerned primarily with the interaction of Indonesian and Javanese and contrasting uses of both languages in ethnically distinct Javanese and Chinese subcommunities. The broad focus of their work required more general data which could be drawn from a corpus of observed use. But the central concern here is not with the community of Javanese speakers as a whole, or even with ethnic Javanese, but with a small subgroup of ethnic Javanese; the systematic data required from members of this particularly small group must be obtained by other means.

This is not to say that observed and recorded speech was not gathered for this study; whenever and wherever possible, observed occasions of speech level use were recorded from informants, friends, and acquaintances. Although the presence of a microphone has a tendency to create formality in a situation and so affect speech in Java, as in many other situations studied by sociolinguists, its presence during interaction over a long period of time (sometimes more than a year) reduced its importance as a conditioner of language use.[9]

Although data of observed use will not bear the weight of a general description (as will become clear in chapter 4) they offer a valuable means for corroborating points drawn from and supported by other kinds of data.

Written sources

Another obvious source of data is Javanese literature: novels and stories, written by Javanese for Javanese, which are both easily accessible and at least partially representative of the spoken idiom. Treatments like Uhlenbeck's (1978) and Walbeehm's (1897), for instance, are based to different degrees and in different ways on the evidence of written use. It should be noted right away, though,

---

[9]Bax (1974:ii) reports, however, that his presence made all people speak more formally, despite the length of his stay in a village in south-central Java; he found also that he was never able to make villagers disregard the presence of a tape recorder.

that renderings of spoken language in such sources are really instances of reported use made by an author, and are based on his/her knowledge or belief that some type of speaker represented by a fictional character speaks in characteristic ways in certain types of situations. The accuracy of such reported usage must be evaluated as possibly reflecting authors' normative or ideal-typical conceptions of a character; and this can be done with extratextual information which is not always available.

An author is also a speaker, a member of a community and subcommunity, who has beliefs and prejudices about how members of various social subgroups speak; these may quite naturally be reflected in such reports of speech. Sources which apparently exemplify spoken usage may thus turn out to fit with prescriptions or stereotypes of how an author believes language should be or is used. When reading a text, just as when conversing with a speaker, one is confronted with the problem of gauging the accuracy of reports and observations, and the possible influences of norms or stereotypes on them. Oral reports can at least be elicited more systematically, questioned in a variety of ways, and checked more thoroughly with other speakers. That a given character in a novel speaks in a certain way may indicate as much about the author as about the character being portrayed; without information on author's background, interpretation may be difficult and at best tentative.[10] A student of the speech levels who reads novels to acquire data must beware of taking projections of authors' prejudices in examples of fictitious persons' speech as entirely accurate specimens of oral use.

As a reader, one also has to have a feel for the accuracy and naturalness of written language which ostensibly represents natural speech. Like other speakers, authors vary in their ability to capture the realities of use, and are more or less accurate renderers of the spoken idiom. An author is essentially anonymous for the reader—more so, certainly, than any informant—and his or her talent for capturing the realities of everyday speech may be difficult to evaluate. Given the highly stylized and didactic roots of recent

---

[10]This is why Labov (for instance) is very concerned about the social background of the authors of texts which he uses in his study of post-vocalic /r/ (1972:285-7) and is so skeptical about the use of novels as sources of data.

Javanese prose literature, and the relative recentness of a "natural" prose genre ostensibly faithful to everyday life and language, it would not be surprising to find that written usage deviates from reality as a result of literary convention.

Similarly, one needs a fairly clear idea of what the character speaking is like: what his/her repertoire might be, who is present at an occasion of use, and so on. Some sorts of contextual information are nearly always available, but it is not always clear what repertoires should be attributed to characters whose speech is written down.

Other problems for evaluating written representations of Javanese involve the place of orthographic convention for use of Javanese script; Javanese spellings, like those in English, do not always accurately reflect the pronunciation of colloquial and informal variants of speech.[11] When written examples of an informal variety of speech such as madya are compared with written examples of informal varieties of krama, it is sometimes difficult to judge whether an author's choice of orthography was constrained by a reluctance to adapt "normal" spellings of words to reflect their true pronunciation. This also depends to some degree on an author's taste and talent, and cannot be directly gauged by the reader to whom that author is anonymous.

All of these problems notwithstanding, written texts offer very real and unique advantages. Most important, there are numerous and accessible written renditions of usage which date from the last century, and even if these are not as complete (in any of the ways mentioned above) as one might wish for, they are very valuable for developing a historical perspective. The obvious if partial solution to the problem of evaluating the accuracy of language in a written text is to compare it with others, searching for examples which corroborate each other. The same procedure is used when working with informants: checking observed and reported usage, and looking for samenesses and differences in use and evaluations of use. But written sources must be considered

---

[11]For instance, there is no standardized way to write the informal varieties of the English affirmative response which has the formal alternant "yes." The traditional syllabary and modern Javanese alphabet are, to be sure, far more accurate means for rendering Javanese speech than is English orthography for English speech.

with an eye to the ways the medium of presentation, and their author's prejudices, might make for deviation from the reality of actual use. I thus do not deny the validity of a sociolinguistic approach to written language; it is certainly legitimate to distinguish between the media of expression of spoken and written language, and to treat them as related but autonomous (Abercrombie 1967:17-18, Romaine 1982:14-22) since the focus here is on oral expression, of which written sources provide less-than-ideal representations, the latter can be used only with caution.

Native speaker judgments and evaluations

Another research strategy is to draw speakers' attention to and question them about aspects of the ways they and others speak. Much recent linguistic research has been predicated on the assumption that native speakers are in fact able to draw on their knowledge of their language to judge well-formedness and potential semantic and pragmatic significances of examples. Their statements are reports of use which, unlike those in literature, are elicited directly from speakers whose social background can be studied in detail, whose reliability can be tested and checked against other speakers of similar background, and whose attention can be drawn to relatively precise points of form and use.

A common criticism of this approach is that speakers have social biases and prejudices: partial, subjective views of language and language users which condition what they say about language. But when language is studied primarily as a part and indicator of broader perspectives on society and social relations, then those judgments are in and of themselves quite valuable if the underlying biases are recognized.

Questions put to speakers of different ages within the priyayi community were designed to gain information on the structure of level use—what combinations of elements were acceptable and unacceptable—and their functions—in which contexts the speech styles were appropriate. These are general rubrics encompassing large numbers of questions, answers to which were provided by a sizable, stratified sample from the priyayi community. By selecting one's informants rather than using what happens to be available in the literature, one can (within obvious limitations) gather information on particular issues. Patterns of variation in speakers' responses can be taken as evidence at least of changing attitudes to language, speech contexts, and speech partners, but also (I will argue below) as evidence of actual change in forms and functions of language use among priyayi.

Informants' reports, like written sources, can be cross-checked against each other for consistency and reliability, but unlike written sources, they can also be checked against the observed usage of informants themselves. In this way social biases with no basis in fact can be detected and dealt with appropriately.

Since there is no omniscient observer or describer of a speech situation, there can be no perfect source of data for analysis of language use. Like the authors cited above, I have relied on the types of data best suited for my purposes, but I make use of other sources when and if they are available and appropriate. It is clear that Wolff and Poedjosoedarmo (1982) (and, apparently, Uhlenbeck[12] as well) adduced a few native speakers' judgments on various topics and I, conversely, compare conclusions and evidence from observed and written reported use where possible and appropriate. The nature of these problems and their importance for the research is taken up more specifically in chapter 4.

CLASSIFYING SPEAKERS

To characterize variation and changes in the structure and functions of Javanese linguistic politesse, usage will be described with respect to three different but related social contexts, and three groups of priyayi speakers. In this way patterns of speech are linked to milieux in which priyayi have used and continue to use linguistic etiquette; traits of language use can thus be allied with attributes of speakers of different social strata, and with periods in Surakartan history.

When speakers are referred to below as "traditional," "conservative," or "modern," these labels are intended to link differing aspects of the structure, function, and evaluations of

---

[12]In his brief consideration of madya (1978:311) he indicates that he checked an earlier description of madya vocabulary with a native speaker.

speech level repertoires with broad differences in the social milieu in which users of those repertoires have grown up and lived. They are adopted as descriptive rubrics and heuristic abstractions for making social sense of linguistic change and variation, serving as parts of an expository strategy, not as labels for discrete, clear-cut stages in the history of the Javanese language or Surakartan speakers. They cannot be fully justified with exhaustive documentation, nor can they be used to classify all types of variation in priyayi speech exhaustively or totally accurately. But an ideal analysis of an ideal corpus of data would, I believe, confirm the validity of the basic approach, and show that a tripartite view of a century of Surakartan priyayi sociolinguistic history would prove useful for understanding variation and change. Each label is associated with features of language use "typical" of speakers said to live in and belong to different eras. Chapter 2 is devoted to historical background of different generations of speakers, and general aspects of language use within those contexts. This approach highlights the role of the speech levels in social context, and provides a perspective on the linguistic details dealt with in chapters 3 and 4.

Speakers and speech patterns called "traditional" are known primarily from written records dating from 1848 up to about 1900, the year the eldest of my own informants were born. Living informants' recollections of their parents' and grandparents' language use are valuable—especially since they tend to corroborate each other and yield a general picture of traditional priyayi society—but they are not as detailed as are their descriptions of their own usage gathered by elicitation and observation of spontaneous use. The common substance of their recollections complements written sources, and provides insight into the intimate relations of traditional etiquette and social structure.

Speakers called "conservative" here are informants born as early as 1900, as late as 1940, with whom I was able to work. Their reports on linguistic usage among their predecessors and on the social history of Surakartan priyayi are (within limits) consistent, and confirm each other well enough to be a valuable source of information on usage dating from the turn of the century. Their reports indicate personal status was traditionally defined in terms of "distance from a king," and from this basic definition followed a principle of "status fade-out" manifested in variation in patterns of speech level use within different strata of priyayi society.

These speakers provide a living bridge with a recent but somewhat enigmatic past, and make up the majority of informants to be called "conservative." Many grew up during the last part of the reign of Pakubuwana X, who is generally recognized to have been the last great king of Surakarta, a living symbol of traditional Surakartan priyayi culture. They also witnessed the last phases of the progressive diminution of the realm and profound changes in Surakartan society which accompanied it. Conservative speakers provide partial, socially biased, but nonetheless valuable perspectives on a major shift in priyayi/non-priyayi relations which came about early in the century. This had effects on speech level use, unobvious but ubiquitous and important correlates of an elite response to social change.

Many priyayi of this period were instrumental in bringing about basic social and attitudinal changes in Surakartan society, and were in part responsible for social changes which deprived them of their traditional social position. It is important, then, to remember that the designation "conservative" is used here in a restricted, semi-technical sense, convenient for identifying these persons with respect to their speech and evaluation of speech. In no way is it to be taken to impute or attribute to them any sort of broader political belief or ideology. From this generation of priyayi, indeed, came many of the most prominent participants in and leaders of the revolution against the Dutch.

Because the label "conservative" is used here for features of language use and evaluation, it applies also to some younger speakers, although they are a minority in this group. They are of more recent generations of priyayi living in Surakarta, of ages between 15 and 35, and not coincidentally are of high noble and official status. Through their parents they are still much involved with and close to what remains of the traditional courtly circles, and these younger speakers can no more be automatically labeled socially "old-fashioned" or politically conservative than can their parents and grandparents; in their case too the designation alludes primarily to common features of use of the speech levels.

Age-mates of these young conservative speakers who differ significantly with respect to speech level use are called "modern," in an analogous semi-technical manner. These younger priyayi speakers had been born as early as the last days of the revolution, and as recently as 1965; all grew up in a modern and at least incipiently egalitarian-ethic, nationalistic social milieu. Modern speakers' awareness of their traditional priyayi heritage vary, but taken as a group, they contrast with their conservative parents and grandparents in their patterns of language use. Those differences can be taken as indications of differing perspectives on social relations, and differing ways of dealing with other members of urban society, that is, determining who counts as a peer, a superior, or an inferior. Evidence of change in speech level usage in contemporary Surakarta can be inferred from a large group of data collected from informants, who are grouped on the basis of language use and evaluation of use presented in chapters 3 and 4.

Variation in the structure and function of speech level use among these speakers can be shown to reflect different responses to changing social relations between Surakartans. I will argue that the place of younger priyayi in modern society, at once linked to and distinct from those of their parents and grandparents, is reflected in the ways they evaluate speech level varieties as parts of their own repertoire of registers. "Modern" speakers' use of speech level repertoires differs from their elders' in that it does not so much mark status differences (priyayi versus non-priyayi, commoner versus noble) in asymmetric speech level use as they mark relative formality of relations in accordance with less specific social criteria. In this way they are assimilating into a new educated urban group which is relatively heterogeneous and fluid compared with that in the Surakarta of even twenty years ago.

Proceeding from a brief description in chapter 2 of the history of the priyayi class—different milieu in which priyayi have lived during the last century—we consider the forms of different repertoires of ngoko and krama speech styles in chapter 3. In this way the range of styles called madya is simultaneously circumscribed for discussion in chapter 4. Madya has been the least understood type of speech style, and some reasons for difficulties in dealing with it will be adduced by comparing speakers' classifications of examples of krama and madya as non-ngoko language. It turns out that the criteria speakers use to identify styles differ significantly from those found in the literature, and correlate moreover with their own status in, and perspectives on, society.

Some but not all young priyayi tend to disassociate themselves from the social circles and language of their parents and grandparents; they base choices between speech styles on different kinds of evaluations of social situations, of relations to speech partners, and of appropriate uses of their repertoires. Their identifications of styles thus provide evidence of broad differences in attitudes to language use and users among speakers in the priyayi class, and suggest ways of interpreting the variation found in judgments on the well-formedness of madya examples which are discussed in chapter 4.

The regular variation which appears in informants' judgments on well-formedness of examples fits with their identifications of examples discussed in chapter 3. Where more conservative priyayi tend to draw a well-defined line between krama and madya as "standard" versus "substandard" non-ngoko language respectively, modern speakers' judgments and use allow for no such clear-cut distinction between them. For these latter speakers, krama and madya thus appear to be segments on a continuum of politeness, registers between which modern priyayi (and non-priyayi) speakers choose on the basis of criteria different from those used by conservative speakers. These latter perceive (and to all appearances use) madya as a social dialect which they use essentially to members of what they see as an outgroup; the younger generation of speakers does not.

If the structures and functions of speech level repertoires of so-called "modern" priyayi are in fact coming to resemble those of their non-priyayi educated peers (as will be argued), then linguistic variation in this community provides insight into changing perceptions of social relations between speech partners, and views of sociolinguistic subgroups. It appears that since the turn of the century, speech level usage among the priyayi called "traditional," "conservative," and "modern" has changed, reflecting the progressive linguistic assimilation of priyayi into the larger educated urban class, and their adoption of different ways of using linguistic etiquette.

2

PRIYAYI SOCIETY AND LANGUAGE IN TRANSITION

From the middle of the eighteenth century to the end of the nineteenth century, Surakartan priyayi enjoyed a stability which they owed, paradoxically enough, to the same foreign presence which was progressively restricting their domain. The founding of the royal polity of Surakarta was one upshot of a power struggle which rehearsed a recurring pattern in indigenous dynastic history. It nonetheless signaled a new era in Javanese politics, insofar as the Dutch played a crucial role in its establishment (Ricklefs 1974, 1983). The basic structure of traditional courtly society was preserved well into the twentieth century as a final instance and elaboration of traditional elite social organization informed by traditional (if largely anachronistic) conceptions of royal power.

In the traditional kingdom power was delegated by a king to locally based nomarchs through stratified hierarchies which corresponded largely, if not perfectly, with Weber's model of the patrimonial state (Schrieke 1957:120ff.). As Anderson puts it:

> According to this model, the central government is essentially an extension of the ruler's personal household and staff. Officials are granted their positions . . . and they may be dismissed or degraded at his personal whim. . . . Payment of officials is allotted by the ruler for the period of tenure of each particular office. Within the central government latent or overt tension persists between the royal descent group . . . and the . . . high ranking officials of common origin who have risen to power on the basis of their administrative capacities and personal loyalty to the ruler. . . . While the power of the ruler in the

immediate environment of his capital is unquestioned, the poor quality of communications and . . . financial difficulties make it difficult for him . . . to maintain tight administrative control. . . . He must inevitably attempt to coopt regional notables and to devolve a great deal of informal power to them. . . . The ruler has also to face the danger that a *ministerialis* assigned to govern some remote province may develop such roots there that he assumes leadership over, or is coopted into, the group of local notables. . . . (1972:33)

Power was traditionally conceived to devolve from the palace *(kraton)*, becoming at once concrete and relatively autonomous within self-regulating spheres which centered around the king; because his direct control decreased further from the royal center, his relation as central ruler to subject became looser in proportion to the distance between them.[1] The concomitant of personalized power was a particular kind of social relation between persons at hierarchically distinct levels: the patron-client relation. Strong vertical connections came into being at the expense of horizontal ties between members of a single stratum in the hierarchy, such that their relations with an immediate superior across social strata were closer than their relations with peers and fellow clients.

The quality of this type of relation, the feeling of "diffuse, long standing, affect-laden mutual obligation . . . [and] personalistic power accumulated through the role of influencer as provider, protector, educator, source of values" (Jackson 1972:435) is still expressed by Javanese in the idiom of familial relations.[2] Intimate stratified relations built on person-oriented loyalty, often likened

---

[1] The traditional Javanese polity is an instantiation of that more general areal phenomenon called by Tambiah (1976, chapter 7) the galactic polity. Virtually all of the characteristics he attributes to that form of political organization may be found in the Surakartan case which, if it came to resemble the strong version of the galactic polity was, as Tambiah suggests (1976:124), highly unusual, and in fact artifical.

[2] For more detailed analysis of the nature of patrons and clients in Southeast Asia see Scott 1972.

to the bond between father (*bapak*) and child (*anak*), permeated traditional priyayi society as a means for understanding social relations. This ideal image of the dyadic relation was exemplified and rehearsed at various levels throughout the elite, informing the social structure of their community.

In the traditional Javanese view the kingdom was an image of the universe writ small, in which the the king stood less as a premier administrator or patrimonial chief and more as a mediator between man and god. Aligned with and representative of the magico-spiritual powers of the universe, his spiritual potency and efficacy were greatest at the source, the royal person, and gradually diffused as they radiated out and away from him. As Anderson (1972) has pointed out, a consequence of this conception is that one's relation with a king, that is, one's proximity to the source of royal power, was directly related to the one's potential to absorb power from its source, and so to one's place in the social hierarchy of which he was the center and apex.

Traditionally a priyayi's status correlated with his or her distance from a king, and depended on kin relations and/or official position. Since personal and relative status were key determinants of the patterns of respect behavior priyayi adopted with each other, speech level use can be generally and preliminarily characterized by examining the different dimensions of status, the official and familial social axes along which distance from a king was measured. Social conduct did not just bear the marks of status differences among social interactants; it served to modulate the impact of one's actions on others, and marked one's inward awareness of one's place in the social and natural order of things.[3]

ETIQUETTE IN TRADITIONAL SOCIETY

The complex code of priyayi etiquette governed virtually every aspect of personal appearance and movement, but the precise and explicit rules for dressing, making obeisance, walking, and much else will be glossed over here. What follows is a brief summary and exemplification of how general principles of status

---

[3]Geertz's interpretation of priyayi etiquette in relation to world-view and ethos (1960 and 1976) is reconsidered and discussed in Errington 1984 and 1988.

differentiation affected the particulars of linguistic usage. The most general criteria for evaluating persons are outlined below in descending order of their breadth of applicability, and relevance to social conduct among priyayi.

To adapt a pattern of speech level exchange with someone—answering the implicit questions verbalized by the gentleman quoted in chapter 1 as "Who am I? Who are you to me?"—was to gauge personal status as the basis of relative status. For a priyayi this meant determining what one had in common with and how one differed from a speech partner. Minimally, two priyayi shared some common kingly ancestor, but their respective genealogical distances from a most immediate kingly forefather might differ. Among those of equal descent, genealogical seniority, calculated on the basis of birth order of their respective ancestors, would be unequal. If they shared just one progenitor, other status differences would exist. If they shared both progenitors, they would still necessarily differ in birth order, which made for status differences and particular uses of etiquette.

At the same time, two interactants might share responsibilities and rights in the same or different offices of the royal government, and they might hold identical or different ranks. The basic norms governing face-to-face interaction thus reflected personal and relative status, calculated in terms of "distance from a king." The elaborateness and overtness of the patterns of behavior adopted to mark these status differences varied, the latter more finely drawn and the former more overtly marked among those who stood closer to the royal center.

Rights to descent titles illustrate this latter principle clearly enough to deserve brief description. Overt titular distinctions existed for descendants of kings down to the fifth generation, a group called the *putra sentana dalem*. More distant descendants in traditional Surakarta were marginal members of the elite classes, at least in terms of descent status. At the highest level of descent, titles differed for offspring of the queen (the *padmi*) as opposed to offspring of concubines (the *selir*), and, among sons of the queen, between eldest and younger siblings. One level "down," titular usage for grandchildren of a king (wayah dalem) differed only among males: the eldest son of a prince by a first wife was titularly distinguished from all other offspring. No titular differences marked analogous distinctions among great-grandchildren of a king. Titles of those of relatively low descent status "further" from the king, marked less finely shaded status of differences, reflecting a kind of "status fade-out" marked likewise in patterns of language use and speech level exchange according to status differences.[4]

Among those of high social status, who were members of and interactants within circles close to the apex of society defined by the king, very small differences in status engendered overt differences in behavior. If patterns of use reported in the literature are compared with reports by older conservative priyayi, it seems that such status differences—different mother than, younger sibling/elder sibling, etc.—gave way to less overt, more flexible marks of deference further "down" the social strata and "away" from the royal center.

Descent

All priyayi trace their descent in at least one way (and usually more) to a common noble ancestor: Sultan Agung, founder of the latter Mataram empire. Those of his descendants who acceded to the throne likewise became 'sources' (*pancer*) of noble lines, and more immediate points of reference for calculating descent status. Two priyayi of different degrees of descent from a common royal ancestor were of unequal status, but the significance of that difference for etiquette depended on the general level of elitehood involved. Deference shown by a grandchild of a king for an offspring of that ruler would be far greater, for instance, than that shown (say) by a sixth generation descendant of some king for a fifth generation descendant from that same "source."

Genealogical seniority: the awu relation

Collaterals sharing a common degree of descent from a common closest kingly ancestor were differentiated by another criterion. Relative status of two grandchildren of the same king, for instance, would depend on the birth order of the siblings from

---

[4]Compare what Haas (1951) calls "declining descent" in Thailand, and what Geertz (1980) calls "sinking status" in Bali.

whom each was distinctly descended, at the point their respective lines of descent split. A priyayi whose grandparent stood as biological elder sibling to another priyayi's grandparent would therefore stand as genealogically elder sibling (in Javanese, older in *awu*). Since the relation between ancestral siblings was superimposed, as it were, on a collateral relation, the genealogical senior would address the other as 'younger sibling,' give ngoko, and receive a kin term glossable as 'male elder sibling' or 'female elder sibling' together with polite, deferential speech.

Physical age would be a mitigating factor only among those at levels of descent relatively more distant from a royal source. Although genealogical seniority would be relevant for determining seniority and kin term usage at all levels in priyayi society, the overtness of patterns of etiquette adopted on that basis would differ in proportion to overall distance from a king. Closer to the center of the elite society, differences in physical age of inter-actants would be relatively less important.

Status of mother

Half-siblings typically shared a father, not a mother; their statuses were calculated on the basis of status of their pro-genetrixes. Like the king, male priyayi of the higher ranks often had more than one wife, one of whom was recognized as "official" or "first" wife (*padmi*) while others were accorded the status of second wives (*selir*). Jural motherhood accrued to the first wife, and reports from conservative priyayi indicate that in at least the first two generations of descent from a king, wives' statuses were sharply differentiated and marked in patterns of speech style use among themselves and with their husband's offspring. All children gave the most deferential forms of krama to the first wife, and received ordinary ngoko in return, whereas (at least at high levels) they gave ordinary ngoko to other wives, often including biological mother, and received krama with deferentials in return.[5]

---

[5]One of many important details otherwise ignored in this summary must be mentioned here. In traditional society, there were two kin terms for 'mother': one a deferential (*ibu*), given to first wife, the other (*mbok*) to concubines. This formerly standard address pattern is now virtually obsolete among priyayi.

This pattern of exchange often represented a specific instance of the general principle of differentiation by descent status. A first wife's descent status was usually comparable with that of her husband, and thus combined with the kin relation of mother/child to reinforce the asymmetric social relation between mother and child. Other wives were usually more distantly descended from kings, or perhaps had no descent status at all; because they were of lower descent status, they were obliged to speak "up" to the king's children and be spoken "down" to in return. An example of this principle in operation is worth mentioning: an elderly priyayi acquaintance of mine was a grandchild of a king by a woman of the fifth generation of descent from a king. The difference in their relative descent ranks (he third generation, she fifth) was counterbalanced by the kin relation of mother and child: the upshot was that they exchanged krama. Both of course gave highly deferential krama to their husband/father, a prince of the realm, who returned ordinary ngoko to them.

Relative status of biological mother likewise determined language use among half-siblings, since those born of a first wife were superior regardless of age or birth order. Again, the degree to which status differences between half-siblings affected their conduct with each other varied across social strata, and had more overt impact in the higher elite circles.

Birth order

Finally, we can consider relations between those who shared both father and mother, be the mother first wife or concubine. In these cases etiquette and speech patterns in the high circles keyed to differences in birth order, the elder giving ordinary ngoko to his/her junior, and receiving deferential krama in return. Even a few days difference in age between those born of concubines was significant in this regard. Again, the overtness of linguistic marks of status difference appear to have been greater among high noble elite than among those "further" from the king.

For an older priyayi in Surakarta to specify a kin term used by one priyayi to another is usually tantamount to specifying the entire pattern of verbal behavior, since it follows necessarily for them that one speaks deferentially to those who count as one's elder (siblings, parents, parents' siblings) and receives deferential speech from those who are one's junior. More than once, such speakers responded to my questions about language use with the simple mention of a kin term for address, which for them was a sufficient indicator of etiquette patterns.

Affinal seniority: the ipean relation

Affinal relations were another factor which could affect the calculation of relative status. To younger siblings of his wife, for instance, a man would stand as elder sibling, regardless of relative physical age; similarly, his wife would stand as elder female sibling to his own younger siblings. Speech level use, at least in the highest circles, followed that relation, usually making for an asymmetric pattern which keyed to differences in relative status.

The criteria for distinguishing status are thus of varying generality, ranging from the broadest commonalities of descent to the most specific criterion of birth order, but all served in traditional Surakarta to distinguish status of persons who were relatively distantly or closely related. More specific principles were applied more rigorously and had more overt impact on conduct within the upper strata of priyayi society, among those "closer" to the king; there, asymmetric patterns of exchange were the rule, rather than the exception, marking status differences between persons.

Physical age

Further down the hierarchy these types of criteria for differentiating status became less important for choice of a style of speech to a relatively close relation; patterns of language exchange loosened up "further" from the king, and asymmetric use became restricted to situations in which more pronounced status differences existed. At the same time, physical age, the most general attribute of all, gained in salience as a determinant of conduct. A difference in physical age often would have had negligible impact on interaction within the highest circles. A twenty-year-old prince would speak ordinary ngoko to a forty-year-old grandchild of a king and receive highly deferential krama return, and a fifteen-year-old grandchild of a king would speak ngoko to a thirty-year-old child of his father's younger sibling.

But age differences would be much more important (for instance) in the household of a fifth-generation descendant of a king, whose children might well exchange ngoko with each other (perhaps with krama inggil given by younger to older), give krama to their father, but perhaps only ngoko with deferentials to their mother, regardless of whether she was first wife or not. The existence of collateral and/or affinal relations between two priyayi at these levels might lead the lower status speaker to address his/her genealogical/affinal elders with a term meaning 'elder male sibling' or 'elder female sibling,' but other asymmetries in language use might be less overt, and might not extend to asymmetric exchange of ngoko and deferential krama. Further down the familial hierarchy, what speech partners shared—same family as, same sibling group as, etc.—became relatively more important.[6]

This sketch of priyayi language use indicates just the most general principles of etiquette exemplified by patterns of usage reported by and observed in use among older conservative informants, as well as in older written sources. It is impossible here to move beyond the broadest aspects of linguistic etiquette—asymmetric or symmetric exchange of ngoko and krama speech styles—to even a few of the ways speakers could shade the expression of respect and deference by choice an expresion for referring to addressee (title, name, personal pronoun), use of formulaic expressions, intonation, and other stylistic subtleties. (See Wolff and Poedjosoedarmo 1982:40-49, Errington 1988.)

The basic point is that all things being equal, patterns of speech level use within different segments of the elite community varied according to status calculated in terms of distance from a king. Things were however rarely equal, and social relations were in fact rarely so simple; priyayi were often related to each other in

---

[6]This is not to say that a great disparity in physical age could not play a decisive factor in speech level usage, even in relations involving a high elite member. Padmasusastra (1896:42-43) gives an example of such usage between a low-level priyayi official and a young prince. The official speaks ngoko with deferentials to the prince, and receives plain ngoko in return.

several distinct ways which could contraindicate appropriate role relations and patterns of speech level use.

MADYA USAGE IN TRADITIONAL SURAKARTA

Discovering the precise forms and social functions of madya usage in traditional priyayi society is difficult for several reasons. First, madya was spoken to speech partners to whom one stood in a relatively complex relation, and served to mark status differences which were mitigated by other factors. Second, nineteenth century accounts of madya usage are incomplete, in some respects inconsistent, and disagree, moreover, with reports provided by the oldest priyayi informants living in Surakarta today. These discrepancies result in part from speakers' differing perspectives on users and uses of madya in different eras and social milieux, and it is not easy to resolve many problems thus involved in understanding the place of madya in priyayi etiquette. Changes and variation in structure and functions of madya repertoires can be linked to changing patterns of social interaction in Surakarta. The brief outline which follows provides sociohistorical background for the more detailed analysis of madya in contemporary Surakarta in chapters 3 and 4.

Speech level repertoires of priyayi and non-priyayi Surakartans have always varied, and that variation is partially responsible for madya's contrasting functions in different social and linguistic subgroups. The traditional educated elite speaker controlled and defined the standard style of krama speech; commoners or "little people" (*wong cilik*) as a rule did not. Then, as now, commoners' non-ngoko repertoires extended only to styles of madya, which they used in ways which distinguished their linguistic etiquette from that of priyayi. Commoner madya usage, like priyayi krama usage, counted as polite speech insofar as it was distinct from ngoko; it could either be exchanged asymmetrically with ngoko to mark status differences, or symmetrically in relatively formal situations.[7] Differences in the structures of priyayi

---

[7] The parameters for differentiating status likewise differed, centering more on differences in age and/or kin relations.

and non-priyayi repertoires were directly related, then, to appropriate uses of styles in those repertoires.

Even when commoners spoke to a priyayi—who was not only of markedly higher status, but also exemplified just those forms of conduct normatively adopted by inferiors in his/her presence—they could often muster little more in the way of "high" or "polite" language than some version of madya, and this resulted in an unhappy situation for all concerned. The view of madya commonly held by conservative priyayi in Surakarta today is based on this social attribute of a segment of the community: it is the non-ngoko language of the uneducated, and as such marks social status of its users. In this way, and for these speakers, it counts as a social dialect.

On the basis of their recollections, elderly conservative informants report with remarkable unanimity that examples of speech styles answering the structural description of madya were not used by their parents or grandparents, either to other priyayi or to non-priyayi. With the latter sort of speech partner, who traditionally was of lower status, priyayi would use ngoko and generally receive in return the best sort of non-ngoko language that non-elite speech partner could produce. Conservative priyayi attribute to their predecessors their own evaluation of madya usage as typical of their outgroup, the non-ngoko speech style of uneducated persons who do not know any better.

Such was the distastefulness of madya for at least one conservative informant's father, it seems, that in order to avoid being actually addressed with such language by nonnoble inferiors, he took his young daughter (my eighty-year-old informant) with him when he inspected land holdings in the country; she acted as his "interpreter" or surrogate addressee when he had to converse with "little people" who could not address him in krama. Such unabashedly expressed biases, reported likewise by Geertz (1960: 253-254) and Wolff and Poedjosoedarmo (1982:17), are common in descriptions of traditional priyayi speech level usage given by their conservative descendants.[8] But according to the older

---

[8]Geertz reports on a rural area in eastern Java in the 1950s; Wolff and Poedjosoedarmo describe Yogyakarta in the 1970s. The sort of persons Wolff and Poedjosoedarmo call "hyperconservative" priyayi are similar to but distinct from those to whom I refer as conservative here.

literature, traditional priyayi used madya in ways which conservative speakers do not report. We can infer the general functions of madya styles from a few descriptive and prescriptive sources by drawing common situational features from examples of priyayi use presented there and considering a few explicit remarks on its use. In his work on Javanese language and literature *Urapsari* (1896), Padmasusastra, "the greatest figure in the field of Javanese language teaching around the turn of the century" (Ras 1979:9), provides a fairly systematic account of speech level use between priyayi officials of different ranks. Padmasusastra's descriptions of priyayi madya usage cannot be represented here in any detail, much less compared with other treatments, but will be taken as a kind of paradigmatic source.[9]

There is one common feature in all the types of situations for which Padmasusastra describes (or prescribes?) the use of madya by priyayi speakers: among priyayi, madya styles were asymmetrically exchanged with either krama or ngoko to mark in muted fashion differences in status mitigated by some other aspect of the relation between speech partners. Consider in this respect Padmasusastra's description of the madya style he calls *madyangoko* (1896:9-10), distinguished from other madya styles insofar as it consists of madya alternants to ngoko and krama forms, ngoko in each slot for which a distinct madya equivalent is not available, and never contains deferentials for reference to addressee. Beyond this, he says, it is further characterized by the use of a particular second: *ndika*. *Madyangoko*, says Padmasusastra, is the non-ngoko style typically exchanged by market-sellers (*bakul*), and his example of its use in symmetric exchange between non-priyayi contrasts significantly with his examples of priyayi use of other styles of madya. Furthermore, it is significant that Padmasusastra carefully identifies a feature of personal pronoun use as typical of non-priyayi madya speech. Examples from *Urapsari* and other sources show other madya styles to be exchanged asymmetrically by priyayi to other priyayi for some style of ngoko or krama.

---

[9]Other treatments written by and for Javanese include Dwidjosusana et al. (n.d.), Soebroto (n.d.), and Dirdjosiswojo (1957). Some may well have been intentionally patterned on Padmasusastra's work.

Contrasting functions of priyayi and non-priyayi use of madya can be considered through examples which are grouped according to two general types of contexts. Some contexts are "official," in the sense that they involve functionaries in the royal government, while others are "familial," involving interaction between persons related as kin. In both types of context, use of madya is described (or prescribed) in asymmetric patterns of exchange to mark in relatively muted fashion a difference in status between speech partners; madya styles can then be treated as kinds of surrogate krama or ngoko styles used in asymmetric exchange.

Madya in official relations

Padmasusastra gives examples of two styles of madya in use by priyayi, both of which, he writes, are distinct from *madyangoko*. One is called *madyakrama*, and consists of madya and krama forms, plus krama inggil deferentials and the second person pronoun *sampéyan* for reference to addressee. The other madya style he calls *madyantara* in *Urapsari*. This consists of madya and ngoko elements, but unlike *madyangoko*, it also requires the second person pronoun *kang sarira* or a kin term for reference to addressee (1896:9-10). *Madyantara* thus resembles but is distinct from *madyangoko*, and Padmasusastra describes and exemplifies its use by a younger to an older speech partner who is nonetheless of lower status.

In Padmasusastra's examples of *madyantara* in official contexts it is used by officials to their subordinates if relative descent status or relative age contraindicate the use of ngoko presupposed by the difference in official status. So if it happened that the prime minister were to speak to a cabinet minister,[10] an immediate subordinate of high rank, who was of high descent status, (i.e., of the fifth generation of descent or higher, a *sentananing ratu*) or appreciably older, *madyantara* might be used rather than ngoko. The person receiving this style of madya would apparently return krama and refer to his official superior with krama inggil. In this way the status difference would be

---

[10]'Prime minister' and 'cabinet minister' are used here as translations for the names of offices held by the *adipati* and *bupati* respectively.

marked by the asymmetric exchange pattern but the superior would nonetheless "raise" his/her speech from ngoko to a "higher" intermediate madya style.

But an example which Padmasusastra provides elsewhere in the same work (1896:25) has a prime minister addressing a lower minister in *madyantara* with the second person pronoun *ndika*. *Ndika*, Padmasusastra writes elsewhere in the same work, is outgroup usage. In a footnote, he notes that he himself had observed the prime minister speaking in this way. This explicit reference to corroborating evidence of observed use is unusual enough in Javanese descriptions of Javanese language to draw one's attention; it indicates first that use of *ndika* by priyayi to priyayi was unusual, and second that alternations between second person pronouns were a crucial means for distinguishing ingroup from outgroup madya usage, that is, between commoner use of a substandard social dialect, and priyayi use of a semi-polite stylistic register. The fact that Padmasusastra gives an example of and comments on this uncommon usage is doubly significant, since it shows that some priyayi usage failed to conform with prevalent norms for priyayi linguistic etiquette. It indirectly shows something about those norms for madya usage.

Madyakrama, on the other hand, is exemplified in speech by subordinates to superiors when the difference in official rank was offset by a significant difference in age or descent status. But Padmasusastra's description (or prescription) for use of *madyakrama* seems to be focused primarily on different kinds of social relations and contextual criteria involved in family circles.

Madya in familial contexts

In another very valuable work, the *Serat Tatacara* (1907), Padmasusastra provides a lively and detailed portrayal of Surakartan customs and beliefs, largely in the form of dialogues between friends, family members, and others. Among these are dialogues between priyayi couples in which men of (apparently) middling to high official rank speak in ngoko to their wives in return for a variety of madya which contains krama forms wherever possible and full deferentials for reference to husband/addressee.

Now in the preface to the *Serat Tatacara*, Padmasusastra gives an example of madya answering his own description of *madyakrama* in *Urapsari*. But in the *Serat Tatacara* he names it *madyantara*, the label he used in the *Serat Urapsari* for a madya style incorporating ngoko words. There is terminological wavering here which bespeaks at least an absence of normative focus on madya within in the speech community, but also quite possibly a more basic, underlying problem in classifying speech styles and evaluating Padmasusastra's treatments. In *Serat Urapsari*, Padmasusastra says that madya speech with krama words and deferentials for addressee (i.e., *madyakrama*) is typical first of usage from wife to husband,[11] and secondly of "little priyayi in the country"[12] (1896:10). Given the author's evident concern in this passage with contrasts in priyayi/non-priyayi usage, it seems curious that he is vague about the status of couples he alludes to in the first phrase—are they priyayi or non-priyayi?—especially in light of his careful restriction on use of the style in other, apparently nonfamilial, contexts to nonurban priyayi. These latter priyayi, of low status by the standards of the court and royal polity, lived relatively far from the urban centers of power; it seems that here, too, Padmasusastra ascribes to a non-urban elite community, really another outgroup, a pattern of use which was presumably "incorrect" outside of the narrow range of situations involving spouses. This lack of precision in an otherwise systematic, careful description may be attributable less to oversights on the author's part than to a kind of ambiguous social significance accruing to madya usage, which is manifested in this vacillation and/or ambiguity in his treatment (and perhaps in others). There is indirect evidence here that Padmasusastra himself, despite his keen ear for the actualities of colloquial use, was not immune to certain prejudices which were probably widespread within the priyayi community about the use of madya speech styles. Nonetheless,

---

[11]"*Punika kathah tembungipun tiyang èstri dhateng ingkang jaler.*" The phrase I interpret as meaning 'husband and wife' is literally 'female person to the one which is male', but this commonly used phrase for a married couple is intended to refer to just that type of social relation. Certainly the example of this style he gives in *Serat Urapsari* (1896:53) involves such a relation.

[12]*utawi priyantun alit ing dhusun.*

madya was sometimes used by priyayi to priyayi in the Surakartan community.

In Winter's *Javaansche Zamenspraken*, a well-known prescriptive source, is a dialogue between a prince (*pangéran*) and "two elderly Javanese of lesser status" (1848:139-144). The prince gives a style which combines madya with ngoko forms to his speech partners, and receives in return a most elegant and deferential krama style. Lack of contextual information makes the case less illuminating than it might be, but from the dialogue's content—the only source of any detail on the social situation—it seems clear that at least one of the lower status speakers is familiar with the prince, at least to the extent that he feels comfortable asking to borrow archery gear. One or both of these speakers might be taken to be related to the prince but of far lower status.[13] Another example worth mentioning can be drawn from one of the earlier novelistic works written in Javanese, called *Dwikarsa* (Sastraatmaja 1930) about a low-ranking Yogyakartan priyayi family in the country. The wife gives madya with krama and deferentials to her husband (as Padmasusastra describes in *Serat Urapsari*), and receives ngoko in return. More interesting is usage between the husband (the title character) and his father-in-law, a high ranking official in the Yogyakartan court, who lectures Dwikarsa in a madya style mixed with krama without krama inggil for addressee; he receives in return full krama with deferentials.

Despite the unavoidable difficulties caused by lack of contextual information for these examples and descriptions, taken singly or as a group, one feature shared by all of them can be drawn out. In each, madya speech is part of an asymmetric pattern of exchange, given in return for either ngoko speech without deferentials for reference to addressee, or for a variety of krama. I have found no examples of symmetric exchange of madya between priyayi, and take this to indicate something about the function of madya in all the situations where it is used asymmetrically. In each case madya use marks a difference in status which is nonetheless mitigated by some other factor: intimacy, age difference, or other contraindicative aspects of social relation between speech partners.

---

[13]They might be offspring of a sibling of the prince's mother, for instance, who in turn might be a concubine of low descent rank.

A wife speaks madya to her intimate but socially superior husband, a prince uses a form of madya to his lessers to mark a status difference which is perhaps at odds with age difference and intimacy. The high official of the Yogyakartan court similarly marks relative intimacy with a son-in-law who is also his official inferior with madya.

In each case madya usage in the priyayi community is illustrated as a kind of compromise speech style for asymmetric exchange. Speakers in traditional society apparently capitalized on its structurally interstitial position in a continuum of styles, arrayed between "full" krama and ordinary ngoko, to use it in contexts which presupposed asymmetric exchange keyed to status differences. As such, it allowed for a shading of formality/respect in the face of overriding status differences. Speech styles which combine madya forms with ngoko or krama forms are, as Walbeehm (1897: 19) points out, really styles of ngoko (a "raised" version) and krama (a "lowered" version) respectively.

In this view, madya styles are registers "between" krama, which is "higher," and ngoko, which is "lower," and as such stand as surrogate ngoko and krama styles used in asymmetric exchange. This apparently complemented madya use by non-priyayi as a non-ngoko language which could be exchanged symmetrically, which as such was substandard from the traditional priyayi point of view. Since (by all accounts) traditional priyayi did not speak madya to commoners under normal circumstances, madya use by commoner to commoner would count as a functionally distinct speech style, chosen from a structurally distinct type of speech level repertoire. Among priyayi, on the other hand, madya styles lent a delicacy to the differentiation of status which could be marked in speech, and as such did not function as a distinct style-type independent of ngoko and krama varieties.

But the formal comparability (if not identity) of some styles of madya used by priyayi and non-priyayi appears to have engendered a potential tension or ambiguity in its use, evinced in ambiguous if not contradictory statements about who uses madya to whom. Padmasusastra, for instance, relegates to "little priyayi in the country" patterns of madya usage which he also attributes to Surakartan priyayi. Madya's interstitial nature is reflected in the peripherality it seems to have in the literature, and in inconsistencies which exist in descriptions and exemplifications of its structure and function.

Similar discrepancies which exist between these traditional written sources and conservative informants' reports reflect the same dual interpretability of madya: on one hand, some madya styles served as registers in traditional priyayi interaction; on the other, madya now counts for conservative speakers as a social dialect or a substandard non-ngoko langage spoken by commoners. A pattern of exchange in which wife speaks to husband with full krama (rather than madya) and receives ngoko in return, can still be heard in some high-ranking conservative households today, but analogous use of madya, such as that reported by Padmasusastra is, as far as I am able to determine, nonexistent among conservative priyayi in contemporary Surakarta.

To reconcile the situation described in the literature with that in Surakarta today, we must consider social changes which have affected traditional priyayi views and uses of madya, and disturbed this implicit balance between two disparate ways of evaluating such speech. These reflect broader social changes which have occurred within the traditional elite, and in Surakartan society as a whole. Linguistic changes which have occurred over the last century can be treated as consequences of changing social attitudes and social relations which have given rise to the speech level variation in the contemporary community discussed in chapters 3 and 4. As criteria for gauging social status have changed, so too have the linguistic structures and functions of priyayi speech level usage.

PRIYAYI SOCIETY IN TRANSITION

The 1920s and 1930s could be called the golden age of the house of Pakubuwana. The tenth king of that family was ruling over a city which, in the words of the Dutch resident in 1918, was to Java what Paris was to western Europe: the major center of classic culture and home of some of the most educated people on the island (Jakarta 1918). Even if the king's tremendous wealth came from Dutch profits on the plantations being exploited in his own domain, his ostentatious display of royal well-being and generosity insured the continued celebration of the modern cult of glory. His death in 1939 marked the end of a financial and political era; the Dutch imposed on Pakubuwana XI a drastically reduced budget and further restricted his already limited powers within the kingdom. This was one of the more obvious moves by the Dutch to undermine or at least transform the traditional elite, and to incorporate them into a colonial governmental organization.

Besides introducing new forms of government, they also introduced a new educational system and new languages. These foreign influences on the traditional elite of Surakarta, dating from the end of the nineteenth century, had already wrought less obvious but profound changes on priyayi and their language. They can be dealt with under three rubrics. Social change affected conceptions of and criteria for priyayi status, the nature of social and linguistic interaction between priyayi and non-priyayi, and (apparently) the ways priyayi family members evaluated their relations with and spoke to each other. All resulted indirectly from the introduction and gradual acceptance of a rationalization of traditional governmental structure, a move towards a democratization of social interaction, and at least a partial shift from aspects of status (high/low) to formality (intimacy/nonintimacy) in social relations as salient criteria for choice of speech style.

The "purification" of Javanese

The Hollands Inlandsche Scholen (HIS) established in 1914 offered many children of priyayi families an opportunity to learn from and about the West. As early as 1875, when a medical school opened in Java, it became possible for priyayi to procure a western-style education in the Dutch language from their colonizers. The value of this was quickly perceived by many priyayi, and in the early twentieth century many nobles of the Surakartan court received advanced educations both in Java and the Netherlands. As western education became a new symbol of and avenue to elite status, Pakubuwana X did what he could to see that less well-off nobility had access to it, subsidizing the school costs for their children. The name of the school near the palace attended by children of priyayi court circles—the *Sana Kasatriyan*, "place for (the teaching of) qualities of nobility"—echoed traditional values, but the content of studies there were almost entirely western. Dutch was the language of instruction, to which Javanese was subordinated as a secondary language studied under Dutch instructors.

The result was that an early and immediate threat to the primacy of the traditional priyayi came from within the priyayi class itself. The Dutch did not just erode the traditional patrimonial system by taking over the king's land, but also indirectly created a new sort of native elite which used their language and enjoyed an achieved status different from that traditionally ascribed to priyayi. This was a focal point for tension between a literati and a new intelligentsia (Geertz 1960:235-8), and a split between what Scherer calls conservative and progressive priyayi.[14] With the growth of a Western-educated elite and the shift to a rationalized bureaucratic style of government, priyayi who were educated in the traditional manner as apprentices in government offices lacked newer skills and languages (Dutch and Malay), and found themselves in a new sort of competitive situation.

> In the Surakarta *kepatihan* [the government's central office], newly graduated students from the HIS who could scarcely even sit properly on the floor, and who could not speak good Javanese nor write it well, were immediately appointed to jobs with a salary of 10 guilders a month, and they received a monthly bonus of 15 guilders in recognition of their HIS diploma. . . . You can just imagine the feelings of assistant clerks who had been in service for 10 years, but who could only speak Javanese. (Jasawidagda 1957:48, quoted and translated in Quinn 1983:18)

Priyayi who "could not speak good Javanese" were doubtless able to manage little more than some variety of madya, which served them as "polite" language as it did non-priyayi: it was a non-ngoko speech style. Hostility towards them as a threat to traditional rights and values had for a symbolic focus progressive priyayi use of foreign languages at the expense of Javanese, and their misuse or neglect of proper Javanese linguistic etiquette. As a result the

---

[14]Scherer 1975 cited in Quinn 1983:16. More detail on this process is provided in both sources; see also Sutherland 1979. Note that Scherer's use of the term "conservative" differs fundamentally from mine in discussion below of members of the present day speech community.

Javanese language and in all likelihood the speech level system, quintessentially the province of "true" priyayi, became a special symbol of the traditional elite status, and in all probability underwent a compensatory prescriptive elevation. By 1912, and possibly much earlier, "something was amiss with Javanese" (Jasawidagda 1957:46, quoted in Quinn 1983:17) as the result of a new linguistic heterogeneity in a formerly homogeneous (but hierarchical) subcommunity.

The consequences of a heightened self-consciousness among traditional priyayi are not difficult to imagine; an enhanced awareness of what set them off not just from commoners but also from the new breed of literate elite would have led to new prescriptive rigor in evaluation and use of the speech levels. If, as Jasawidagda reports (1957:49, quoted and translated in Quinn 1983:18), improper use of the levels elicited ridicule and abuse from traditional priyayi, the compensatory reaction would have been to "reform" or restandardize speech level use. And if madya was the most commonly known non-ngoko speech style, a kind linguistic common denominator as far as non-ngoko speech was concerned, and was used among the Western-educated priyayi as their "polite" Javanese, it would therefore have been a natural target of criticism. Madya would appear then less an intermediate sort of speech style and more a sloppy, substandard non-ngoko style spoken by commoners and those literates who had not had a "proper" education.[15] If proper use of the speech levels became a symbol of traditional priyayi values and allegiance, then its use within that group would have been correspondingly purified, quite possibly resulting in a revaluation of the status of madya as a social dialect, rather than an intermediate register. This is how conservative priyayi in Surakarta today evaluate it.

---

[15]One wonders, in fact, if Padmasusastra's *Urapsari* might have been written in normative reaction to this incipient change, to assert traditional speech patterns and values, and teach them to modern priyayi who "didn't know any better." It may be significant in this respect that as early as 1911, Rinkes noted in the introduction to Padmasusastra's *Layang Basa Solo* that this little textbook was needed to replace Winter's *Javaansche Zamenspraken*, which was already outdated.

One symptom of the speech levels' symbolic value as a social dialect used by those with traditional good breeding and awareness of proper (i.e., traditional) status distinctions, was the founding in 1917 of a group called *Djawa Dipa*, whose progressive elite members wished to abolish all non-ngoko forms of Javanese entirely (see Bonneff 1981). The polarization of the indigenous elite on this linguistic issue can likewise be seen in the countermovement started in response by members of the traditional courtly circles, a group called *Krama Déwa* which espoused the policy that krama should be maintained at the expense of ngoko. The latter policy was even less feasible than the former, but as a symbolic reaction to incipient modernization its very existence suggests the new normative impetus being brought to bear on the speech levels, and on madya in particular. Like other traditional priyayi responses to Dutch encroachment, this was a symbolic move, adopted in lieu of more direct responses.

Changes in Surakartan society

Progressive priyayi hardly did away with the speech levels, but did transform them by instigating fundamental changes in patterns of social interaction between elite and nonelite. Nationalistic and incipiently democratic ideals were being propounded by the anticolonial groups which had developed by 1900, and these were to a significant degree well-received and fostered among members of the small but influential progressive native elite. Many priyayi returned from Dutch schools outside the kingdom to find that their own hopes for a united noncolonial archipelago were consonant with nationalistic ideas spreading among their newfound anticolonial compatriots.

In the 1920s and 1930s forward-looking members of this same elite, upheld by a foreign colonialist power and largely isolated from the "little people," were beginning to form a receptive audience for radical ideas of independence and sociopolitical reform. The western idea of *liberté* came to be associated with *egalité*, and the notion of social equality (at least in the abstract) became widespread and increasingly acceptable among the more progressive elite. In linguistic interaction the idea came gradually to be implemented through a kind of lip service. Comparison of conservative priyayi reports on usage with the evidence of written sources indicates that some time after the turn of the century, priyayi began to make increasingly frequent use of madya in symmetric exchange with nonintimate commoners.

The context of appropriate use of madya speech styles thus changed in important ways. It came to be exchanged more or less symmetrically; whether or not relatively lower and higher styles were used, they were all distinguished as madya by distinct madya alternants. And it was being used to persons who by traditional Surakartan standards were markedly inferior to priyayi of any rank. The use of non-ngoko language by priyayi to nonintimate inferiors conformed with new views of social interaction, and new principles for use of linguistic etiquette. To treat a commoner as an ostensible equal meant engaging that person in some symmetric pattern of speech level exchange; because non-priyayi typically did not control "proper" or standard krama, the non-ngoko speech styles commonly shared by priyayi and non-priyayi speech partners were styles of madya. Ngoko, the language exchanged by intimates, and given by superiors to inferiors, was totally unacceptable in the ears of priyayi from nonintimate commoners; for a priyayi to speak good krama and get madya back would be to effectively place that commoner in a higher status position than himself/herself, which was equally unthinkable. Madya was thus the only real alternative to traditional patterns of use.

Since the formal intermediacy of madya makes for a range of structurally allied but distinct substyles, total reciprocity was by no means inevitable. If nothing else, asymmetric exchange of ngoko and krama elements in madya, and perhaps the use of some krama inggil by commoner for reference to priyayi, would mark the social gap between speech partners. Reports by older priyayi informants indicate this change in usage patterns was certainly complete by the mid-1930s, and possibly earlier. Even today a few old priyayi, something of an embarrassment to other priyayi, still begrudge commoners madya, and insist on speaking ngoko. But clearly the trend had started in the 1920s, if not sooner, and most of my older informants, who were born late in the first or early in the second decade of this century, remember the transition and themselves grew up using this speech pattern with commoners.

As early as 1924, it is clear that nobles of no less a rank than prince of the realm had adopted the newer style.

Djojohadikusumo, himself of high nobility, writes in his memoirs of Kusumayuddha, a son of Pakubuwana X:

> Although he was a *pangéran* he was not an arrogant snob. I noted this above all in his relations with the village people. He would always call the head of a village *Pak Lurah* (thus not the usual lurah) and also use Madya-Javanese (not Ngoko, or low-Javanese). . . . (1970:59)

This observation provides particularly valuable clues to the general sociolinguistic situation as well as one prince's usage. That Djojohadikusumo found such usage remarkable in the first place indicates that it was not typical, and implies that at least some priyayi were still commonly using ngoko to non-priyayi. Given his own egalitarian political sentiments, his phrase "arrogant snob" speaks as much for a progressive social group as for the author himself, and carries an implicit criticism of those who maintained traditional use of "low" Javanese to their traditional inferiors.

Such speech level use by a prince of the realm is notable not just because it indicates the degree to which the new usage and views of noble/commoner social relations had penetrated the highest court circles; it shows that powerful forces within the traditional priyayi community were being exerted to bring about social change. A prince's subordinate—and that would be almost anyone—who persisted in using ngoko in situations like those in which the prince used madya would be indirectly placing himself/herself above the prince, or at least asserting his/her own view of the nature of the relation over the prince's. By adopting new patterns, high traditional elite could exert indirect but significant pressure on their inferiors to do the same.

This shift in outgroup madya usage doubtless affected ingroup madya usage, and may have been largely responsible for the increasing abstinence from use of madya to shade markings of status differences with other priyayi. It is clear that nowadays conservative priyayi do not use madya as an ingroup code; they report unequivocally and unanimously that they use madya with members of what they conceive of as their outgroup. Observation of and participation in language use with members of families of these speakers over a period of eighteen months corroborates their statements.

It is crucial for an understanding of the dynamics of priyayi speech level usage to recognize that madya is for conservative speakers a social dialect, one which they use only to people they consider to be uneducated or at least improperly educated, and not members of their group. This attitude and its linguistic correlate are major foci of the next two chapters. The functional ambiguity of madya as substandard commoner versus priyayi usage would obviously have been affected, as it became the norm for interaction between priyayi and nonintimate commoner, especially in symmetric exchange in highly stereotyped, and usually transient relations.

The upshot would be that priyayi might find themselves using madya speech styles to nonintimate commoner and to intimate superior or inferior; the significance of madya thus shifted, becoming for traditional priyayi then what it is for conservative priyayi now: an outgroup code used to outgroup speakers, rather than peers or superiors. This attitude appears clearly in conservative speakers' evaluations of sentences.

Changing priyayi social relations

A final relevant aspect of rapid social change during this period involves the nature of relations in the priyayi community itself. If solidarity was in fact being promoted within the traditional Surakartan elite, it may well be that norms for use of speech levels were simultaneously changing among priyayi. There are differences between observed and reported conservative priyayi usage on one hand, and their reports of usage among their parents and grandparents on the other, which indicate that a shift has occurred in the aspects of social relations marked in speech. Criteria most salient for speech level use have shifted from status differences to intimacy, from positional to personal aspects of social relations.

This appears most clearly in changing patterns of familial use. Where the large majority of conservative priyayi wives I knew speak to their husbands in ngoko with deferentials for reference to him, all but one reported that their own mothers spoke to their husbands in krama with deferentials. I did not observe or hear reports of informants, informants' relatives, or acquaintances using madya in asymmetric exchange with spouse, parent, offspring, or sibling. Whether or not their reports on the past are colored by sociolinguistic prejudice, a comparison of their own usage with examples in the literature indicates that there has been a shift from non-ngoko styles—krama or madya—to ngoko styles in such situations.

If this change was occasioned by changes in their social milieu, it likewise marks a shift in the dynamics and perceptions of personal relations which resemble those reported by Brown and Gilman for contemporary Western Europe, where intimacy is generally ascendant over status differences for a choice between T and V forms. What persons share has become more important for determining choice of a pattern of speech level exchange than what distinguishes them. Insofar as a shift appears to taken place away from asymmetric use of krama (or madya?) and ngoko between (for instance) siblings, affines, and other relations, it could be that madya fell out of use as an ingroup priyayi register. Degrees of status differentiation marked by use of madya have themselves lost relevance in day-to-day priyayi interaction. Several older priyayi parents and grandparents complained to me that their children and grandchildren preferred to speak to each other in ngoko, as if they were just ordinary people, when they should show proper respect for their elder siblings by using krama.

I am suggesting then, that a formal simplification of priyayi repertoires in at least some ingroup contexts resulted from changes in the ways priyayi evaluated social relations with each other. This may have complemented the general shift in usage to commoners which made madya inappropriate for speaking to another priyayi. The shift from ngoko to madya in priyayi address of commoners would have simultaneously resolved the social-functional tension which had previously accrued to the use of madya. A priyayi woman (for instance) who found herself obliged to address her husband in substantially the same way she spoke to a market seller would feel the brunt of that double significance and react accordingly. To avoid talking to her husband "as if he were a pedicab driver," as one conservative priyayi lady retorted to my suggestion that she might speak in this way, would be to avoid speaking madya. This would likewise be to avoid the implication that those she addressed with madya—commoner pedicab driver and priyayi husband—were somehow the same.

When the balance between disparate social significances of madya in the Surakartan speech community was upset by relatively sudden social change within and outside the traditional elite, so speech level usage between priyayi changed. These three aspects of change may have had complementary effects on linguistic etiquette used in different situations within different segments of the priyayi community, conspiring, as it were, to create new patterns of use and attitudes to use. But similar ambiguities still accrue to use of madya, as will be shown in the description of ongoing language change and variation in modern Surakarta in chapters 3 and 4.

SURAKARTA NOW

Surakarta is known as the city that never sleeps, but for all of that is more of a sleepy town than Jakarta, Semarang, or even Yogyakarta. Although its population has grown to about 450,000, and it is a district capital, it has less of the feeling of modernity than does Yogyakarta, the city of students. Like all Indonesian cities, Surakarta is growing, and that means it is sprawling. The houses of some of my older acquaintances which adjoined rice fields fifty years ago now look out on a six-lane highway, complete with street lights and traffic lights, one of the major channels of traffic to and from the west.

Reminders of the old days are present everywhere, although the relatively undeveloped tourist trade (again compared with Yogyakarta) makes it necessary to look a little bit harder to see them. Areas in the old part of town all take their names from the noble families which once lived there, and behind some of the dirty whitewashed walls in the crowded residential blocks (*kampung*) still stand some of the traditional houses in which those nobles lived. Many have fallen into disrepair because costs are rising, and owners often cannot afford to maintain them properly. Many have been sold to wealthy merchants. Living in a traditional house with an open front requires enough surrounding space to preserve some measure of privacy, and this too is increasingly impractical in a city located in one of the most densely populated nonurban areas of the world.

Social and political change has created pervasive and powerful pressures on the traditional priyayi elite to adapt to a new sort of urban society, and the most important aspects of this transformation are relevant for an understanding of differences between speech level use by different generations of priyayi speakers today. The impact of modernization on Surakartan priyayi will be treated here in three respects, as having affected the size and cohesiveness of the traditional priyayi community, conceptions of elite status, and the numbers and functions of languages in the urban speech community. The traditional priyayi community has diminished in size, the new priyayi elite is less clearly distinguished as part of a class more permeable to upwardly mobile non-priyayi, and Javanese, which priyayi traditionally standardized, has been relegated to an essentially secondary role in governmental and official contexts.

The priyayi community in transition

By no means is the term "priyayi" used nowadays exclusively or even primarily with the meaning "persons close to the king." During and after the Japanese occupation many priyayi left Surakarta to serve in the armed forces, or to participate in the *pro tem* local government for the provisional republic. The revolution brought Surakarta quite abruptly into a national context and a new political reality. What had been a unique province of traditional Javanese culture became a subprovincial center in one of twenty-seven provinces, governed via the provincial capital in Semarang from the new center of power: the national capital of Jakarta.

Since the establishment of the national government, power dynamics have largely superseded and to an extent subsumed the traditional elite of Surakarta. After the revolution the priyayi class became a major source of educated professionals and experienced bureaucrats, and so its members have had an important place in forming the new state apparatus, and organizing and leading the new nation. The sultan of Yogyakarta, a leader in the revolution and former vice-president of the republic, is probably the best example of an old elite member who entered the struggle on the side of the nationalists, and so became part of the new elite which holds real power in modern Indonesia. To this day, the sultan is still administrative head of the area around Yogyakarta.

But post-revolutionary Surakarta saw an all but total separation of the traditional elite from the royal houses. Members of that elite who had fought in the revolution found new roles in the ongoing process of nation building; they had lost symbolic supremacy in the Javanese community, but gained political power at the panethnic, national level. No longer Javanese nobles ruling by right of descent, they became (at least within the nationalistic ideology) servants of the people within a democratic republic. Traditional priyayi have maintained or lost their membership in the new elite class in proportion to their willingness and ability to use their education and experience to find new niches in the national framework.

Before the war a priyayi served the king; now the priyayi image is less of the royal servant than a "federal employee" (*pegawai negeri* in Indonesian). The prestige attached to government work remains, even if the bureaucracy is vast, complex, and ethnically heterogeneous. Rising in rank nowadays still means getting closer to the center, but now that center is Jakarta, and young priyayi continue to look away from Surakarta. Put briefly, the traditional elite have been leaving Surakarta in droves since the mid 1940s, and most of them have moved to Jakarta.

A simple and effective way of demonstrating this is to cite the circumstances of one extended priyayi family. One of my informants is a retired English instructor at a teacher training school in Surakarta, a priyayi in the traditional sense who still works part-time at the Mangkunegaran palace. He has made a hobby of tracing the whereabouts of his and his wife's extended families as far back as four generations. By making contacts over a period of three or four years, he procured the names and addresses of about three hundred relatives. In table 2.1 can be seen general trends in changes of residence among these descendants of traditional priyayi.

Obviously there has been a flow of priyayi to larger cities; Jakarta is the home of almost half of them, more than Surakarta and Semarang combined. Less than one in eight lives in Surakarta. This same pattern is reflected in residences of members of the other families with whom I became acquainted while living in Surakarta.

Of the ten other families for which I have complete data on whereabouts of offspring—a total of 66—42 percent are in Jakarta, 28 percent are in Surakarta, 13 percent are in Yogyakarta, and 15 percent are elsewhere. Moreover, the number living in Surakarta in all probability will decrease in the next few years, as a significant number of those living in Surakarta who are still in high school and grade school will, like their elder siblings, continue their studies or work elsewhere in a few years' time.

Table 2.1
RESIDENCES OF AN EXTENDED PRIYAYI FAMILY

Location	Number of Residents	Percent of Total
Jakarta	123	41.0
Surakarta	7	12.3
Semarang	35	11.6
Surabaya	33	11.0
Bandung	17	5.6
Madiun	9	3.0
Other*	45	15.0
Total	300	99.5

*This includes residents in Sumatra, the outer islands, and abroad; no more than two are in any one location.

Changing notions of "priyayi" status

Gradual change in the conception of priyayi-hood, and the meaning of the word "priyayi," can be glimpsed in the ways the word is used in ordinary day-to-day language; these reflect very real changes in what traditional priyayi think "being a priyayi" means.

I was struck by the way Javanese would sometimes refer to me as the "priyayi from America" or the "foreign priyayi"; these are descriptions which, given the traditional definition of priyayi I had learned, seemed somewhat ludicrous if not contradictory in terms. I usually wrote it off to an inclination to compliment me because I was, however clumsily, speaking polite Javanese and trying to "act like a priyayi" (*mriyayèni*). It turned out, though, that this was not always hyperbole; for many Javanese, elite and otherwise, it seems rather that the word "priyayi" has become, like the word "gentleman" in English, a term of respect which no longer necessarily implies anything about the descent (noble or otherwise) of the person so referred to. It indicates something about a person's manners, bearing, and occupation, rather than about his descent. Such use of the word is definitely nonliteral for older traditional elite members, but not for their offspring.

One of my young informants, himself a priyayi in the traditional sense of the word, told me a story about visiting an uncle (his father's brother, an ex-ambassador) who lived in a far suburb of Jakarta. His uncle had hired a new chauffeur, and my informant asked where the chauffeur was from, referring to him as a *priyantun* (the krama equivalent of *priyayi*). As he related the incident to me:

> My uncle was silent a moment, and then said that a chauffeur is not fittingly called a priyayi; 'person' (ng:*wong*, k:*tiyang*) is fine. Well I just took it. But that's the problem, *Mas* [referring to me]. For me it's nothing, but as for my father and others of his generation, they're still very careful.

Criteria for membership in the class of persons designated by the word "priyayi" are becoming less clear-cut, and losing the implication of ascribed status it still carries for some members of older generations. If the new political arena in which the old elite find themselves is enormous compared with the old, for that same reason they are working within a much more heterogeneous group. This is true in Surakarta, even if in that city as in no other (with the possible exception of Yogyakarta) the word "priyayi" carries particularly traditional connotations.

So the younger members of traditionally priyayi families are assimilating into a new social milieu and adopting different sorts of criteria for gauging their social status in relation to others. These are the younger people who count as modern speakers and who, I will argue below, have their own views on who their peers are, and how linguistic politesse is to be used when speaking Javanese.

Languages in change since the revolution

Changes in knowledge and use of languages in Javanese society generally, and in Surakartan society particularly, have been both obvious and subtle. Changes in the status of the non-native languages used before the revolution—Dutch and Malay—certainly cannot be passed over entirely. By the 1920s Dutch had become a widely-known language among priyayi as the medium of the schools and Westernization. It was commonly used in priyayi circles (and in other elite subcommunities in Indonesia) as an ingroup code, particularly when topics of discussion became intellectual. Within the elite group, it also came to be used as the code largely free of the socially significant distinctions embodied in the speech levels of Javanese; thus it was a code which allowed speakers to "opt-out" of a choice between speech levels when dealing with another priyayi. This was not uncommon among the elite whose own bias in the direction of westernism often made the use of Dutch much more congenial than Javanese.

Malay too became a language of urban speakers, and although it was not accorded in any way the same prestige as Dutch, it also functioned as an avoidance code, especially for those who did not know Dutch. In a treatise on etiquette, Sastrawirya offered a rule of thumb for dealing with people with whom one's relative status was unclear:

> If you are asked a question by someone, what language should your answer be in? Use the language of the questioner. But if you cannot speak that language, use Malay. (1932:60-61)

The availability of these two languages as linguistic vehicles made for indeterminancy or free play in usage which had previously been unavailable. In this sense Dutch was not only a new means for communicating new ideas, but also permitted communication largely free of precise, unambiguous marks of status differences.

The fate of the two languages was very different: when the Japanese occupied Indonesia they banned Dutch, and although it has to a limited extent been maintained as an ingroup language of the prewar elite, it still carries the stigma of the colonialist elite in larger society.[16]

Malay has evolved into Bahasa Indonesia, the national language, which has taken over all the functions of Dutch originally served and much more: it is the language of offices (or at least of officials acting in official capacities), of schools, and the vast majority of the media. It is the language of intellectual discourse, the mushrooming "national" culture of Indonesia, the vehicle of what is modern: movies, novels, most pop songs, television, are all provinces of the national language. The growth and acceptance of Indonesian by people of all strata of Indonesian society, and the rapidity with which it is spreading even to the rural areas, is one of the more remarkable aspects of the process of nation-building in the archipelago. (See on this point Alisjahbana 1971.)

Between two Javanese, and two Surakartans in particular, Indonesian offers the same option Dutch and Malay did, without identification with an extra-national, colonial power. In the pre-war days the use of Malay between Javanese carried a feeling of stiffness, formality, a lack of ethnic identification and intimacy. It wasn't *luwes* ('supple'). Even by the late 1950s, hardly more than a decade after the declaration of independence, this change was remarked on by one Javanese observer:

> When I was young . . . if I heard people speaking Malay I felt it was as if they were treating each other as different kinds of people; it lacked intimacy, they weren't 'treating the other as a sibling' [*sumanak*]. Unless one was talking with a friend of the same level, using krama was too formal, ngoko was too coarse, and in that situation one would use Malay. Is it still that way? Not at all. (Prawirohardja 1958:32)

As early as 1958, Indonesian had become widely accepted as a language appropriate between two Indonesians who might also be

---

[16]See on this point Tanner 1967. It is still quite common for some of my older informants when talking with older friends to freely intersperse their Javanese with Dutch.

Javanese. Indonesian is less of a non-Javanese language and more of a national language.

The introduction of Indonesian to the repertoire of virtually all urban Javanese is in large part responsible for change in and descreasing knowledge of the speech levels of Javanese. It has taken on official functions and offers a simpler way of mediating relationships with other people. As almost everyone (including youngsters themselves) commonly say, these days young people don't use polished Javanese as much—they run to Indonesian. The impact of Indonesian on the use and knowledge of Javanese is an acknowledged and documented phenomenon in modern Java (see Wolff and Poedjosoedarmo 1982). Less commented on but no less profound are changes in speech level use which have indirectly resulted from changes in social contexts of use. With the transformation of the social milieu, two major kinds of linguistic changes have come about, corollaries, as it were, of the changes in the elite class.

First, members of the traditional priyayi class are no longer universally recognized as the class of speakers who use what counts as "good" language. While they are commonly acknowledged to be the "best" speakers of "good" non-ngoko Javanese, it no longer follows that they are necessarily models whom others are particularly concerned to emulate. Secondly, the collapse of traditional elite society has resulted in new kinds of criteria for determinating relative status as marked in speech.

It is oversimplistic to say that the speech levels of Javanese are dead, or even that, taken as a whole, they are moribund. Rather, they are undergoing radical changes and simplification resulting from changes in the community in which they are used. Non-priyayi use of the speech levels has developed independently of elite usage, resulting in (among other things) the gradual appropriation of formerly highly deferential forms which once were the province of priyayi alone. As one priyayi wrote in the late 1950s:

> Probably all the old-time priyayi would feel amazement and dislike if they heard market sellers or village people talking. . . . Market sellers who once used to use madya or plain ngoko are using krama, and even krama inggil. (Seto 1958:40)

According to older priyayi, it is wrong for a commoner to use krama inggil for a commoner, but they have to admit that it is usual: they have no power to prevent it from becoming the norm. Such errors in usage are not just 'wrong' (*salah*), these priyayi say, but are 'errors which are widely accepted' (*salah kaprah*), not felt to be errors as such by the vast majority of speakers. The number of *salah kaprah* in Javanese today (say older conservative priyayi) are numerous; some are discussed in chapters 3 and 4. The point here is that members of the traditional priyayi speech community must accept such usage whether or not they adopt it themselves.

Priyayi's loss of actual status as definers of proper usage leads them to accept if not use new criteria for speech level use in the larger community. The extended network of familial and professional interrelations between members of the elite has broken down to the point that only the members of the innermost circles of nobility really continue to make use of them in the old way. Status within the royal government, purely symbolic, and basically immaterial to status in society at large. It is ignored by many of even high noble descent.

Status within society is still of primary importance in determining proper linguistic usage, but now depends more on occupation in a different society, and on phyical age. Affinal and *awu* relations likewise are increasingly irrelevant to use of the speech levels among the contemporary elite in dealing with members of their own group and others. To a great extent, the ascendant parameters supplanting them are physical age and familiarity within a relation.

> Now the use of language depends only on age and occupation. It is not like the old era when one had to pay attention to whether [the alter was] *Radèn, Radèn Mas*,[17] and so on. (Seto 1958:49)

Many younger priyayi are not as conscious of any special status they have as standardizers of a language, or holders of special social or linguistic privilege. Linguistic change which reflects this far-reaching, unconscious, and deep-seated transition are the foci of the next two chapters.

---

[17]*Radèn* and *Radèn Mas* are priyayi descent titles.

3

STRUCTURES AND FUNCTIONS OF SPEECH STYLES

Chapter 2 provided general sociohistorical and linguistic background, a sense of living priyayi's ties with the Javanese past and Indonesian present to which the labels "conservative" and "modern" are intended to allude. We consider here particulars of conservative and modern priyayi linguistic etiquette: the structurally distinct styles which make up speech level repertoires, and the ways priyayi use and evaluate use of the speech levels. This chapter deals primarily with the structure of ngoko and krama speech styles, and with speakers' descriptions and conceptions of the social functions of ngoko, krama, and madya. Discussion of structural and functional aspects of the speech level system is needed to describe variation in the structure of madya speech styles dealt with in chapter 4.

The first part of this chapter deals with variation and change in priyayi use of ngoko and krama speech styles: the range of acceptable patterned combinations of lexical alternants—ngoko, krama, and krama inggil—which make up parts of their repertoires. Inferences about change in the structure of priyayi repertoires are difficult to draw, because there are basic discrepancies between informants' evaluations of examples and descriptions found in the literature. Nonetheless a picture can be developed of contrasts between priyayi and non-priyayi repertoires in contemporary Surakarta. At the same time, the range of structurally interstitial, functionally ambiguous madya speech styles can be preliminarily delimited by determining the "lower" limits to krama styles, and "upper" limits to ngoko styles, since these are also the boundaries to variation in madya speech.

Structurally distinct styles which make up parts of priyayi repertoires will be treated in the second section as objects of speakers' talk about talk, their evaluations of styles' social significances in use. It will be shown that patterns can be found in speakers' classifications of examples which reveal social attitudes toward language use and users, and that these patterns of contrast provide a first basis for classifying priyayi speakers as "conservative" and "modern." The characteristics of examples which different speakers find salient when they identify usage point to more general views of the nature of linguistic interaction, and so also of social interactants. Recurring meanings of speakers' labels for examples of speech styles can be drawn out and dealt with as more than simply "native" (not "scientific") descriptions; these names for examples of linguistic conduct can be shown to presuppose a few basic, underlying classificatory criteria which can be abstracted from them and shown to reflect in turn contrasting socially based conceptions of etiquette.

This provides an entree into the nature of fundamentally different classificatory perspectives on madya, and a way of interpreting the particulars of variation in acceptability of examples of madya discussed at length in chapter 4. By treating madya here as a negatively defined rubric covering lexemes and speech styles, we assume operationally that structural variation within madya can be ignored in order to better understand its place in speech level systems.

THE STRUCTURE OF SENTENTIAL LEVEL REPERTOIRES

In the following description frequent mention is made of members of a paradigmatic set which cannot be ignored. Second person pronouns are especially important objects of and instruments for description because they make up the single most complex repertoire of ways of speaking of addressees, and do not really match up one-to-one with the speech styles (i.e., with unitary syntagmatic combinations of the other kinds of alternants). Choice of a second person pronoun can thus lend extra qualification or delicacy to a speaker's evaluation of a social relation with an addressee as marked in linguistic conduct.

This is one reason native speakers can regularly use personal pronouns as part of their metalinguistic vocabulary, as a means for talking about talk. To the most neutral sorts of questions about speech level use—for example, "How do you speak with X?" where

X is the name of an acquaintance, family member, or description of some hypothetical and "typical" speech partner—speakers typically respond with a specification of personal pronoun and nothing else.[1]

The special place of personal pronouns in this description can also be attributed to their unique species of referential meaning. Like titles, proper names, kin terms, and definite descriptions, personal pronouns can be used to speak of persons. But unlike all of these, they refer to persons by virtue of the role a person has as referent vis-a-vis the act of speech of which the pronoun is part. The meaning of "you" in English, for instance, is 'the person who is being addressed by the message containing this occasion of use of "you"'. So a description of different speech styles as combinations of ngoko, krama, and deferential krama inggil lexemes like those given below fails to capture finer, more subtle distinctions which are available when choosing a way to speak of a speech participant with a personal pronoun.

Further terminological complications stem from different uses of semi-technical labels—"ngoko," "krama," "krama inggil," and so on—by scholars and "naive" native speakers. All will be used here in the "standard" senses discussed above, and in their paradigmatic and syntagmatic senses alike. But a further qualification of their meaning must be made, since they can be used for syntagmatic patterns of sentential speech levels which are structurally allied, but also structurally distinct.

Syntagmatically, the labels "ngoko" and "krama" can be used to refer to particular, "standard" or "canonic" versions of ngoko or krama. But authors and "naive" speakers sometimes use these same terms to refer to other speech styles which they count as "kinds" of ngoko or krama because they share some structural trait(s) with the "regular" version of each, but are nonetheless distinct in some other respect(s). So, "ngoko" and "krama" can be used syntagmatically as umbrella terms for several related but distinct speech styles. With an awareness of these added terminological ambiguities, "ngoko" and "krama" can be used with appropriate qualifications on one hand as cover terms for

---

[1]Bax (1974:20) similarly reports that peasants he studied would regularly explain differences between the levels by alluding to various personal pronouns.

related varieties of speech styles which share such traits, and on the other for what can be thought of as the "ordinary" or "plain" varieties of each.

Varieties of ngoko

The term "ngoko," then, is regularly used in the literature to speak of the "basic" language: speech made up entirely of ngoko lexemes. Other styles of ngoko contain ngoko lexemes, but are nonetheless distinct due to the presence of other types of non-ngoko lexemes, krama or krama inggil. As Walbeehm (1897:29) points out, it is misleading to use the term "ngoko" as if it names a speech style which is on the same footing with non-ngoko speech styles. Ngoko is the basic language itself, upon which the edifice of linguistic politesse is erected.

Most traditional treatments like those cited in chapter 2 deal with ngoko speech in terms of three categories:

1. ngoko: all ngoko words and affixes
2. *antyabasa*: ngoko words and affixes, but deferentials used for reference to addressee
3. *basaantya*: ngoko with deferentials used for reference to addressee, but also certain krama words

The most crucial and ubiquitous features which distinguish "plain" ngoko from "polite" ngoko are alternations between second person pronouns. In ordinary ngoko, *kowé* ("you") is used together with the corresponding possessive suffix *-mu* and verbal prefix *kok-*.[2] In "polite" or "non-plain" ngoko speech the simple presence of some second person pronoun other than *kowé* will suffice to mark respect for an intimate addressee, and so set of a classificatorily relevant type of variation in language use.

Even the preliminary task of establishing just how these two putative types of polite ngoko called *basaantya* and *antyabasa* in the literature might be distinguished is problematic, since examples of polite ngoko used and judged as acceptable by speakers in contemporary Surakarta differ in some respects from

---

[2]A colloquial variant on this latter is *mbok-*.

examples found in the literature. Informants rejected examples of the style called *basaantya* taken from written sources, and I never observed any occasion of use of ngoko by any speaker fitting descriptions of it. It does happen, however, that polite ngoko speech contains krama lexemes, but this style can be shown to be functionally distinct from *basaantya*. As will be shown, this latter type of ngoko is a subvariant of the style called *antyabasa* in the literature, and to further complicate matters is variably acceptable among priyayi and non-priyayi.

Antyabasa

We can consider first the structure of examples of polite ngoko unanimously accepted and usable by informants; these conform with descriptions of *antyabasa* in the literature. All informants, priyayi and non-priyayi, modern and conservative, accepted examples of ngoko containing krama inggil deferentials for reference to a respected addressee. Several informants spontaneously noted that this version of ngoko always involves a second person pronoun other than *kowé*, either *panjenengan* or *sliramu* or *kang s(a)lira*, a somewhat literary variant on the latter).

On this much the informants' judgments of examples agree with descriptions in the literature, but the situation is more complex for two reasons. It does happen that krama lexemes are used in polite ngoko speech by some speakers, but they function then only as supplementary or surrogate deferentials. They are used in accordance with structural rules and for social functions which ally the style in which they appear with *antyabasa*, rather than *basaantya*.

The crucial restriction on krama words used in ngoko is that they be used only for reference to a deferred-to person, and have no krama inggil equivalent. They thus function in place of a deferential, standing as a non-ngoko surrogate for a nonexistent krama inggil forms, as a supplement to the deferential vocabulary. The structure of the paradigmatic set of alternants from which a krama lexeme might be chosen is thus directly relevant to the possibility of its use in ngoko speech.

Geertz noted that krama lexemes could be used in ngoko speech styles but did not mention this crucial structural constraint, writing only that there is an interstitial polite ngoko style set off by the presence of krama lexemes:

> As these krama words employed in ngoko sentences occur in the same meanings as the special honorifics, they might be called "low honorifics," in contrast to the special "high honorifics," such as *dhahar, panjenengan*.³ (1960:253)

Uhlenbeck has pointed out the crucial qualification:

> It is true that *krama*-terms may function as honorifics, but this is possible only in the absence of a corresponding *krama inggil*-term. This means that as honorifics *krama*-terms fulfill only a supplementary function. (1978:309)

Thirty informants' evaluations of examples of ngoko examples containing non-ngoko lexemes indicate that Geertz was partially correct in calling polite ngoko something of a "priyayi specialty" (1960:253), since this special use of krama lexemes appears to be restricted to priyayi repertoires. All priyayi and non-priyayi speakers accept and use examples of polite ngoko with deferentials, but the acceptability and use of supplementary deferential krama covaries with status of a speaker as a priyayi (in the traditional sense of the word). Both modern and conservative speakers use krama lexemes to supplement the deferential vocabulary when speaking ngoko, and in this respect no variation exists

---

³As will be shown below, *panjenengan* does not count as a "high honorific form" among contemporary Surakartan priyayi; it is the second person pronoun normally used in krama. It is difficult to evaluate Geertz's description because there are probably real differences between speech level usage in Modjokuto in the 1950s and Surakarta in 1979 and 1980. Possibly (as Geertz reports) *sampéyan* was used in ngoko in Modjokuto, and likewise in Surakarta during an earlier era. To complicate matters, it appears that use of *sliramu*, discussed above, is restricted to such ngoko speech, but that its use may vary in the community. For further discussion see Errington 1988 and sources cited there.

between their speech level use. Evaluations of ngoko sentences which contain the krama word for 'stand watch' *njagi* (as in sentences 1 and 4 below) rather than its ngoko equivalent *njaga* (as in sentences 2 and 3 below) show this variation quite clearly. (In these and other examples of ngoko speech, krama lexemes are italicized.)

1. *Panjenengan*, ta, sing arep *njagi*?

2. *Panjenengan*, ta, sing arep njaga?

3. Bapak, ta, sing arep njaga?

4. Bapak, ta, sing arep *njagi*?
   Oh, so you're the one who's going to stand watch?

One and 4 were accepted by all priyayi informants save one younger "modern" informant (see below), whereas all non-priyayi informants rejected (1) and (4), most spontaneously indicating that one had to use the ngoko word instead.

In sentences 1 and 2 the addressee is referred to with the personal pronoun *panjenengan*, but in sentences 3 and 4 the kin term *Bapak*, glossable as "father," is used. It is indefinite with respect to the relative status of addressee (save as an adult male). Contrasts in speakers' evaluations of these four sentences show first that krama lexemes are not obligatorily used in polite ngoko as are "regular" deferentials, and second that choice of term of reference for addressee is a relatively crucial marker of social relation in linguistic conduct. *Panjenengan* alone as in sentence 2 marks the sentence as polite ngoko, and renders use of *njagi* supplementary. "Plain" ngoko kowé, on the other hand, could never be used together with njagi. Priyayi reported that sentence 1 was acceptable, and for some, 'normal' (*biasa*) polite ngoko. If a speaker chooses a kin term, such as *Bapak* in (3) and (4), rather than a personal pronoun to refer to an addressee, he/she does not explicitly mark deference in a term of address and then, priyayi informants reported, it is particularly felicitous to use *njagi* as an explicit marker of deference. Independently of any actual or hypothetical context of use, eight of these priyayi speakers noted that example 4 was more deferential in comparison with (3) than was example 2 in comparison with (1).

So acceptability of krama lexemes as surrogate krama inggil in ngoko speech vocabulary varies in the Surakartan community, but the use of deferentials in polite ngoko speech does not. The special use of krama words makes available for priyayi an added degree of refinement and flexibility in speech level use.

The status of basaantya

The major question regarding the style of ngoko called *basaantya* is not whether it is in use now—it is not—but whether it has ever been widely used within or outside priyayi circles. No example of such usage has ever been observed by myself or (apparently) by other researchers (see Poedjosoedarmo 1968, Wolff and Poedjosoedarmo 1982). In an effort to find cases of *basaantya* which are (or at least were) indubitably acceptable, I borrowed examples from Padmasusastra's *Serat Urapsari* (1896:21), numbers 5 to 7 below, and Poedjosoedarmo's description (1968:15), example 8. (Krama words and their glosses are italicized.)

5. Nanging aku ora *saged* mesthekaké *angsalé* sing *saé*.
   But I *can*not guarantee (we'll) *get good* ones.

6. Sa*sumerep*ku ana *tiga*.
   As far as I *know*, there are *three*.

7. Takdandan *rumiyin*.
   I'll dress *right away*.

8. Iki anak *kula* Tini sing takaturaké mau.
   This is *my* child Tini I told [deferential] you about just now.

There is implicit disagreement even between these two sources: Poedjosoedarmo's example contains the krama first person pronoun *kula* which Padmasusastra excludes from all varieties of ngoko.[4] No informant—young or old, conservative or modern, priyayi or non-priyayi—accepted any of these examples, finding them pragmatically uninterpretable.[5]

One can plausibly conclude, then, that this style may never have been in common use, and has continued to be mentioned in the literature largely by virtue of the prestige accorded early prescriptive sources. If this style was in fact in use at one time (presumably among priyayi) then its loss as a means of shading the social meanings of polite ngoko (intimate, but deferential) can be taken as an indication of decreasing relevance of such distinctions for mediating social relations through speech. And in this case, the loss would complement the apparent loss of madya as an ingroup priyayi style.

It might seem that contradictory statements have just been made, that examples of what was called *antyabasa*, as in statements 1 and 4, do not really differ from *basaantya*, as in statements 5 to 8, since they all contain krama lexemes. But this is not the case. First, the krama vocabulary in Padmasusastra's examples of *basaantya* is not restricted in referential range to persons, whereas it is limited in this way in *antyabasa*. In example 6, moreover, a krama word is used *sasumerepku* to refer to speaker, meaning something like "as far as I know." *Sumerep (=sumerap)* means "know, see," and has ngoko equivalents *ngerti*

---

[4]Padmasusastra's examples, unlike Poedjosoedarmo's, do not contain deferentials for reference to addressee, but Padmasusastra does specify that they must be so used whenever the occasion arises to mark respect for addressee. This is the basic motivation for the further refinement of adding krama items in the first place.

[5]But Bax (1974:23) reports that his informants accepted the example provided by Poedjosoedarmo (number 8 above), and examples of usage answering the description can be found in at least one relatively recent source, a novel entitled *Djodho kang pinasthi* (Sri Hadidjojo 1952:31). The son of a "little priyayi in the *désa*" speaks to his mother in this style, for example (with krama forms italicized): Mesthiné ya *naté* lara barang, nanging sarèhné *saged* diraosaké sadurungé *sanget*, lan *sumerep* tambané, mbok menawa dadi kemajuan *sawetawis*. 'Of course *sometimes* one would get sick, but since one *could feel* it before it was *very* great, and *know* the cause, probably it would be *a bit of* an improvement.'

and *weruh*, and a krama inggil equivalent *pirsa*. Now if in polite ngoko speech one may use krama words only as surrogate honorifics for a person deferred to and referred to, this use of *sumerep* should be subject to restrictions analogous to those governing use of krama inggil. Native speakers' reactions to sentences like 9 show this to be the case.

??9. Aku sing arep *njagi* mengko bengi.
I'm the one who's going to *stand watch* tonight.

The question marks are not to indicate that the sentence is ungrammatical or semantically uninterpretable, but that it is unacceptable by virtue of the social meaning which would accrue to its use. Priyayi evaluate the use of the krama word *njagi* for self-reference in ngoko as tantamount to using a krama inggil deferential for self-reference. In this way one implicitly places oneself "above" an addressee, and acts *digsura* ('haughty'), the most censured form of conduct. Sentence 9 is unacceptable, then, not because it is structurally wrong, but because it is rude. This demonstrates the functional unity of krama and krama inggil lexemes when used in ngoko, and indicates that krama words in the polite ngoko style called *antyabasa* in the literature function in different ways than do krama words which may have been used in the style called *basaantya*.

Native speakers' judgments of the sort given on the examples presented above indicate that their ngoko repertoires correspond in only a few respects with traditional descriptions; I never observed or heard a report of an occasion of use of any style of ngoko which answered descriptions of these unacceptable examples.

TYPES OF KRAMA

For the sake of conciseness, the features of krama speech styles which are specified in most written sources are given schematically below. We thus gloss over differences between those descriptions which are not directly relevant to the central focus here.

1. *mudhakrama*:	krama words with deferentials, and the
    ('young krama')	personal pronoun *panjenengan* for reference to addressee

2. *kramantara*:	krama words without deferentials for
    ('between	reference to addressee with the
    krama')	personal pronoun *panjenengan*

3. *werdakrama*:	krama words with ngoko affixes and no
    ('old krama')	deferentials for reference to addressee

4. krama inggil:	krama words with deferentials and either *sampéyandalem* or *panjenengandalem* as second person pronoun

But again there are basic problems in reconciling these older treatments with the modern situation. Comparison of the facts of contemporary use with examples from the older literature indicate that *sampéyan* was at one time the "regular" polite second person pronoun in the krama speech styles which otherwise answer these descriptions of *kramantara* and *mudhakrama*. *Sampéyan* has since been displaced in krama by the new pronoun *panjenengan*.[6] In contemporary Surakarta virtually all speakers use *sampéyan* only in varieties of madya speech.[7]

---

[6]The structure of personal pronominal repertoires have changed over the last century both in structure and function, but the details of such changes will be ignored here in favor of ad hoc characterizations which help to explain native speakers' reports of use. *Panjenengan* is the standard spelling of this form, and represents its regular or formal pronounciation. It has reduced, less formal variants *penjenengan* and *njenengan*, on which see chapter 4.

[7]It does still happen, however, that some old, conservative speakers will use *sampéyan* in varieties of krama answering the description of *kramantara*, although these speakers and the occasions on which they do this are not so common as to merit further consideration here. Wolff and Poedjosoedarmo report (1982:46) that in East Java *sampéyan* can be used in all speech styles.

The name of the style *mudhakrama* (lit. 'young krama') correctly indicates that deferentials are normatively used in krama speech by junior to elder, but the same speech style is normatively used by inferior to superior. This style is the basic style of polite expression, showing respect and perhaps social distance if used symmetrically. In comparison with *mudhakrama, kramantara* is a "lower" speech style, expressive of formality, politeness, but not deference.

According to several sources the speech style called "krama inggil" is distinguished from *mudhakrama* by a single crucial alternation between the second person pronouns *sampéy andalem* and *panjenengandalem* on one hand, and *panjenengan* on the other. This demonstrates the crucial role of pronominal alternations as markers of relative politeness of speech, and in this special case the term "krama inggil" is applied syntagmatically to a style distinguished solely by special second person pronouns.

Sampéyandalem is traditionally the form of address used to the king, and only to the king; it distinguishes the "highest," most deferential sort of Javanese there is. On the scale of language ranging from "lower" (less deferential) to "higher" (more deferential) speech, there exists "between" *sampéyandalem* and *panjenengan* an intermediate deferential second person pronoun, *panjenengandalem*, which has less formal (and perhaps more frequently used) variants *nandalem* and *ndandalem*. These latter were normatively used within the highest noble ranks to children of the king.

The differences in deferentiality which are marked with these alternants fit with the structure of krama speech styles in which they are used. *Panjenengan* may be used in krama speech with deferentials to those of high (but not the highest) status, or without deferentials to an addressee with whom one is in a formal relation but whose status is lower than or roughly equal to one's own. To use the "higher" pronoun *panjenengandalem*, on the other hand, is always to presuppose speaker's deference for addressee, and so likewise to presuppose appropriate use of deferentials when speaking of him or her.[8]

---

[8]The range of vocabulary reserved for the highest of the noble elite actually extends to a few super-deferential alternants to "regular" krama inggil forms. These are discussed briefly in Errington (1982). The

Werdakrama

The one variety of krama described in the literature which is not used by any member of the contemporary Surakartan speech community is called *werdakrama*. It will be dealt with here as described in the literature to determine the "lower" structural limits on variation in krama speech styles, and the point of demarcation between krama and madya. If a variety of krama answering descriptions of *werdakrama* has ever actually been used in Surakarta it is now obsolete, and quite possibly has never been in any kind of common use among speakers of any Surakartan subcommunity.

As described by Padmasusastra, for instance, the distinctive mark of *werdakrama* is the use of ngoko rather than krama affixes: *-aké* rather than *-aken* (causative/benefactive verb marker), *di-* rather than *dipun-* (passive verb marker), and *-(n)é* rather than *-(n)ipun* (genitive marker/nominalizer). In Padmasusastra's description of its use, which is echoed by other authors, it is described as a style of formal language used by an elder to a junior of equal status, but with whom there is a relatively distant social relation.

The strategy used for studying *basaantya* was also implemented to determine whether *werdakrama* is usable by anyone in contemporary Surakarta. Examples taken from Padmasusastra (1896:21), (10) to (12) below, and Poedjosoedarmo (1968:62), example 13, were presented to speakers. Here too one is hard put to reconcile the distinguishing features which each author implicitly or explicitly attributes to style. Poedjosoedarmo's example contains the ngoko relative clause marker *sing*, which he thereby implies is obligatory in *werdakrama*.

Padmasusastra, on the other hand, claims that the ngoko elements used in *werdakrama* are limited to just the affixes mentioned above, and so implicitly requires that *ingkang*, the krama alternant to *sing* be used.

---

availability of *sampéyandalem* as a title in fact makes its status as a personal pronoun problematic, but this problem must go undiscussed here. Speakers all "naturally" treat it as being of a type with *panjenengandalem* and other forms.

10. Kala menapa dhatengé kèngkènané saking Semarang?
    When did the messenger arrive from Semarang?

11. Inggilé menapa jangkep kalih meter?
    Is it a full two meters tall?

12. Mboten wonten ciriné.
    There are no indications.

13. Menika anak kula Tini sing kula cariyosaké wau.
    This is my child Tini I told you about just now.

Poedjosoedarmo indicates that *werdakrama* is little used and that he was unable to find any examples of it in the actual data he recorded for research he carried out with Wolff (1982). Informants' judgments indicate that this style type is not just little used, but unusable: each of the twenty-three informants who judged examples 10 to 13 rejected them, some spontaneously modifying them so as to fit with structural features of "ordinary" krama or madya. They converted syntagmatic elements of krama to their madya equivalents—e.g., *menapa* to *napa* ('question marker') in (10) and *wonten* to *ènten* ('there are') in (12)—or substituted for ngoko affixes their krama equivalents—e.g., *-ipun* for *-é* in statements 10 to 12.[9]

If *werdakrama* was at one time a formally and functionally viable, structurally distinct speech style, it appears that its loss would have resulted in a further decrease in the delicacy of priyayi repertoires of linguistic politesse. At the same time, the structural distinctions between krama and madya speech styles would have become more clearly defined, since an obvious contrast between them is that ngoko affixes are always used in madya, but never in krama.

Such conjecture aside, some clear conclusions are available about the structural properties of ngoko and krama speech levels, which are essentially identical to those made by Uhlenbeck as follows:

---

[9]Bax (1974:23) reports that his informants accepted Poedjosoedarmo's example, number 13 above.

1. speech in which no *madya*-elements are used and in which *krama inggil*- or *krama*-elements occur only for respectful reference to third persons

1A. speech in which no *madya*- or *krama*-elements are used, but with regular use of *krama inggil*-terms also for reference to the addressee

2. speech in which the speaker avails himself of all possibilities for using *krama*-forms

2A. speech in which the speaker avails himself of all possibilities for using *krama*-forms and for using *krama inggil*-forms for referring to the addressee. (1978:312)

Perhaps Uhlenbeck ignores the status of styles called *werdakrama* and *basaantya* because he doubts (as do I) that either has ever been in common use; he may believe that they are properly treated as parts of the range of styles called madya, which fall between krama and ngoko. But native speakers' rejections of examples such as (5) to (8) and (10) to (13) because of their structural ill-formedness indicate that they are part of no speakers' repertoire, and can be ignored in further discussion.

To establish the limits on variation in the structure of ngoko and krama speech styles is to indirectly establish the structural limits of madya variation as well. Encoded constraints on combinations of paradigmatic alternants turn out to vary marginally among Surakartans who control krama, regardless of their age and status as priyayi or non-priyayi. The social significances of use of styles can now be further considered in preparation for a study of the structure of madya in the next chapter.

It does not necessarily follow from any identity of or comparability between the structures of repertoires of different speakers that they use the styles which make up those repertoires in identical ways. To study variation in the social functions of speech styles requires some knowledge of the typical kinds of use which speakers of different social backgrounds make of them, and the different ways they evaluate examples of different speech styles.

To deal with this issue, we make recourse to the sort of classification which speakers provide when asked for broader evaluations of examples. When asked to evaluate the well-formedness of examples, they answer questions about use and conceptions of use of repertoires in ways which turn out to vary significantly within the community. As objects rather than instruments of analysis, speakers' classifications suggest ways of treating priyayi speakers as "modern" and "conservative" and reveal basic biases towards madya speech. These biases are in turn directly relevant to the study of the structure of madya repertoires.

FOLK CLASSIFICATIONS

By using judgments on the well-formedness of sample sentences to study the structure of speech style repertoires, we assumed that speakers are capable of discriminating between those examples of speech styles which conform with their own usage and those which do not. Responses made at various times to questions about a variety of examples asked over a long period of time were so consistent as to justify this assumption. Furthermore, during eighteen months in Surakarta, I never observed or participated in an occasion of language use in which a speech style typified by the rejected examples was used.

We have simultaneously broached the problem of how "ordinary" speakers who are not authors of systematic descriptions like Padmasusastra's classify, compare, and distinguish between examples of level usage. Since examples of styles exhibit various structural and functional traits which are shared with or distinct from traits of other styles, several kinds of attributes can be alluded to in order to identify examples of styles. Different kinds of labels can be used in order to name them or pick them out. This is true of "naive" native speaker classifications to be discussed below, but also of more "technical" metalinguistic vocabularies already discussed. From written sources of the sort discussed above, for instance, three general types of properties can be drawn:

    1. SENTENTIAL STRUCTURE: Some metalinguistic terms implicitly allude to structural characteristics of the styles or classes of styles they refer to. The word "krama" is used as a cover term for distinct but related speech styles, for instance, because it is understood that styles so designated share structural features: the

obligatory presence of certain classes of krama lexical alternants.

2. POSITION IN A REPERTOIRE SYSTEM: Some terms identify styles' positions within a repertoire which is conceived to be arrayed along a continuum between the "highest," or most polite, and "lowest," or least polite, forms of speech. The term "madya," for instance, which means 'middle,' identifies style(s) of speech which fall in the middle of the continuum by virtue of their sentential structures. Similarly, the term *kramantara* alludes to the intermediate position of that speech style between "lower" and "higher" speech styles which also count as krama.

3. FUNCTION AS A REGISTER: Some terms allude directly or indirectly to features of a situation of use in which the style they designate is deemed appropriate. The term "ngoko," for instance, derives historically from an old second person pronoun *ko-* (cf. modern *kowé*) and is comparable in meaning to the French *tutoyer* 'to say *tu* to someone' (Wolff and Poedjosoedarmo 1982:4). *Mudhakrama* alludes to an attribute of a person who is at least prescriptively its user, that is, the youth of a speaker in relation to an addressee.

It turns out that speakers classify or name examples of usage by alluding to or identifying similar sorts of characteristics, and they do so, moreover, in ways which vary significantly within the community.[10] But they frequently make use of a fourth sort of criterion largely or entirely unused in written descriptions:

---

[10]This analysis of classifications differs from Wolff and Poedjosoedarmo's (1982:29); they found speakers could accurately classify sentences with pre-given labels alluding primarily to structural criteria and position in a repertoire. The focus here is on speakers' own labels.

4. FUNCTION AS A DIALECT: Speakers often link an example and the style it typifies to some segment of the community, members of which they associate with that style as its "typical" or "characteristic" users. In so doing they link the style as a social dialect with some subgroup of the community from which they usually dissociate themselves, either implicitly or explicitly.

In fact, it can be shown that different speakers evaluate different kinds of examples as registers, keying to situation of use (criterion 3 above) and as dialects, keying to social characteristics of a user (criterion 4). There is a pattern to these contrasting classifications which correlates with informants' social backgrounds and social perspectives. From these classifications can be developed a picture of contrasting perspectives on linguistic etiquette, each model "a partial, specific, though not inaccurate, perception that closely partakes of the phenomenon it is intended to describe" (Fox 1974: 81).

The result, then, is not a series of categorical, unambiguous, mutually exclusive labels which exhaustively classify examples, but subjectively based and contextually variable categorizations of language and, indirectly, language users. Because we are dealing here with knowledge for governing conduct in everyday life, rules for interpreting specifically linguistic aspects of social reality and for acting accordingly, this classificatory study represents a specific, narrow, but nonetheless suggestive essay in the sociology of knowledge. It provides some preliminary insights into the functions of madya speech styles, which are discussed in more detail in chapter 4.

Terminological issues

There are two complementary ways of asking native speakers about language use, proceeding from either side of the dichotomy of language use and context of use. One can work from a social context—actual or hypothetical, described in varying degrees of detail by or for an informant—to the language which that informant reports to be appropriately used in it. This procedure was used to gather much of the information about the traditional social milieu summarized in chapter 2. On the other hand, informants can be presented with (or may themselves provide) an example of use which can be classified as somehow typical of a speech style and characterized vis-a-vis appropriate or inappropriate contexts of use. These are two distinct conceptual spheres involving different sorts of elicitation frames and if, as Frake (1980) tells us, frames should be plied only with care, we need to understand the differences between them.

Choice between personal pronouns, for instance, is relatively crucial for linguistically mediating one's social relation with a speech partner, and since the second person pronominal paradigm is more complex than descriptions in the literature might lead one to believe, we must consider them as special parts of linguistic conduct. When asked: "How do you speak to X?"—whether X is the name of a relative, an acquaintance, or a description of a hypothetical or actual member of a certain social class—informants generally respond by specifying some first or second person pronoun. They "naturally" focus on such aspects of speech as crucial parts of linguistic interaction.[11] Alternatively, they say either that the style they use to X is ngoko or *basa*.

The term *basa* is ambiguous. It can be translated most broadly as 'human language'—the Javanese language is *basa Jawa*, and English is *basa Inggris*—but is used more specifically in talk about Javanese speech styles to refer to non-ngoko language. In these latter contexts it can be applied (as can the terms "ngoko," "krama," etc.) to both paradigmatic and syntagmatic aspects of the speech levels: a non-ngoko word counts as *basa*, as does a sentence which could be more particularly classified as madya or krama. So, for example, a person can express his surprise that a young boy in a television drama addresses his father in krama by saying: *Kok nganggo basa?!* 'Why is it that he is using *basa*?' The causative verb created by affixation of *basa* with the causative verb marker *-aké* in ngoko,[12] (*-aken* in krama) may mean 'put into

---

[11]This very interesting and important phenomenon lies outside the scope of this work. For discussion see Errington (1985, 1988).

[12]So, for instance, the ngoko sentence *Omah yèn dibasakaké, dalem* means "The word 'house' (*omah*) when made *basa* is *dalem*." The nonspecificity of *basa* with respect to the distinction between

words, express in language,' but also 'to express in non-ngoko language.'

It should not be surprising, then, that informants' answers to an investigator's questions regarding usage in particular situations frequently lack the precision one might hope for. Insofar as the term *basa* has the meaning 'non-ngoko language,' it is really a negative classification which fails to specify which of several distinct non-ngoko substyles it is being used to refer to. If asked to be more specific about non-ngoko usage with a question such as "What sort of *basa?*" people usually resort to a simple adjectival qualification, adding a word such as *alus* ('refined'), *saé* ('good'), *biasa* ('usual'), or some other description which is vague and unenlightening from a structural point of view. It gives no clues to exactly what linguistic characteristics of speech make that language 'refined,' 'good,' or 'usual.'

It seemed to me at first that insofar as informants were apparently unable to distinguish between speech styles in their descriptive remarks, they were not particularly conscious of the range of expressive styles they actually controlled and used. But as work progressed, a pattern gradually emerged which showed how different informants were, from their own points of view, accurately and consistently distinguishing between important stylistic elements of their own repertoires. When different speakers say of a social relation between themselves and someone else, "We exchange *basa"*—often the relation is called *basan* or *basanbinasan*—they may be referring to one of several specific types of level usage, and doing so in a fairly precise manner if one understands the proper, and to them obvious, social presuppositions. When examples are presented to speakers, rather than elicited from them, their responses reveal a great deal about the language they and others use, and so, about themselves and their relations with others.

If speakers use a native metalinguistic vocabulary ambiguously or vaguely, then it can be risky to use questionnaires or other elicitation techniques without preliminarily checking on what people intend to refer to with such terms. And because the

---

krama and deferential lexemes makes it possible to say with equal accuracy that the *basa* of *omah* is *griya*, the krama equivalent of the deferential krama inggil *dalem*.

terminology commonly used by "naive" speakers overlaps with that found in the literature already discussed, complications arise for comparing both sorts of descriptions. One cannot automatically assume that all native speakers (or writers) will use a given term in identical ways to talk about the same things.

When one is concerned with sociolinguistic variation, a study of folk taxonomies is ideally based on classifications elicited from a large and socially heterogeneous group of Surakartan informants with a variety of backgrounds: old and young, priyayi and non-priyayi. Surakartans are all aware of the unique status of the language they speak, and it was not at all difficult for me as a foreign student of Javanese to steer conversations with even casual acquaintances around to the speech levels: how many there are, what their names are, how to tell them apart, and so on. So data presented below on native speaker classifications were obtained from a wide range of Surakartans. It sometimes happened that informants would raise this topic spontaneously with me, providing their own examples, which I would develop and work around.

VARIATION IN CHARACTERIZATIONS OF EXAMPLES

Early on during the research period I began to ask speakers to provide names for and examples of the ways they spoke to other people, and conversely, I presented examples of speech which I asked them to identify. These latter classifications, presented in table 3.1 as sentences 14 to 19, were elicited for a set of sentences I kept as invariant as was feasible to avoid inadvertently changing some overlooked but significant variable. These basic examples are listed at the heads of columns, speakers are identified by numbers, and their classifications are arrayed in rows.

Sentences 14 to 18 are all versions of the very common greeting 'Where are you going?' chosen first for its commonality—more than one informant provided some version of it spontaneously—and second because in the madya variant there is no slot in which ngoko and krama terms with no distinct madya equivalents might alternate. Madya styles can be treated unitarily here by ignoring class-internal differentiation.

Table 3.1
INFORMANTS' CLASSIFICATIONS OF EXAMPLES

Group A	EXAMPLE 14 Nandalem badhé tindak pundi?	EXAMPLE 15 Panjenengan badhé tindak pundi?	EXAMPLE 16 Panjenengan badhé dhateng pundi?	EXAMPLE 17 Sampéyan ajeng teng pundi?	EXAMPLE 18 Panjenengan arep tindhak ndi?	EXAMPLE 19 Inkang agengipun semanten menika
1.*	krama inggil	krama	kramamadya	krama désa	ngoko alus	krama, krama inggil
2.	krama inggil	kramamadya	kramamadya	krama ngoko	ngoko alus	krama
3.	krama inggil	kramamadya	kramamadya	basa pasaran	ngoko alus	
4.	krama inggil	kramamadya	kramamadya	krama kasar	ngoko karo krama inggil	kramamadya
5.	krama inggil	kramamadya	kramamadya	krama kampung	ngoko alus	kramamadya
6.	krama inggil	kramamadya	kramamadya	kramamadya	ngoko alus	
7.	krama inggil	krama		krama désa		kramamadya
8.	krama inggil	kramamadya		basa pasar		krama
9.	krama inggil	krama	krama	krama désa	ngoko urmat	krama
10.	krama inggil	krama biasa		basa andhap	ngoko ngajêni	krama jangkep
11.	krama inggil	krama	kramamadya	kramamadya	basa campuran	krama inggil
12.	krama inggil	kramamadya	kramamadya	krama andhap	ngoko ngajêni	krama alus
13.	krama inggil	kramamadya	kramamadya	basa bakul	krama ngoko	kramamadya
14.	krama inggil	krama		basa madya	ngoko ngajêni antyabasa	krama inggil
15.	krama inggil	krama	krama	basa pasar		krama, krama inggil
16.	krama inggil	krama		krama désa	ngoko urmat	krama

90

Table 3.1 continued

Group B	EXAMPLE 14 Nandalem badhé tindak pundi?	EXAMPLE 15 Panjenengan badhé tindak pundi?	EXAMPLE 16 Panjenengan badhé dhateng pundi?	EXAMPLE 17 Sampéyan ajeng teng pundi?	EXAMPLE 18 Panjenengan arep tindhak ndi?	EXAMPLE 19 Inkang agengipun semanten menika
17. 18.	krama inggil krama inggil	krama inggil krama inggil	kramamadya kramamadya	basa kampung basa bakul	mudhakrama ngoko mawi krama inggil	krama krama inggil
19. 20.	krama inggil krama inggil	krama inggil krama inggil	kramamadya krama	basa désa basa pasar	ngoko alus ngoko ning ngajèni	krama inggil kramamadya, krama inggil
21. 22. 23.	krama inggil krama inggil krama inggil	krama inggil krama inggil krama inggil	krama krama madya	krama andhap basa désa basa orang kampungan		krama inggil krama inggil

91

Table 3.1 continued

Group C	EXAMPLE 14 Nandalem badhé tindak pundi?	EXAMPLE 15 Panjenengan badhé tindak pundi?	EXAMPLE 16 Panjenengan badhé dhateng pundi?	EXAMPLE 17 Sampéyan ajeng teng pundi?	EXAMPLE 18 Panjenengan arep tindhak ndi?	EXAMPLE 19 Inkang agengipun semanten menika
24.	basa miebet	krama inggil	krama biasa	basa kasar	ngoko alus	krama
25.	basa kraton	krama inggil	krama lugu	basa pasar	ngoko alus	krama jangkep
26.	basa kraton	krama inggil	krama	basa padinan	ngoko alus	krama, krama inggil
27.	basa kraton	krama inggil	basa umum	basa umum	ngoko alus	krama inggil
28.	basa kraton	krama inggil		basa padinan	ngoko alus	krama inggil
29.	basa kraton	krama inggil		basa kasar	ngoko alus	krama, krama inggil
30.	basa kraton	krama inggil	krama biasa	krama kasar	ngoko alus	krama inggil
31.	basa kraton	krama inggil	krama	krama biasa	ngoko alus	krama inggil
32.	basa kraton	krama inggil	krama biasa	kramamadya	madya	krama inggil
33.	basa kraton	krama inggil	krama	basa campuran	ngoko alus	krama, krama inggil
34.	basa kraton	krama inggil	krama	basa padinan	ngoko alus	krama inggil
35.	basa kraton	krama inggil	krama	basa kasar	ngoko alus	krama inggil
36.	basa kraton	krama inggil	krama	kramamadya	ngoko alus	
37.	basa kraton	krama inggil	madya	madya kampung	ngoko alus	krama jangkep
38.	basa kraton	krama inggil		basa pasar	krama madya	
39.	basa inggil	krama inggil	kramamadya	basa bagongan		
40.	basa kraton	krama inggil		krama pasar	antyabasa	krama inggil
41.	basa kraton	krama inggil	kramamadya	kramamadya	ngoko ngajèni	

*The numbers in the left-hand column identify the informants, informant number 1, informant number 2, and so forth.

Sentence 19 was introduced only towards the middle of the research period after I realized that some speakers sometimes use the term "krama inggil" to refer to lexemes which are not deferential, and to sentences which contained no deferentials. After making this admittedly serendipitous discovery, I began to ask speakers about this elliptical sentence which means 'As much as that,' and contains no words which refer to any person whatsoever, and no paradigmatic slot in which deferential lexemes could possibly alternate with non-deferential krama or ngoko equivalents.

Varieties of ngoko

Although there is little socially significant variation in speakers' classifications for example 18, the first three classificatory parameters mentioned above can be seen to underlie three different sorts of classifications of sentence 18.[13] This and other ngoko sentences containing deferentials (or for priyayi krama words functioning as deferentials) were termed *ngoko alus* by more than half of all informants, nineteen out of thirty-five. They thus opposed example 18 to "plain" ngoko by the refinedness accruing to the former, and implicitly allude to a continuum of linguistic polish and politeness ranging from the "low," "crude," and "familiar" varieties of ngoko to the "high," "polished," and "polite" varieties of krama. This spatial metaphor of a continuum of elevatedness or polish, along which styles differ in structural makeup, proves as congenial for speakers' as for analysts' metalinguistic discussion. But no speaker contrasted example 18 and "plain" ngoko with terms which mean "high" or "low," (for instance, calling (18) something like *ngoko inggil* 'high ngoko'). We will return to this point.

Seven speakers identified example 18 in terms of its contextual appropriateness, and so, in terms of its function as a register. They alluded to its "politeness" with labels like 'respectful

---

[13]The "plain" ngoko version of this example, *Kowé (me)nyang ndi?*, and its less formal alternate, *Nyang ndi?*, are not provided because informants classified both as ngoko, or sometimes *ngoko lugu* 'plain ngoko.' *Lugu* was a word commonly used to distinguish and contrast 'plain ngoko' with sentence 18, *Panjenengan arep tindak ndi?*

ngoko' *(ngoko ngajèni, ngoko urmat)*, focusing on the speaker/addressee relation presupposed for its use.

A few informants characterized example 18 by alluding to its sentence internal structure. One older priyayi referred to it as 'mixed language' *(basa campuran)*. (Note that here the word *basa* must be interpreted in its wider sense of [Javanese] language.) Others were more specific, calling it a mixture of 'ngoko with krama inggil' *(ngoko karo krama inggil, ngoko mawi krama inggil).*[14]

Although there is no obvious correlation between these classifications of ngoko examples and the ages and backgrounds of speakers who provided them, I will suggest below that the relative heterogeneity of labels used by group A speakers is significant when considered as parts of more general classificatory patterns, and offers indirect evidence that conservative and priyayi speakers have different conceptions of norms for using linguistic etiquette. But variation which does exist for classifications of varieties of non-ngoko language, or *basa*, suggests right away some obvious contrasts in conceptions of "polite language."

"Krama inggil" vs. "Palace language"

Speakers whose classifications of examples are presented in table 3.1 are subgrouped on the basis of their classifications of the most "polite" examples, (14) and (15), which both exemplify krama styles, but contrast by virtue of a second person pronoun alternation between *nandalem*[15] in (14) and *panjenengan* in

---

[14] Here they used "krama inggil" to designate deferential lexemes; by classifying examples of ngoko such as sentences 1 and 4 in the same way, these speakers indirectly affirmed the functional unity of krama with deferentials when used as surrogate krama inggil in ngoko. Only two informants made use of the term *antyabasa*. One of these, as it turned out, was something of a buff on Javanese literature who had read several old grammars; the other studied the levels and their names while a student in the Netherlands.

[15] This is a short and more commonly used alternant of *panjenengandalem*, treated classificatorily by all speakers as its equivalent.

(15). There is a clear contrast between speakers who classified example 14 as "krama inggil" and are grouped under headings A and B, and other speakers who identified example 14 in one way or other as 'palace language': *basa kraton, basa kedhaton, basa mlebet*. These speakers are in group C.

It is significant that this difference in classifications correlates closely with these informants' reports on their own usage, which are, as far as I was able to determine, accurate. Those who classified (15) as "krama inggil" themselves have occasion to use the second person pronoun *nandalem* to show deference to certain esteemed addressees, whose high status stems from high traditional courtly positions. The priyayi called "conservative" in chapter 2 are represented here by all the speakers in groups A and B, who tacitly recognize example 14 to be representative of their own usage, and worthy of their allegiance.

Those who classified example 14 as 'palace language,' on the other hand, have little if any occasion to address people in this way, although they recognize its linguistic meaning and social function. This is a fairly heterogeneous group of old and young, priyayi and non-priyayi speakers, but all associated use of *nandalem* with a social milieu they perceive to be in some way distinct from and peripheral to their own. Especially striking in this respect are cases of young modern offspring of conservative priyayi, informants 24 to 30 and 33.

The terms used for example 14 by members of group C all reflect what was called above "classification by outgroup"; these speakers classified example 14 by alluding to a social group of which they do not count themselves as members, even if they occasionally use the style themselves. Speakers of different social backgrounds, with different perspectives on the composition of society thus apply this principle to identical or similar examples with varying results. We will see later how the same principle was applied by other speakers to the example of madya, and how this classificatory complementarity extends to other speech styles, and suggests deeper differences in priyayi views of the composition of Surakartan society.

The group of priyayi called conservative has been further subdivided into groups A and B on the basis of their classifications of example 15. Some informants (1-16, group A) used labels like "krama," *"kramamadya,"* or (in one case) *"krama biasa"* ('usual krama') for sentence 15. All these labels contrast with those used for example 14, which they called "krama inggil." But the conservative speakers, numbered (17) to (23) in group B, identified sentence 15 in the same way as (14), with the label "krama inggil." In this respect they agree with group C speakers, who also called (15) "krama inggil," but identified (14) as outgroup usage.

Speakers of group B are conscious of the social correlate of this implicit double perspective they adopt on language and society; in explicit descriptions and prescriptions of use they indirectly allude to the fact that they straddle a kind of social dichotomy between speakers like those in groups A and C. They are aware of these two related but distinct norms for appropriate language use, which they regard as equally valid but differentially relevant in various kinds of speech contexts.

Consider, for instance, informants 18 and 19, who are of high nobility (their father, informant 15, is a prince) but are also relatively young (seventeen and twenty-one years old respectively, at the time of the research). Although they have frequent contact with their relatives among the nobility still close to the palace, they are also in frequent contact with members of the new educated urban class, many of whom are their non-priyayi friends and schoolmates. In the modern bureaucratic framework, it happens that non-priyayi are often their superiors. *Nandalem* is part of these speakers' working repertoires, but is appropriately used only with "old-fashioned" high-status speakers. Informant 18 made this point quite explicitly when I asked her about examples 14 and 15:

> If I talk with a teacher at school, I want to honor him *(ngajèni)*, but I can't use *nandalem*, that's not fitting *(pantes)*. But if I meet my cousin who's a prince, of course I have to use *nandalem*.

Another case in point is informant 20, a grandson of a king in his early sixties who works as a high level functionary in Jakarta but keeps his household in Surakarta. He contrasted sentences 14 and 15 by saying:

> If you meet the president [of the republic] you could use *panjenengan*, that's O.K. But some of the high

nobility still feel it is fitting to use *nandalem* to them, and so you should.

These classifications of examples 14 and 15 are suggestive about speakers' views on their (and others') linguistic usage, since they allude to the importance of their connection to the center of the traditional elite social group, the palace.[16] Others in group B (speakers 17, 21, 22, and 23) are all *priyayi cilik* ('little priyayi') of low traditional rank who, unlike *priyayi cilik* in group C discussed below, have frequent contact with the court. Three are low-ranking royal servants *(abdidalem)* while the fourth has freqent social contact with the princely house of Mangkunegara. These informants also use the term "krama inggil" in two different senses, which reflect the ways they adjust their speech to different understandings, uses, and norms for use held in the speech community at large.

"Krama inggil" vs. "Ordinary krama"

This clear-cut variation in speakers' classifications of statements 14 and 15 contrasts with the apparent homogeneity of labels they gave for example 16, which, as a group, appear to be fairly consistent. But these more or less similar labels cannot be assumed to be equivalent before they are compared as parts of larger systems. As a classification of an example of one style which is itself part of a system of linguistic etiquette, each characterization must be systematically compared with others. When a given label is examined together with labels for other styles given by a speaker, it may turn out to have a "meaning" which differs from its "meaning" for some other speaker.

---

[16]Padmasusastra and several other authors have used the term "krama inggil" for the style appropriately addressed to the king, unambiguously marked as such by the use of *sampéyandalem*. Speakers of groups A and B classified sentences containing *sampéyandalem* as krama inggil, generally adding a spontaneous qualification to the effect that it was "special." Members of group C treated those examples, like 14, as *basa kraton*, that is, 'language of the palace.'

Consider first classifications elicited from the conservative speakers of groups A and B; the majority (thirteen out of seventeen) named sentence 16 and structurally allied examples *kramamadya*. The other four simply call it "krama." Among members of group C the most commonly used labels were krama (six of fourteen respondents); others qualified it as being 'plain' *(lugu)*, 'everyday' *(padinan)*, or 'usual' *(biasa)* krama. Two respondents used the label *kramamadya*.

Within group A speakers' classifications, these labels seem to lump the style exemplified by example 16 together with the style exemplified by (15), as "non-krama inggil" over and against the style represented by example 14, which counts as "krama inggil." When members of groups B and C, on the other hand, use labels like "krama" and *"krama(madya)"* for example 16, they explicitly distinguish it from example 15. The commonality group A speakers implicitly impute to sentences 15 and 16 reflects what is (for them) the privileged function of the alternation between *panjenengan* and *nandalem* as opposed to the alternation between deferential krama inggil verbs like *tindak* (in sentences 14 and 15) and nondeferential krama verbs like *dhateng* (in example 16). Even though these verbs alternate in and distinguish (15) and (16), that difference is classificatorily less crucial for group A speakers than is the alternation between personal pronouns.

Speakers of group C, on the other hand, who make little or no use of *nandalem*, have *panjenengan* as the second person pronoun of choice whether or not they use a deferential like *tindak*. The absence in their working repertoires of *nandalem*, and so of an opposition between *panjenengan* and *nandalem*, makes the presence or absence of a non-pronominal deferential referential like *tindak* the crucial marker of different krama speech styles, and this is reflected in their classifications.

Relevant here are examples with no available slot for alternating deferential and nondeferential lexemes, like 20:

20. Panjenengan saking pundi?
    Where are you (coming) from?

In this sentence the slot in which deferential and nondeferential verbs might alternate is elided, and so example 20 falls into two classes for speakers of group C: both krama inggil or *krama(madya)*. For speakers of group A, however, it is only *krama(madya)*, since what counts for them as krama inggil speech would necessarily include *nandalem* or some equally and markedly deferential alternant. As figure 3.1 shows, the apparent similarity of labels used by all informants for sentences like (16) belies an underlying difference in those labels' places in different taxonomic subsystems.

Figure 3.1

CONTRASTS BETWEEN CLASSIFICATIONS AND REPERTOIRES

GROUP A LABEL		EXAMPLE	GROUP C LABEL
krama inggil	(14)	nandalem + tindak	(OUTGROUP)
krama(madya)	(15)	panjenengan + tindak	krama inggil
	(16)	panjenengan + dhateng	krama(madya)

Madya: substandard or intermediate?

Sentences like (17) in table 3.1 exemplify the speech style called madya in the literature, and were labeled in generally complementary ways by a significant number of speakers in group C as opposed to those in groups A and B. This classificatory difference itself complements the general differences in their classifications for examples 14 and 15 discussed above, since each case involves classifications by outgroup criteria which are themselves symptomatic of more general social attitudes.

Conservative speakers of groups A and B do not use the term "madya" as do authors; those who use it apply it to one or more varieties of the speech style exemplified by sentences 16 and 20, either alone or in a compound term like *kramamadya*. In fact, only seven of the entire group of forty-one informants (three in group A, four in group C) used some label for sentence 17 which included the term "madya," although it would count as madya by criteria used in the literature.

Conservative speakers (groups A and B) most commonly label (17) by associating it with what counts for them as an outgroup. Fifteen of these twenty-three conservative speakers applied labels to example 17 which allude explicitly to the social class and/or context of use they associate with the speech style it represents: 'village krama' (ng:*krama désa*, k:*krama dhusun*), 'neighborhood krama' (*krama kampungan*), 'market language' (ng:*basa pasar*, k:*basa peken*), 'seller's language' (*basa bakulan*). They identify the example through attributes of the people who commonly use that language, or to the contexts in which they believe it is typically heard.

Again, this is not to say that conservative speakers do not actually use this sort of language; even old, conservative priyayi will speak this way, but only when dealing with members of the sociolinguistic outgroup and in speech contexts they identify with these labels. Their classifications reflect an underlying bias toward madya as the substandard speech of those who, by their own conservative standards, are undereducated.

Other labels which were used by speakers in groups A and B are ambiguous outside of the context of elicitation, because they may be interpreted in accordance with different uses of the metaphor of verticality: social worth of user vis-a-vis addressee, or linguistic refinedness of usage vis-a-vis a repertoire. On one hand, they can be seen as descriptions of the social status ("high" or "low") of members of some group of speakers who use this language or to whom it is used, and on the other as allusions to the position this speech style occupies along the continuum of language types between crude and refined. Informant 4, for example, identified example 17 as *krama kasar* ('rough krama'), and added by way of elicited explanation that the language was *kasar*, as were the people who used it. Similarly, the three informants of groups A and B who called (17) 'low' language[17] (10, 12, and 21) likewise explained that the language is 'low' (i.e., less polite than the style of example 16) but the people who use it are socially low (ng:*wong (ce)ndhèk*, k:*tiyang andhap*), that is, of non-priyayi status. This dual or ambiguous use of the metaphor

---

[17]This use "*krama andhap*" differs from that in the literature, where it refers to deferentials which exalt one person in use for reference to someone else of lower status.

of verticality—on one hand for social status of speaker, on the other for systemic position of an example—will be discussed below.

The relatively heterogeneous classifications of sentence 17 given by speakers of group C can be subgrouped and shown to correlate with the social characteristics of those who gave them, since their social backgrounds fit with and help explain their responses. Consider first those who classify example 17 by outgroup, informants 25 and 37 to 40. Some called sentence 17 *basa pasar* or *krama andhap* and indicated, as did the conservative speakers discussed above, that they were referring with these designations to typical contexts of such usage. Similarly, informant 37, who called sentence 16 madya, called sentence 17 *madya kampung*, alluding as did conservative informants to the 'language of the neighborhood'. Informant 39's classification of this sentence as *basa bagongan* represents a curious allusion to the language used by royal servants of the heroes of *wayang* dramatic presentations of stories from the classical literature. This informant pointed out that these clowns speak the language of the "common people" even at their most polite.[18]

All five informants thus allude in one way or other to a speech community other than their own, and four share a social background which sets them off from other members of group C, but also from speakers of groups A and B. All but informant 25 are relatively older than other members of group C—none is younger than forty-five—and all count as *priyayi cilik*, that is, persons with relatively distant or tenuous connections to the centers of traditional noble society in the palace. All are conscious of and take pride in their priyayi heritage, but the language of the palace (like example 14) is nonetheless "not theirs," as one put it. Their classifications of example 14, like those from other speakers grouped under C, indicate as much. At the same time, they set themselves off from the part of the speech community they perceive to be composed primarily of people who know no better style of non-ngoko language *(basa)* than madya, such as in

---

[18]There was at one time a special vocabulary used in royal audience by servants for address of each other often called in Surakarta *basa kedhaton*. A brief description of the history and use of this vocabulary is provided in Errington 1982.

sentence 17. In this respect they resemble speakers of groups A and B more than those in group C.

The remaining fourteen speakers of group C (including informant number 25) are all relatively young, between the ages of fourteen and twenty-five. Nine are priyayi of relatively high traditional status; five are not priyayi in any traditional sense but do control full krama and, as college students, are of relatively high status by contemporary Surakartan (and Indonesian) standards. In this subgroup only one informant, number 25, identifies example 17 as speech of an outgroup; all others allude to its systematic characteristics in a repertoire ('middle'), its structural characteristics *(basa campuran* 'mixed language'), or its function as a register appropriate to certain contexts of use independent of an outgroup identification.

All four who used some phrase involving the word *kasar* ('rough')—three young priyayi (24, 29, and 30) and one non-priyayi (35)—explained that it was *kasar* because it was less *alus* ('polished') than other speech styles. Just as important, they indicated that it was used when one is too familiar with one's partner for polished language which is 'too refined' *(kalusen)*, but not familiar enough to use ngoko (see chapter 4). Similar opinions on use of these examples were expressed by other modern speakers, and contrast as a group with those of conservative speakers. They fit, for instance, with informant 32 and 36's use of the term "madya" for example 17, and with their explanations that it was "middle" language: higher than ngoko, but lower than krama.[19]

The characteristic of example 17 most commonly alluded to by these modern speakers is its "usualness," as can be seen in labels like 'usual krama' *(krama biasa)* and 'everyday krama' *(krama padinan)*. Three younger priyayi and two younger non-priyayi informants gave such identifications. So for them the most salient social-functional trait of example 17 (and the style called madya in the literature) is the fact that in the Surakartan community as a whole it is the most common type of *basa* heard. The same criterion of "usualness" adduced by a member of group

---

[19]These in fact are almost the only native speaker classifications that fit with use of descriptive labels in the literature.

A (informant 10) to distinguish (15) from (14) is used by a member of group C (informant 31) to distinguish (17) from (16).

Among classifications given for (17) by these members of group C there is a general and significant absence of labels which allude explicitly to an outgroup. There is a conspicuous agreement or concensus between the labels young, modern priyayi and non-priyayi provide for such speech, and a corresponding lack of fit between these young modern priyayi labels and those given by their elders. These classificatory contrasts and complementarities strongly suggest two basic views on the speech levels, contexts of language use, and speech partners.

This implicit difference in social perspective is particularly striking in contrasting classifications given by members of different generations in a single family. Pairs of siblings—(24) and (25), (26) and (27), (28) and (29)—contrast in this respect with their parents (4), (7), and (20), respectively. At the same time physical age is clearly a major but not the sole correlate of patterns of classifications. We have seen that informants 18 and 19 are young but nevertheless conservative speakers who are still close to the palace; they classified example 17 in a manner similar to their mother (informant 1) and their father (informant number 15). Like their parents, they evaluate examples of madya as substandard social dialect. "Little priyayi" on the other hand are of distant descent but considerably older; they too dissociate themselves from the palace on one hand, but also from the "common" language of uneducated non-priyayi on the other.

CONTRASTS IN PRINCIPLES OF CLASSIFICATION

Classifications may appear vague or inconsistent to one who is unaware of norms for evaluating speech and features of contexts of speech which speakers presuppose when they identify salient features of examples with classificatory terms. Speakers differ in what they take for granted in identifying examples of styles, according to their various social perspectives on madya as ingroup/outgroup speech, on *panjenengan* as polite and/or deferential address, and so on. When for instance a conservative speaker says "I speak *basa* to my father," she may assume as a matter of course that I know non-ngoko language like example 17 is outgroup speech to which she could not possibly intend to refer. If she responds to a request for more detail by saying "I use *nandalem*," or "I use krama inggil," she assumes "naturally" that I know that *nandalem* will only be used with deferentials, or that by "high" she alludes to her father's higher social status and his asymmetric relation with herself. The differences in classifications which are most obvious and also most significant for understanding the uses of madya styles can be treated as functions of differing social perspectives.

It is worth reconsidering the ubiquitous metaphor of verticality which appears in different classificatory systems. Conservative speakers of group A commonly use adjectives which mean 'high' and 'low' to allude to differences in the status of speech partners. Modern speakers, on the other hand, use the same adjectives, together with others which mean 'refined' and 'rough,' to pick out examples of styles along a continuum of linguistic refinement which is independent of context of use.

This double applicability appears also in classifications of sentence 19, which requires a general review and comparison of classifications of the other examples. Like sentence 20, 19 contains no lexical items which function as krama inggil deferentials, but unlike examples 14 to 17 and 20, it also has no slot for an alternation between pronouns which refer to (and might mark deference for) addressee. A significant number of informants, and the majority of group C speakers, nonetheless classified it as krama inggil, or said it was both krama (or *kramamadya)* and krama inggil.

Two informants from group A classified it only as krama inggil; ten called it some other variety of krama: krama, *krama jangkep—*'full, complete krama,' thus alluding to structural criteria— or *kramamadya* (example 15), or *krama alus*. Two called it both krama and krama inggil. All but one informant in group B said sentence 20 was krama inggil, one adding that it was also *kramamadya*. On the other hand, no less than eleven of fourteen informants of group C said it was krama inggil, three adding that it was also krama.

It is clear from this example too that the modifier *inggil* can be understood to refer to two things: either to the systematic position of the example vis-a-vis other level variants, or to an aspect of the social relation between speech partners presupposed for its appropriate use, namely, that addressee is of superior, or "higher" status. So (19) was called by one conservative informant the *basa* which is 'highest' *(inggil piyambak)* and the *basa* used to those who are 'higher' *(langkung inggil)*. Neither criterion involves a sentence internal structural feature of the example per se; indeed, it contains no lexemes which count as deferentials.

An informant who says example 19 is both *kramamadya* and krama inggil may thus be taken to refer to the social relation presupposed for appropriate use of that style: it is 'middle/high' krama in the sense that it may be used to either an equal or to a superior. At the same time, he/she may be referring to 19 as occupying both the 'middle' and 'high' points along the continuum running between ngoko and the most polite possible language. The metaphor of verticality is ubiquitous in speakers' classifications of examples in part because of this double applicability.

The image of examples of styles occupying points on a graded continuum of levels—'high,' 'middle,' 'low'—is often invoked with other terms which allude to them as relatively 'refined' *(alus)* and 'rough' *(kasar)*. But unlike *alus* and *kasar*, words which mean 'high' (k:*inggil*, ng:*dhuwur*) and 'low' (k:*andhap*, ng:*cendhèk*) can also be used to describe aspects of a social relation between speech partners with which it fits: one party to speech interaction can be thought of as sufficiently "higher" or "lower" than the other to warrant the use of relatively "higher" or "lower" speech.

Sentence 19 is important because it diverges structurally and functionally from the type of example on which native speakers typically focus, in which speaker refers to addressee. Sentences which contain no deferentials and have no slots in which deferentials might alternate with other forms show that native speakers generally allude either to an example's position vis-a-vis stylistically distinct, referentially identical alternants, and/or to aspects of the presupposed conditions of its appropriate use. It becomes clear from such examples, then, that for some speakers the label "krama inggil" applies to more than deferential words and sentences containing elements of the vocabulary of krama inggil.

The classificatory trends within these groups can be further seen to indicate differences in kinds of evaluations of contexts of use. Given the traditional priyayi concern with personal and relative status as determinants of behavior discussed in chapter 2, it seems sensible that conservative speakers' classifications should fit the basic organizational principle of the traditional social order in which the standard speech level repertoires were used. The most important determinants for speech level use in traditional circles were after all status relations, which naturally lend themselves to description in Javanese (and English) as "high" and "low," or "up" and "down" in asymmetric speech exchange. When an informant refers to a sentence like (17) as 'low krama' *(krama andhap)*, he/she can be taken to allude to the vertical "direction" in which an utterance metaphorically "moves," determined by relative status of addressee vis-a-vis the speaker.

The same metaphor was used to classify proper forms of conduct in a didactic treatise on etiquette written by a Javanese priyayi for Javanese in the early 1930s, entitled *Tata Krama Jawi* (Sastrawirya 1931-32). In a diagram like that shown in figure 3.2 Sastrawirya presents characterizations (running along the arrows) to show the kind of feeling *(rasa)* a speaker should have when dealing with others in any of these three types of relations, and the demeanor one should normally assume in each case. Here patterns of conduct are ranked as "low" to "high" in relation to each other as interactants are related to each other. It is simple to apply this model to speech level use, by substituting in the names of speech styles which were most commonly given by speakers of group A (figure 3.3) which can be seen to name aspects of a status relation between speech partners, that is, the relative status of the addressee to whom each is appropriately used. This fits the image of vertical hierarchy which informed traditional priyayi conceptions of social organization, etiquette, and interpersonal relations. Here is one way names of speech styles can be seen to fit a schema of social stratification, picking out what count as relatively salient contextual features of situations of use for conservative speakers: differences and equivalences in status.

Conservative speakers' use of the word *inggil* to describe a social relation is clear in the case of sentence 14. The second person pronoun *nandalem* is always and only for one's superior and so is appropriate only as "high" language for "high" addressee in an asymmetric pattern of exchange. *Panjenengan* in krama with deferentials (example 15) or without (example 16), is "lower" in the repertoire, and used to people of status comparable with speakers of "middling" rank in symmetric exchange, or perhaps but not necessarily with superiors in asymmetric exchange.

Figure 3.2
SASTRAWIRYA'S CONCEPTION OF ETIQUETTE

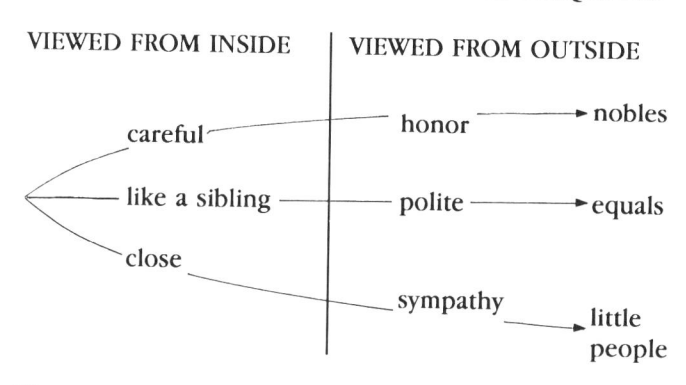

VIEWED FROM INSIDE	VIEWED FROM OUTSIDE
careful	honor ──→ nobles
like a sibling	polite ──→ equals
close	sympathy ──→ little people

The presence of krama inggil deferentials "raises" the level, but not enough to mark a difference in status sufficient for conservative speakers to distinguish it classificatorily. Since sentence 19 can be used in both contexts it could potentially be classified as both, although only three speakers in group A do so. Ngoko in this scheme is language spoken "down" the hierarchy to inferiors in asymmetric exchange, or to intimate equals in symmetric exchange. The focus on status, "high" and "low," goes together with a concern with asymmetric use.

Figure 3.3
CONSERVATIVE LEVEL USE AND ETIQUETTE

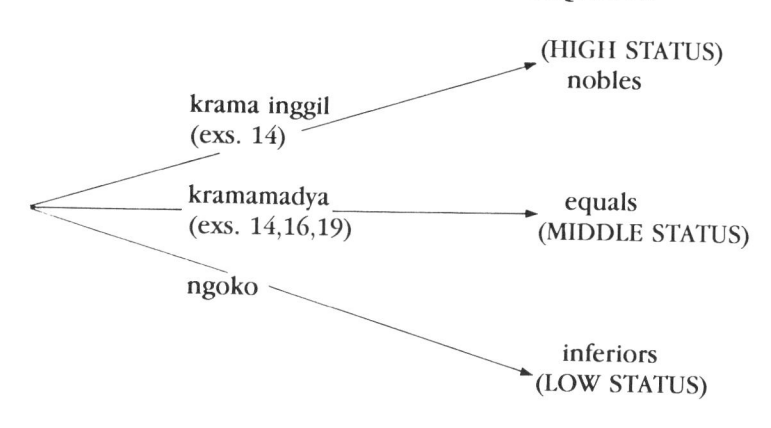

krama inggil (exs. 14) ──→ (HIGH STATUS) nobles

kramamadya (exs. 14,16,19) ──→ equals (MIDDLE STATUS)

ngoko ──→ inferiors (LOW STATUS)

The two styles which do not neatly fit this schema of social hierarchy are exactly those for which there appears to be relatively great variation in the labels used by speakers of group A. Polite ngoko (sentence 18), which contains deferentials for addressee, marks intimacy with a nonetheless high status addressee, and in this sense it always keys simultaneously to both status relations and intimacy. It is therefore relatively unsusceptible to classification in a scheme of unambiguous social stratification. For examples of this style, there is a striking degree of heterogeneity in the labels which otherwise consistent speakers of group A provide. Similarly, the style called "madya" in the literature—used by conservative priyayi in more or less symmetric patterns to members of an outgroup who are, by their standards, of lower status—is categorized most generally as an outgroup dialect. This style marks a different, nontraditional type of status relation, equality of a sort which does not fit into this more traditional view of language and social context.

It is worth noting that speech styles described in the literature which have apparently fallen out of use among priyayi during the last century—varieties of madya and, perhaps, of krama *(werdakrama)* and ngoko *(basaantya)* as well—served to differentiate with relatively greater delicacy those status differences which were mitigated by some other aspect of a social relation (relative familiarity, age, and so on). The dropout of these madya styles would have made for a relative simplification of repertoires, and a concomitant loss of overall potential for finely differentiating status and intimacy in social relations. Conservative classifications appear to be motivated primarily by a conception of appropriate use which is rooted in asymmetric relations, and expressed with a metaphor of verticality and relative status hierarchy which remains after some linguistic nuances have perhaps been lost.

A contrasting principle for classification can be adduced as predominant among group C speakers. First, all but four of the entire group classified example 18 as 'refined ngoko' *(ngoko alus)*. This consistency contrasts markedly with the heterogeneity of classifications given by speakers in group A. Now the adjective *alus* ('refined') can be taken here to be predicated only of the position of examples of the speech style within the repertoire, and not of an addressee or a relation with an addressee. Whether or not a speech partner may be called *alus* there is no direct or intrinsic connection between that characteristic of a participant and a choice of the style they call *ngoko alus*. So example 18 is treated quite naturally by thirteen of the seventeen speakers in group C as a step "up" the ladder of refinedness from "ordinary" to "refined" ngoko, including all the younger modern priyayi and non-priyayi speakers. This contrasts with the speakers in group A, of whom all but five of fourteen speakers allude to sentence internal structure of sentence 18 (i.e., "ngoko with krama inggil," "mixed ngoko," etc.), or what it marks about relation with addressee ("ngoko but deferential," etc.). Only four speakers of group C, on the other hand, did not pick out its place on the scale of refinedness.

Unlike *alus*, the krama adjective *inggil* ('high') and its ngoko equivalent *dhuwur* can be predicated either of a social relation (as shown above) or of the relative position of an example of a speech style vis-a-vis stylistic variants. In neither sense can it be used of example 18, which is not "high" language (it is ngoko, after all) and cannot be used to those of markedly superior status. Now group C speakers' use of *inggil* for both examples 15 and 19 can only be taken to allude to the place of these styles in a repertoire, since those speakers use neither style exclusively to superiors, that is, "up" the social hierarchy. Conservative speakers on the other hand do have such a style in their repertoires, exemplified by sentence 14 which they call "krama inggil."

Example 14 may be "high" language in a contextual and status-oriented sense for conservative speakers, but not necessarily for modern speakers. Examples 15 and 19 count as "high" language for group C speakers only in the sense that they are the most refined, most polite variants available. It is significant, then, that example 19 is called "krama inggil" by only four of thirteen speakers in group A, but eleven of fourteen speakers in group C. Again, the salient criteria for group A speakers seem to be contextual features of "high" addressee status, by which criterion sentences 15 and 19 are not really "high" language as is sentence 14. Since group C speakers evaluate and classify both (15) and (19) according to their places in the repertoire of possible variants, both count for them as "high" language.

In the same way, group C speakers classify example 17 as *krama kasar* to contrast it with "regular" krama like example 16; 17 is a step "down" the continuum of refinedness in relation analogous to that between example 18 which they call *ngoko alus*, and contrast with "ordinary" ngoko as a step "up" the ladder of refinedness. From this perspective the styles exemplified by sentences 17 and 18 are neighbors on the continuum, regardless of their internal structural diversity.

When levels are classified with primary reference to a repertoire system and not a status relation with speech partner, only a continuum of refinedness can be invoked. Underlying notions of appropriate use can also be drawn out of other sorts of observations native speakers make about use. This study of variation in classifications of examples of speech levels does suggest less obvious contrasts in the principles or parameters used by speakers to name and contrast examples of linguistic etiquette. Contrasts between classifications by speakers who are subgrouped primarily on the basis of their use of the principle of classification by out-group suggest basic differences in attitudes towards speech levels, contexts of use, and speech partners which underlie the ways they distinguish and name examples. They provide a classificatory correlate of attitudes to the range of speech styles for which there is more overt, pronounced disagreement: those called "madya" in the literature.

PRELIMINARIES TO THE STUDY OF MADYA

> Javanese experts have never reached agreement as to the actual number of styles to be distinguished. This disagreement was partly due to dialectal differences, but even with respect to the dialect of Surakarta, on which Standard Javanese is largely based, there remained conflicting opinions. The main explanation of this lack of agreement is that there is freedom within clearly fixed limits. It is this *madya*-area which Javanese scholars have in vain tried to classify and systematize. There is here a gradation which cannot be captured by postulating a set of distinct speech styles and/or making finer distinctions between *ngoko, madya,* and *krama*, as has been proposed in the past. (Uhlenbeck 1978:315)

The study of speakers' classifications has obvious implications for these problems, and suggests some other aspects of the issues

Uhlenbeck discusses. Attitudes towards the social functions of styles within the level system, and therefore toward madya speech styles, vary significantly in the priyayi community.

We have thus already touched on some reasons why "madya" is so difficult to deal with: as a category term it refers to a subtype of the sentential levels, subject to different kinds of use. Conceptions of appropriate use within the speech community at large, and among priyayi in particular, can be drawn out to prepare for discussion of structural variation in madya speech styles in chapter 4. Speakers characterize appropriate contexts of use of speech styles with terms very similar to those they use to classify or label sentences, and answers to questions such as "To whom might you use such a sentence [as examples 17]?" provide more explicit evidence of the same basic contrast.

The conservative point of view

Conservative speakers of groups A and B typically answered such questions in the following manner: "To a *wong cilik* ['little person'] who can't use *basa* any better than that to me." Although their characterizations of speech partners varied somewhat, each case specified that addressee was of an outgroup. The very common specification of partner's competence in krama indicates the basic goal is some symmetric pattern of level use when dealing with a member of an outgroup.

The stigma which still attaches to the use of madya among conservative priyayi should not be underestimated; they do not hesitate to voice it in various ways. As the marks of traditional priyayi-hood have become indistinct and blurred in modern Surakarta, one of the few even roughly accurate markers of high traditional social status is control of the speech levels. In this respect, then, use of "high" Javanese functions as a social dialect, marking users' educated status. To quote one young, conservative priyayi:

> Nowadays lots of people think they're priyayi because they work in offices and are well off. They've left the neighborhood *(kampung)* behind, but their language is still bad.

Several suitors of one young conservative speaker were rejected by her parents, she told me, for lack of "breeding," which they betrayed by their inability to speak krama to their would-be parents-in-law, to show the respect her parents felt was their due. The suitors were moreover aware of the stigma which attached to madya in her parents' eyes, and avoided Javanese entirely when speaking with them by using Indonesian.[20]

Since the basic goal in speech with an outgroup nonintimate for conservative priyayi is some pattern of more or less symmetrical exchange, an addressee of relatively low status may justify use of krama by a speech partner simply by using it himself. Consider one young, conservative priyayi's description of an encounter with a "little person" at the market:

> My informant asked the *bakul* (seller): *Niki pinten, ta, Yu?* [madya: 'How much is this, Yu?']. The seller answered: *Menika mirah, Bu, namung tigang ewu kémawon* [krama: 'This is cheap, Bu, just three thousand']. She said to me: "I was so embarrassed, Mas, she spoke good *basa*, and I used *niki-niku* to her."[21]

Older priyayi find the boundary between madya and ngoko to be a thin one in such speech situations; it is, some say, really negligible. As one older conservative informant put it:

> If I'm talking with someone in the market with whom there is a difference of status and age *[kacèk dhuwur,*

---

[20] Inability to use good Javanese, on the other hand, does not necessarily indicate that a speaker is of nonnoble descent; that numerous young priyayi growing up in Jakarta are largely ignorant of Javanese linguistic etiquette shows this. If control of the speech levels is only a sufficient and not necessary condition for claim to (traditionally defined) elite status, it is nonetheless the most obvious in the present-day situation.

[21] The significance of this classification, which identifies two ubiquitous, characteristic elements of madya, will become clear in chapter 4.

kacèk umur ng: 'different height, different age'], I won't use ngoko *kowé-kowé* like that, but I'll use *niku, napa,* so that it's not pure ngoko, like *Kaya niku napa mboten kena?* [madya: 'May it not (be done) like that?']

This reflects the conception of appropriate use common among conservative priyayi: conversation with a member of an outgroup almost always entails use of madya. The other difference between speaker and addressee which might be salient for choice of style is age, although this has somewhat limited impact. Most important is the principle of reciprocity, of giving what one gets; when dealing with a *kasar* person who speaks in a *kasar* fashion, one returns that *kasar* language.

The modern point of view

There is a marked contrast among modern priyayi who, like their non-priyayi peers, treat madya styles as functionally homogeneous parts of their repertoires. For them example 17 is located at an intermediate point on a functionally homogeneous scale of politeness in repertoires, no component style of which is used only to superiors "up" the social hierarchy, or exclusively to members of an outgroup. They view styles called madya in the literature as parts of a grade or range of substyles along a continuum between low and high, crude and refined, *kasar* and *alus* language. This is why the four modern informants who called example 17 *krama kasar* used the term *kasar* to refer to the position of the example in the continuum of possible alternants between which they could choose, and so contrasted it with polished *(alus)* krama speech like examples 15 and 16.

The majority of modern speakers alluded to example 17's "usualness," treating it as something expected, normal language for use in most situations requiring some style of *basa*. For modern speakers the criterion for appropriateness of use of language like example 17 is relative, intermediate familiarity with an addressee, or nonfamiliarity with a speaker who does not control krama. Modern speakers commonly cite the market as one context for use of language like example 17, but also mention another in which they find it to be appropriate. Younger modern informants, priyayi and non-priyayi alike, described use of example 17 with addressees of comparable status, about their age, with whom they felt familiar but did not exchange ngoko. A typical description of the sort of person with whom this symmetric usage occurred is "People of my age and group, who I am familiar with, if (we) don't use ngoko."[22] The way in which such situations develop deserves comment.

MADYA AS DIALECT, MADYA AS REGISTER

When two adult Javanese meet for the first time, it almost never happens that they will immediately begin to exchange ngoko; some non-ngoko style will be used at least initially. The style used varies among speakers: it may be "full" krama, madya, or some mixture of the two. Early on in a developing relationship, a unilateral or symmetric shift "down" may occur; if there is a significant difference in age or status, the older and/or higher status person may switch to ngoko, while the younger, lower partner maintains polite usage. (This was not uncommon for relations between myself, for instance, and older priyayi.) If two people are of approximately equal status and age, the switch will generally be bilateral and more or less simultaneous. The decision to switch in either of these types of situations may be explicitly suggested by a speech partner, or tacitly implemented by interspersing words of the "lower" level, singly or in groups, in one's speech. If a speech partner evinces no discomfort or embarrassment, and/or follows the downward shift, the switch may be said to be felicitous and a relatively familiar relation to be acknowledged and sanctioned on both sides.

But this shift must be made fairly soon after the relation is initiated if it is to be implemented, and there lies the rub. Along with the other situational factors relevant to choice of speech level use between two people, the way in which they have spoken on previous occasions will be highly relevant. If the switch is not initiated soon enough, the fact of use of original speech level will itself make both parties feel awkward about initiating a shift and

---

[22]*Wong sebayak, segolongan sing wis akrab, nèk ora nganggo ngoko.*

disrupting a tacit agreement on linguistic means for mediating the relation. The way one has talked in the past becomes a prime determinant of how one will talk in the future. Tension may be engendered between the actual intimacy of the relation and that marked (or not marked) by level use.

This is not a very common situation, but almost every one of my modern informants mentioned at least a couple of acquaintances—schoolmates, friends, and the like—with whom they were in just such a relation. Thus they find themselves obliged to speak and be spoken to in ways which might seem inappropriate by all parameters other than the established history of usage.

Modern priyayi informants generally feel "safest" initiating language exchange with someone of comparable age and social status with a version of madya, particularly if they believe (as a rule correctly) that the speech partner is not someone who controls full krama. If it comes about that the speakers feel constrained by these kinds of factors to refrain from switching to plain ngoko, the only type of level shift available occurs within madya speech style, i.e., from use of krama referential items (and even, in some cases, krama syntagmatic items) to ngoko referential items with madya syntagmatic items. In such situations, the bottom line or border separating ngoko and madya may be reached. Barring some significant change in personal relations, such "low madya" will become the means for mediating relations in speech. Inappropriate though modern speakers may feel such language to be if a relation grows in intimacy, it may nonetheless serve as an acceptable compromise.

Conservative speakers on the other hand say that they never use madya to one whom they count as a priyayi. If sufficient familiarity does develop, and status differences are not so great as to prevent it, they may switch from krama to ngoko (either "plain" or "polite") or, for that matter, to Indonesian. The mechanics of the shift would be analogous to those just outlined, but would bypass madya. For conservative speakers, use of krama even with a person they know well is preferable to the use of *basa bakulan* ('language of the market sellers'), no matter how familiar the relation. This at any rate is the way they describe their own usage, and I was unable to observe any conservative speaker ever using madya to persons who were not members of their traditionally defined outgroup.

The appropriateness for modern speakers of "low" madya for speech with other members of a more heterogeneous, urban, educated class is a clear indicator of the different conceptions of appropriate use of madya held by conservative and modern speakers. Conservative speakers conceive of a choice between speech styles when dealing with educated people to be an either/or affair involving krama or ngoko. Modern speakers avail themselves of a greater range of possible variation through which they may, so to speak, slide "down" the continuum from formal or "high" types of language to "lower" types. This correlates with the two models which were developed on the basis of the sorts of classifications these speakers made of examples: the status-oriented conservative model, with clear-cut distinctions between krama and madya, as opposed to the modern continuum model, comprising a variable range of mutually determined polish and distance or intimacy.[23]

The basic distinction between social register and social dialect introduced in the first chapter thus becomes relevant for analyzing the entire system of Javanese linguistic etiquette. Insofar as priyayi speakers of different backgrounds perceive different styles either as dialects (associating them with speakers of a given class) or registers (appropriate in particular types of situations of use) they view them in fundamentally different ways. This basic contrast between conservative and modern priyayi, revealed in classifications of examples of styles and in prescribed patterns of use, is the starting point for the study of variation in structure and use of madya in chapter 4.

Conservative speakers conceive of madya as a dialect which they themselves are obliged to use with members of their outgroup. Modern speakers identify such usage in terms of the type of situation in which it is appropriately used, and therefore identify it independently of social status of user. They classify madya as another type of register, functionally integrated with other speech styles and for that reason not closely associated with some precisely defined outgroup. The dual interpretability of

---

[23]The latter conception seems to have been shared by the peasants with whom Bax worked. He reports (1974:34) that they classified madya items as "krama," and made no simple terminological distinction between them.

madya's use reflects an underlying tension between two types of significance which its use (or use of any other speech level) might have. On one hand, it may be treated as an index of a speaker's judgment about a context of use, a social relation with an addressee and, perhaps, a relation with a person referred to other than the addressee. On the other hand, the occasion of use may be interpreted as an indication (perhaps but not necessarily trivial) that the speaker controls and is able to use that speech level.

We can turn to the study of the structure of madya, then, with some ideas about contrasting views on and uses of the speech levels, and some basic expectations concerning variation in madya usage in the priyayi community. We have also developed some ideas about such variation and change in the larger, modernizing, urban context.

4

ON THE USERS AND USES OF MADYA

By first describing the structure of priyayi speech level repertoires, and then preliminarily examining the functions of ngoko, krama, and madya speech styles in those repertoires, we found that norms for speech style functions vary among priyayi, both with respect to the situations in which and the partners to whom styles are conceived to be appropriately used. Since speakers' descriptions of examples of madya speech suggest that social significances of use of madya vary in the Surakartan community, it should not be surprising if a study of syntagmatic structures of encoded madya repertoires turns up corresponding structural differences.

The makeup of the specifically madya vocabulary—that is, the group of alternants to ngoko and krama equivalents which distinguish madya speech—will be shown to vary less among priyayi than do the syntagmatic rules for combining those forms with each other and with distinct ngoko and krama alternants. This variation in madya usage within the priyayi community in turn reflects two aspects of the ongoing assimilation of priyayi into a broader urban educated class.

The most important data for this argument are native speakers' judgments on the acceptability of sample sentences, the use of which is justified in the next section. Examples and judgments on their acceptability are presented under rubrics developed with the metaphor of verticality, which proves so convenient for speakers and analysts alike. First, the basic membership of the madya vocabulary is first studied by looking for the "bottom line" to the range of madya speech styles: what always and necessarily marks madya speech as distinct from ngoko speech. These are forms which must cooccur with each other wherever possible in sentences otherwise made up of ngoko vocabulary. They thus distinguish a non-ngoko speech style which contains ngoko but also madya forms.

Some of these madya elements are distinct in sound shape from both their ngoko and krama alternants, while others are identical to one or the other, but all share a basic sort of linguistic function: they are parts of the grammatico-syntactic and/or the deictic apparatus of the language.[1] None have non-indexical lexical referential meanings of their own. When the results of the present research are compared with other descriptions dating from the last century, it appears that the membership of the obligatory madya vocabulary has changed relatively little over time, although terminological confusions somewhat obscure this fact. At present the obligatory madya vocabulary varies only marginally in madya usage across speech subcommunities; the membership of the set of forms which alternate with ngoko and krama equivalents to distinguish madya speech has been relatively stable.

Having established the vocabulary items which mark the "bottom line" of madya speech as opposed to ngoko speech, we can consider the "top line": the forms of madya, adduced in the manner just summarized, which always cooccur with each other in sentences otherwise composed of krama elements. This is a more complex and interesting issue since it turns out that the line between "krama" speech and "madya" speech, to the extent that one exists, can only be drawn if one recognizes two formally and functionally distinct varieties of krama. This has a parallel in varying ngoko styles as well. Here, then, must be considered the forms and significances of intralevel variation which make ngoko and krama speech more or less formal; the nature of "higher" styles of madya cannot be understood independently of informal krama. Such intralevel variation has been commented on but not exhaustively described in the literature, nor have the ways it makes for speech variation within the level system been considered in any detail. It will be discussed here only insofar as is necessary to make sense of contrasts in modern and conservative priyayi speakers' judgments of acceptability of the relevant madya sentences.

---

[1] Deictic forms function to relate utterances to spatio-temporal coordinates of an act of use in which they are contained.

Put briefly, the evidence of native speakers' evaluations suggests that the speakers called "conservative" in chapter 3 (i.e., speakers of groups A and B in table 3.1) draw a sharp distinction between acceptable examples of informal krama speech on one hand, and of madya speech, which they characterize as an outgroup code, on the other. They reject examples in which appear elements distinctive of both categories; this fits with their opinions on and classifications of examples of speech styles which, we have seen, they treat as distinct. "Modern" speakers, on the other hand, find examples in which elements of informal and formal krama combine with madya elements more acceptable; they treat such examples as arrayed along the graded continuum of refinedness/formality.

If speakers' judgments accurately reflect differences in patterns of their actual use—and examples of observed use corroborate this supposition—then it appears that there have been changes in attitudes to usage and users, which are reflected in encoded syntagmatic rules for combination of madya and krama elements. This would indicate that there are fundamental differences in attitudes to language and language users in the priyayi community. In this sense data to be considered below can be interpreted with an eye to native speaker classifications outlined in chapter 3. If modern priyayi are in fact adopting patterns of use common among non-priyayi, as also seems likely from observed use, this would count as evidence that they are progressively assimilating linguistically and socially into the modern urban community in two respects.

First, they are unconsciously adopting forms of speech and attitudes toward speech which are prevalent outside the traditional priyayi community. Second, this process may be accompanied by increasing use of a different set of norms for use of those repertoires, focusing less on ingroup/outgroup distinctions and relative status within a traditional hierarchized ingroup than on relative formality of relations. This is at least a plausible, socially based interpretation of general patterns which emerge in data of acceptability judgments, which show that there is something of a "top line" to madya styles for so-called "conservative" speakers, but not necessarily for their "modern" children and grandhildren. Given a notion of the "upper" and "lower" limits on the structure of madya speech styles, a problem which remains is what variation might exist "in between." Since the uniquely madya vocabulary is not referential, speakers "raise" or "lower" the refinedness/formality of their speech by choosing between ngoko/krama lexical items; to understand the limits on the range of this sort of variation, then, we must understand limits or constraints on how referential items of the vocabulary can be mixed. This is a more difficult problem because it requires even more data bearing on a still broader variety of relevant factors. Some data was collected during the research period which suggests a few possible approaches to this topic, but also indicates that there is little covariation between informants' acceptability judgments on the relevant examples and their social backgrounds—priyayi or non-priyayi, modern or conservative. This aspect of the nature of madya speech will be disregarded here.

SOURCES AND USES OF DATA

These various problems will all be addressed with constant and crucial reference to native speakers' evaluations of sample sentences, and their responses to requests for judgments on sentences' structural well-formedness. But the validity of such data is questioned by some linguists and sociolinguists, and the risks as well as the advantages of the research strategy must be considered. The obvious prejudice evinced by some conservative speakers against madya, for example, might reflect a basic social bias in the research situation, less a phenomenon to be studied than an insurmountable barrier to accurate elicitation of descriptions of use.

But this approach can nonetheless be justified by the significant and unique advantages it offers. If the structure of various madya speech styles is governed by encoded rules which restrict possible combinations, it should be possible to study them with techniques analogous to those used by linguists to uncover underlying grammatical rules of natural languages. The data of observed usage and reported usage are therefore relegated to an important supplementary, corroborative role here not because they are less useful, but because they are less easily obtained. They can be used in support of systematic conclusions concerning the structure and functions of madya which can be developed with systematically gathered data.

How valid are native speaker intuitions?

The descriptive approach outlined above bears on aspects of the problem of how the speech levels are put together, that is, how they function as parts of a linguistic system. This means that they can be properly investigated only with a systematic corpus of data, which is difficult to gather for several reasons, as brief consideration of an example will show.

I will preliminarily characterize the vocabulary of madya as the set of phonologically and/or distributionally distinct alternants to ngoko forms which cannot appear in acceptable sentences unless other members of the same madya vocabulary also appear, rather than their ngoko or krama equivalents wherever possible, and all other constituents of the sentence are ngoko. This means that crucial evidence which bears directly on cooccurrence restrictions will show the structural acceptability or nonacceptability of sentences which contain non-ngoko forms together with ngoko forms. Consider in this respect three distinct versions of a highly elliptical sentence type; each contains and is set off from the others by distinct members of ngoko/madya/krama paradigmatic sets.[2]

1. Menawi namung menika kémawon kados pundi? (krama)
2. Nèk   mung   niki   mawon   (ke)pripun?   (madya)
3. Yèn   mung   iki   waé   (ke)p(r)iyé? (ngoko)
   IF   ONLY   THIS   JUST HOW ABOUT IT
   How about just this one?

Each sentence can be taken to represent one of the three different speech styles whose names are provided to the right.

How can members of three different vocabularies—ngoko, madya, and krama—be distinguished? If it can be shown that no element of sentence 2 can acceptably replace its conjugate in (1) or (3), then that element is part of the madya vocabulary. By the same token, an element of sentence 1 which cannot acceptably substitute into sentences 2 or 3 counts for that reason as krama.

---

[2]Complications which arise in cases of madya elements which are phonologically identical to their formal or informal krama or ngoko conjugates are discussed below.

This principle for classification of alternants is simple, but if the data bearing on such cooccurrence restrictions were only sentences containing these elements which were observed in usage, as would be ideal, enough cases of cooccurrence would have to be found to show which of a very small percentage of more than two hundred possible combinations for this sentence type were actually usable and acceptable.

The problem is complicated further because some of the paradigmatic slots in sentences 1 to 3 could be filled by still other alternants which make identical contributions to the sentences' referential meaning. One would want to test, for instance, the acceptability of similar sentences containing two other alternants meaning 'only,' *ming* and *naming*. In the slot for elements meaning 'how about it,' one would want to test the "full" and "short"; forms of *kepriyé* and *kepripun—piyé* and *pripun*, respectively—and their other non-ngoko synonym, *dos pundi*. So, the number of possible combinations would increase again. To top it all off, it turns out that some elements function not only as madya but also as informal krama, creating complications dealt with below.

The ideal procedure would involve some test or statistical treatment of occasions of use containing cases of cooccurrence between all the putative madya elements (numbering around forty) and their conjugates. The required occasions of use of speech like examples 1 to 3 which combine relevant paradigmatic alternants would number in the hundreds, and the specific examples of cooccurrence for those sentence-types would number in the thousands. The rigorous application of criteria for discriminating classes of lexemes obviously would involve a multitude of individual facts, because of the relatively large numbers of sets of paradigmatic alternants which combine in a wide variety of syntactic environments.

Let us assume for the moment that we might rely solely on observed occasions of use to glean the crucial data; this would be a corpus large enough to justify conclusions about rules for combining madya elements inferred from "violations" which are observed to be statistically negligible or nonexistent. To have any chance of covering the full spectrum of possible variation—which would, as examples 1 to 3 show, be quite broad—this corpus would have to be very large indeed. And since we saw in chapter 3 that some speakers' attitudes toward madya give firm grounds for suspecting that there is variation in the ways Surakartans use it, that data of observed use would have to be collected in great quantities for a sample of speakers stratified by age and social status.

One such group would be composed of speakers called conservative here, who claim (at least) to use madya, their least-favored speech level choice, in extremely limited ranges of types of social situation. As one conservative informant put it:

> If you want to take a pedicab, and you have to haggle with the driver, you have to use madya. If you speak krama, it will be too *alus* ('refined'); if you speak ngoko he'll think you're *digsura* ('haughty'). You have to use his type of *basa*.

These situations in which conservative speakers report that they use madya—negotiating a pedicab fare, buying goods in the market, etc.—are highly stereotyped, involve predetermined, mutually understood, practical goals, and occur in relatively infrequent interaction with members of an outgroup.

If this is true, then the occasions of use one might hope to observe would be of extremely limited duration, and restricted in range of contexts of appropriate use and topics. And if it turns out that modern speakers use madya as the language of intermediate formality with peers, as they say they do, such usage also might likewise be observed only in very particular types of contexts. As characterizations of use cited in chapter 3 indicate, these would be situations in which the speaker is dealing with a peer with whom he/she is not (yet) familiar, or with whom the pattern of usage has gelled to such an extent that both speech partners are reluctant to switch "down." These appear to be relatively unusual and often transitory situations, and the odds of capturing occasions of such usage would therefore be low.

The other obvious problem involves the role of an observer, especially a foreign observer, present during linguistic interaction, as Labov has emphasized with his Observer's Paradox.[3] To put it another way: we are interested in speakers' capacity to communicate with madya speech styles, but at least some speakers apparently exercise that capacity only rarely, and then in restricted sorts of communicative context. It is doubtful, then, that data of observed and recorded usage would ever suffice for a systematic account.

How then to accumulate enough data to systematically contrast conservative and modern speakers' usage? When dealing with lexical and sentential usage, particularly in limited and stereotyped situations, we do not have the luxury of accumulating sufficient data from observed use to deal with the problems at hand.[4] More than one sociolinguist has criticized studies of language which make indiscriminate use of native speaker intuitions as data, and this criticism is particularly relevant when dealing with a "substandard," stigmatized, and subordinate code, which madya appears to be for at least some priyayi. If madya counts for conservative priyayi as what Labov calls a subordinate dialect,

> the subject may use his knowledge of the prestige dialect to avoid giving any vernacular form which is identical or similar to the standard, and so produce stereotyped forms which are simply a collection of the "most different" or "worst" sentence types. Speakers who have had extensive contact with the superordinate

---

[3] "The aim of research in the community must be to find out how people talk when they are not being systematically observed; yet we can only obtain these data by systematic observation" (1972:209). Wolff and Poedjosoedarmo (1982) chose to solve this problem by recording speech of speakers unaware of the presence of a tape machine. I recorded speech only with the permission of speakers, and found (as have others) that after a long period of time, the presence of a microphone has less effect on speech patterns as it becomes a normal part of the context of use.

[4] As Labov has noted (1972:111), an advantage of working with phonological variation is the relative smallness of the corpus of data sufficient for analysis; here this is not the case.

form no longer have clear intuitions about their
vernacular available for inspection. (1972:214)

On the other hand, in asking speakers who do not control the
superordinate dialect about their "own" subordinate dialect, one
creates what Labov calls a formal situation of use, which gives rise
to other problems:

Whenever a subordinate dialect is in contact with a
superordinate one, linguistic forms produced by a
speaker of the subordinate dialect in a formal context
will shift in an unsystematic manner towards the
superordinate. (1971:450)

Does this mean that the entire problem is in principle inaccessible
to systematic study? I would argue that it is not.

First of all, a large amount of data is required here for the
same reason that data consisting of native speaker judgments can
be used if certain precautions are taken. Silverstein (1977) has
argued that aspects of linguistic usage are differentially available to
native speakers' awareness for characterization and description. He
shows how phonological, morphophonemic, and grammatical
elements are less susceptible than lexical elements to such
objectification by native speakers,[5] and the same may be true of
alternations within each of these structural strata. Since speech
level variation exists essentially at the lexical level, one may
legitimately expect that speakers are better able to inspect and
verbalize their reactions to the structure of such examples more
accurately than to morphological and phonological variation. And
while it is true that speakers do spontaneously provide examples
of madya speech which are (as Labov suggests) the "most
different" from standard krama, it is also true those examples are
entirely accurate exemplifications of madya usage which can be
observed among all kinds of speakers.

Speakers often characterize examples of madya as language
that has no rules; I was told by one person that I did not have to

---

[5]This argument is extended to different aspects of the speech levels
in Errington (1985, 1988).

study it, I could make it up as I went along. But they nonetheless provide examples which are entirely consistent with the actual types of usage that a pedicab driver (for instance) normally uses. The structural coherency of madya emerges more clearly still when informants consider examples as possible utterances in particular sorts of social situations, a task to which their quite overt prejudices are secondary or irrelevant. Even conservative priyayi who made the most caustic remarks about madya and madya users consistently rejected examples of madya which might seem to be minor variations on their own examples, but nonetheless violate encoded rules of cooccurrence. So, for instance, informants provided examples of madya like (4a) and (5a), and rejected the slightly modified versions (4b) and (5b).

  4a. Kula sing niki mawon, Pak.
*4b. Kula sing niki waé, Pak.
     I want just this one, Pak.

  5a. Sampéyan napa seking peken?
*5b. Sampéyan napa saka peken?
     Are you (coming) from the market?

Speakers are able to judge the well-formedness of such examples, and consistent patterns of social variation do in fact emerge from their judgments. Highly uniform results were obtained for judgments on sentences containing madya and ngoko forms, insofar as speakers of all ages and social backgrounds rejected and accepted the same sentences.

    The consistency with which all informants distinguished "good" and "bad" examples like those above, regardless of their own voiced opinion about the lack of rules governing "bad *basa*," stems from the fact that madya is not a subordinate dialect as are nonstandard dialects of other languages. Even conservative priyayi have some occasion to speak madya as a social dialect for dealing with those whom they see as members of their outgroup; this they will readily confirm because their general social milieu is such that all Javanese are sometimes obliged to use, and must therefore control, this subcode. But conservative speakers manifest that competence in spontaneous use only in a narrow range of situation-types, for a limited range of topics and purposes, and in highly stereotyped sorts of role relations.

Further evidence of the validity of elicited acceptability judgments are consistent patterns which do emerge from the data of properly screened informants (see below). When criteria for distinguishing between informants were developed and applied, it turned out that highly uniform results were obtained for judgments on sentences containing madya and ngoko elements. This consistency testifies to the usefulness of the approach, and makes it reasonable, in turn, to treat variation in judgments on examples of mixed krama and madya as accurate indicators of social attitudes to socially and linguistically distinct groups. They may further be real symptoms of differences in the structures and uses of repertoires.

The strongest conclusion to be drawn from the data presented below is that they accurately reflect the encoded syntagmatic rules which govern speakers' usage. The obvious objection is that such regularities as do turn up are simply artifacts of conceptions of proper use, skewed with the reality of spontaneous, unreflective interaction. The data would then simply reflect the same regular differences in attitude toward speech discussed in chapter 3, and would not bear on actual use. But even this weak conclusion would be significant in light of the hypothesis about different perceptions of and attitudes toward madya use and users developed in the previous chapter; it would indirectly parallel and corroborate general views of the place of speech styles in society, and therefore of changing social relations. Aside from that, the stronger conclusion can be supported with examples of observed use which are not so numerous as to independently bear the weight of the arguments being developed by themselves, but as a group corroborate native speakers' judgments and conclusions based on them.

Whatever the practical justification and problems for this approach, its usefulness depends finally on the conclusions to which it plausibly leads. I have in fact tried to get access to the same types of intuitions Padmasusastra relied on when he remarked in his *Serat Urapsari*:

> In *basa madya*, one may not use the krama of these words [listed below] . . . so for instance: *Kula namung*

niki ['I (want) only this one.'] does not work [lit. 'walk']. What works is *kula mung niki*. So with the other terms concerned in this matter. (1896:20)

A similar approach implemented almost one hundred years later yields results that are almost identical.

Other sources of data

As noted in chapter 1, accessible sources of examples of speech level usage (of the sort used extensively, for instance, by Uhlenbeck 1978) are conversations found in Javanese novels. As Labov has pointed out (1972:201) they are problematic since knowledge of the social background of an author is important for evaluating the accuracy of the usage he/she reports: as a member of the community, he/she holds particular linguistic and social attitudes which may be reflected in writing. The same holds for determining the possible effects of geographical varation, which various descriptions (like Padmasusastra's) give reason to believe is an important correlate of level use.

Are the texts from which examples might be gleaned authored by priyayi? By and large those from the first part of the century are, as can be inferred from authors' names and/or titles. But there are other relevant questions: Where is a given author from? How was he or she brought up? To what extent is the author mindful of the standard version of his language, and his/her exemplary role as a speaker/writer of it? How talented an observer and reporter of the natural day-to-day scene is the author? Such information is more difficult to come by. Padmasusastra, after all, noted that some varieties of madya were used by wife to husband, and among "little priyayi in the *désa*" (1896:10). Is this view (accurate or not) shared and acted on by other authors when they put pen to paper? Such social characteristics of an author, and his/her view of behavior among the members of social classes which his/her characters typify, would have to be fully known before examples of usage from literature could be properly evaluated. This is not to devalue such sources, but to point out that one makes assumptions in using them, and that the interpretive problems involved are as great as those involved in using native speakers' statements.

To use both types of data, an obvious and useful precaution can be taken, namely, the cross-checking and comparison of examples from written and oral sources to see if they share crucial structural traits. This is particularly important for the study of change in the paradigmatic sets which contain madya markers.

It may be difficult to obtain many relevant occasions of observed spontaneous speech, but some at least can be gathered to check conclusions developed in other ways. Over the extended period of time I associated with Javanese, I was in fact privy to linguistic interaction between members of their families, friends, and more or less familiar acquaintances. With almost all speakers who had accepted some example(s) which mixed madya and krama, it happened that a situation would arise at one time or another to which I was privy, and in which they spoke in that fashion to a friend, a new acquaintance, or to me. Conversely, it never happened that speakers who rejected such madya and krama mixture used such language, at least when I was in earshot.

Two other sources of data which will be used here are valuable because they share some of the advantages (as well as some of the disadvantages) of both observed and reported use. These are the popular and widely known 'Javanese language plays' (*sandiwara basa Jawa*)—extended soap-operatic plays broadcast regularly on the radio—and comedy skits (*dagelan*) sold on cassettes. Like spontaneous usage, they are oral; because they ostensibly mirror everday usage, they are closer to the "real thing" than written language. Like written language, they are relatively easily obtained and studied, but are also premeditated occasions of use, planned with varying degrees of specificity, and so lacking in spontaneity. Although I was not myself able to determine if actors in *sandiwara* were reading directly from prepared scripts, I was told by a friend who had worked in radio that in fact much was improvised from fairly sketchy outlines of episodes provided for the actors for rehearsal. Comedy skits make up a very rich oral genre. One of the most famous of the comedians working in this format, Basiyo, has recorded many cassettes of live performances in which the use of Javanese is obviously spontaneous and only partially rehearsed.[6]

Another problem with both types of source is that the speech one commonly finds in them is that of non-priyayi, both in reality and in their character-roles; indeed, the actors' personas are often markedly lower class. Speech from these sources therefore cannot be taken as directly representative of any part of my own informant population, but may nonetheless indicate in what ways non-priyayi speak. It would be wrong-headed to ignore the patterns of level use found within the larger society of which informants are members, especially if modern priyayi speakers appear to be assimilating into a different segment of that changing society.

For the same reason, data of observed usage collected from non-priyayi with whom I was in regular contact are considered and presented; these are useful corroboration for conclusions which are also supported by examples of language from plays and skits. Here Labov's characterization of usage by speakers of subordinate dialects and the problem of vernacular shifting is quite relevant. The data presented all come from speakers with whom I had developed fairly informal relations over a year or more, and with whom I was talking about something other than language. As the research progressed, I was able to complement my control of krama and ngoko with facility in madya, such that after dealing with me for a period of time I could converse with people without making them feel uncomfortable. So while it is possible that these speakers might initially have hypercorrected sporadically and unsystematically, this became progressively less frequent.

Using questionnaires

Accumulating data on madya was the single most time consuming task undertaken during the research period; writing, revising, and administering questionnaires, procuring good informants, checking responses, and tabulating data occupied much of my attention from the very start. Questionnaires

---

[6]I owe these examples to John Wolff, who arranged to have them transcribed, to Hadi Sudirman, who did the transcriptions, and to Alan Feinstein, who brought the transcriptions to my attention and kindly lent them to me.

containing examples like (1) to (5) were written to gather judgments on the form of madya speech combined ngoko, krama, and (when they existed) madya elements in various ways. Individual sentences within a given sentence-type thus shared a referential meaning, but were composed of different combinations of ngoko/madya/krama forms. In some cases it was neither possible nor desirable to test every possible combination (as for example the sentence type from which sentences 1, 2, and 3 are taken).

The questionnaires were preliminarily reviewed with a consultant I had known prior to the start of research, who was able to give judgments on the acceptability of examples, and to pick out (and sometimes suggest revisions of) sentence-types which were syntactically awkward or ill-formed. Sentence-types were based as much as possible on actual observed occasions of use, and in some cases on suggestions by speakers.

The results of this procedure indicate that there are obligatory madya alternants for forty-four ngoko forms in the "low" madya speech style which is made up otherwise of ngoko, plus three affixes which are used in both styles. An exhaustive test of just these paradigmatic sets, even in simple pair-wise combinations, would require more than 44-factorial sentence-types. This was clearly impossible to do, particularly since the grammatical functions and meanings of many made it difficult to combine them idiomatically. As far as was possible, the emphasis was placed on different combinations of the same forms to test for consistency and to try to control for any possible syntactic conditioning of cooccurrence restrictions.

By the time the corpus seemed adequate, there were twelve questionnaires containing one hundred and forty-nine sentence types and, in the first stage of the research, some two thousand five hundred sentences. The ngoko versions of these various sentence-types are listed in the appendix. The task of administering and checking responses on questionnaires obviously had to be carried out over a long period of time; most informants met with me regularly once or twice a week for anywhere between eight and fifteen months. In order to quickly minimize the size of the task I was asking these informants to perform without sacrificing thoroughness in cross-checking procedures, I adopted the policy of throwing out sentences rejected as unacceptable by all of the first eight informants who evaluated them. This group consisted of one older conservative[7] priyayi, three conservative younger priyayi, two modern younger priyayi, and two younger non-priyayi; all controlled full krama.

These unacceptable sentences are the primary data for isolating the crucial madya forms which must always cooccur with each other wherever possible in sentences with ngoko referential elements. Informants whom I found to be reliable (by criteria described below) unanimously rejected sentences in which at least one such slot was filled with an obligatory madya element and at least one other was not. The "bottom line" of the sentential repertoire for madya—and so the vocabulary of constitutive madya—is fairly clear, at least for the informant population studied.

This first phase of the research was completed in about eight months, during which time I cultivated relations with a number of other potential informants to whom short versions of the questionnaires were given. Since roughly half of the sentences in the first version were thrown out, the second round of questionnaires, though still divided into twelve installments, was considerably less onerous to complete. They were administered to three older conservative priyayi, one younger conservative priyayi, eight modern young priyayi, and one young non-priyayi who controlled good krama. The same procedure was used, although the entire process took less time.

When six weeks remained in the research period I examined the data tabulated from all completed questionnaires, picked out examples for which there was the most variation in acceptability judgments, and compiled them in a short questionnaire of about eighty sentences. I took this last questionnaire to older priyayi acquaintances I believed would be indisposed to judge one thousand or so examples of what they had told me was substandard language, but would nonetheless be willing to perform this lesser task. In several cases I had helped their children study English, done other favors, or otherwise caught their interest, and so was able to get four of them to take on this briefer task in good will.

---

[7]Henceforth, the labels "conservative" and "modern" are used to refer to speakers classified as such in chapter 3. Conservative speakers are those of groups A and B in table 2.1; modern speakers here are the younger priyayi and younger non-priyayi of group C. None of the 'little priyayi' discussed in chapter three filled out these questionnaires.

At about the same time I found two younger informants, one the child of a high-ranking prince whose judgments turned out to fit the conservative pattern of usage, the other a non-priyayi who spoke good *basa* and fit the modern pattern. As time was short, I asked them to fill out just the short questionnaire. Judgments on the sentences included in this short version form the body of data most relevant for a study of how elements of informal and formal krama combine with elements of madya at the "top end" of the range of madya speech styles.

The total informant population for this last questionnaire thus consisted of eight older priyayi, fifteen young priyayi (modern and conservative), and four non-priyayi culled from a total of thirty-eight prospective informants I had approached at one time or other.

Screening informants

Many speakers were unable to deal with the questionnaires and were disqualified through screening procedures. It became clear early in the research period that I needed some principled way to disqualify those informants who seemed to be giving inaccurate or at least inconsistent judgments.

Since I was acquainted with all prospective informants for some time before asking for help, I had an opportunity to observe their own usage and get an impression of their views on language and the traditional elite. Informants who agreed to undertake the task were first given a copy of one of the questionnaires, which we would go over orally. I would read a sentence, then ask them to repeat it out loud to themselves and decide if they would ever use a sentence like that. I always stressed that the question was neither "Is this a good sentence of *basa*?" nor "Do people ever use language like this?" Those who had trouble grasping the distinction I was drawing usually got the idea after going over a few examples. Several nonetheless insisted on distinguishing between sentences which they themselves would not use, but (they felt) were used by other speakers. Almost all these sentences, as it turns out, are a subset of the sentences for which there is significant variation within the informant population, but their judgments have been tabulated with those of unacceptability in accordance with the original criteria for evaluation.

Ordinarily we would go over about half of a questionnaire together the first time, and the informant was left to judge the rest on his/her own. When explaining how to complete the questionnaires, I constantly repeated a few basic points: do only a few at a time, jump from sentence group to sentence group, and don't rush. Because the pace was not hurried, there was ample opportunity for completed questionnaires to be checked, and I repeatedly stressed that it was best for informants to take their time and do the job accurately, saying each sentence out loud before judging it to get its 'feeling' (*rasa*).

After a sheet was handed back (on the average every one and a half or two weeks) I would check reliability and consistency of judgments by going back over sentences and asking for new judgments on some of them. Since the informant could not see what his/her original judgment had been, the number of sentences being dealt with provided the back-handed advantage of preventing informants from simply repeating a remembered judgment.

This checking process was exhaustive at first, involving the review of at least three-quarters of each of the first two sheets completed; this sometimes took two or three sessions per sheet during the first part of the research. Checking sessions were always broken up with light conversation and talk about other topics, so as to mitigate the repetitiveness of the task. If an informant contradicted himself/herself more than two times in ten in the first two or three questionnaires, I would, however regretfully, refrain from asking that informant more questions. Several informants disqualified themselves during the very first session by claiming that some sentences which they were not able to accurately repeat were acceptable.

During the lengthy process of filling out and checking questionnaires, I was able to get a general impression of how informants felt about the kinds of usage they were examining, and the investigation naturally extended during interviews to discussion of the appropriate contexts of use for sentences judged as acceptable. At the same time, I found myself increasingly using my informants' own descriptive vocabulary in discussion, speaking of the 'feeling' (*rasa*) of sentences as 'fluent' (*luwes*) or 'stiff' (*kaku*), or saying it was *sreg* or not *sreg*. *Sreg* might be least inaccurately translated as 'the feeling of knowing you're right.' Another common characterization was in terms of whether the example 'felt good' (was *kepénak*) or not.

Reliable informants used these sorts of pretheoretical, intuitive evaluations for examples without preconceived notions about what specific structural properties acceptable madya sentences did or should have. Some informants could isolate a single element which disturbed them, saying it was 'very ngoko' (*ngoko banget*) or 'too refined' (*kalusen*), but these too were subjective judgments (with objective correlates) of just the type I was looking for.

Described this way the procedure appears automatized and mechanical, which to a degree it was; but it would be misleading not to acknowledge that my own hunches about informants and their judgments constantly influenced the way in which the informants were checked. Some informants were more consistent and insightful than others, and it did not take too long to figure out which were which. But my suspicions that an informant's judgments did not correspond with his/her own usage were not borne out by back-checking in only one case (an older priyayi), and so I feel compelled by my own standards to include his judgments in the tabulation of data presented below.

THE STRUCTURE OF MADYA

The obligatory madya vocabulary items determined by this procedure are presented in table 4-1, which contains all alternants found to obligatorily cooccur with each other in otherwise ngoko sentences under the heading "madya."[8] Cases of multiple madya alternants for ngoko forms are discussed below. The comparative, historical and structural aspects of madya all deserve brief discussion. There are numerous discrepancies between this and other treatments, which are attributable first to different uses of ambiguous native terms, and second to the lack of a distinction in some descriptions between vocabulary obligatorily used in madya speech, and vocabulary typical but only optional in some dialects of madya speech.

---

[8] Not mentioned in table 4.1 are the affixes *di-*, *-é*, genitive marker and nominalizer, and *-aké*, which are all obligatory madya as well as ngoko.

Comparison of examples of madya usage in literature dating from different eras indicates that the madya vocabulary has in fact been relatively stable over the last century, unlike the vocabulary called *krama désa* with which it has sometimes been conflated and confused. There is evidence suggesting that two madya forms may have come into use (at least among priyayi) relatively recently, having evolved perhaps as a result of the same contraction and elision processes to be discussed later vis-a-vis formal and informal styles of krama and ngoko. These forms may have been in existence among non-priyayi for some time and only recently become part of priyayi madya usage, perhaps as an indirect result of their assimilation into the larger speech community.

Another point which deserves discussion is the doubly interstitial form of madya speech. Since some obligatory madya elements are identical with their ngoko or krama equivalents, certain sentences may be structurally ambiguous in the sense that they simultaneously conform on one hand to structural constraints on madya, and on the other count as either ngoko or krama sentences. Madya is doubly interstital, as informants' classifications show.

Madya vs. krama desa

Numerous discrepancies can be found between different descriptions of madya, among them, Padmasusastra 1896, Walbeehm 1897, Poedjsoedarmo n.d., Wolff and Poedjosoedarmo 1982 (see the summary in table 4.2). But some of these differences are merely apparent, and result from different uses of labels for two distinct types of non-ngoko forms: madya and désa *krama désa* ('village krama'). The meanings of these two terms can be fairly consistently and usefully distinguished in several ways. Most important here are (1) differences in educated urban speakers' evaluations of two different types of words, (2) differing kinds of contributions each type of form makes to linguistic or referential meaning, (3) the types of paradigmatic sets of which they are part, and (4) their susceptibility (or lack thereof) to change in response to different kinds of sociolinguistic pressure.

Table 4.1

OBLIGATORY MADYA VOCABULARY

NGOKO/KRAMA	GLOSS	MADYA EQUIVALENT(S)
aja/sampun	negative imperative	ampun:1,2,3,4 mpun:1,4
aku,-ku,dak-/kula	first person pronoun	kula:1,2,4
ana/wonten	there is, there are	ènten:1,2,3,4 onten:1,2,3,4
apa/menapa	'what,' yes/no question marker	napa:1,2,3,4
ayo/mangga	"let's go," "please"	ngga:1,2,3,4
dudu/sanès	no, not (of nouns)	senès:1,2,4
durung/dèrèng	not yet	dèrèng:1,2,4
iki; kuwi; kaé/menika	this; that; that (over there)	niki; niku; nika:1,2,3,4
iki lho; kuwi lho; kaé lho/menika,lho	this, y'know; that y'know;...(see above)	(ne)gilo; (ne)gélo; (ne)galo:1,2,3,4
isih/taksih	still (verbal aux.)	tasih:1,2,3,4 tesih:1,2,4
iya/inggih	assent marker	nggèh:1,2,3,4
karo/kaliyan	along with	kalih:3,4
kéné; kono;kana/ mriki;mriku;mrika	here; there; over there	ngriki; ngriku; ngrika:1,2,3,4
kepriyé/kados pundi	how about it?	(ke)pripun:1,2,3,4
kowé/panjenengan	second person pronoun	sampéyan:1,2 (sa)mang:1,2,3 ngenengan
manèh/malih	again, more	melih:1,2,4
mangkéné;mangkono; mankana/mekaten	like this; like that; like that (over there)	ngèten;ngoten; ngaten:1,3,4
marang/dhateng	to (a person)	teng:1,2,3,4
mau/wau	just now	wau:1,2,4

Table 4.1 continued

mengko/mangké	later	mengké:1,2,4 ngké:4
menyang/dhateng	to (a place)	teng:1,2,3,4
mung/namung	only (of nouns)	mung,ming:1,2,4
ndi/pundi	interrogative which	pundi:1,2,4
nya/mangga	"take it," "go ahead"	ngga:1,2,4
ora/mboten	no, not (of verbs, adjectives)	mboten:1,2,4
ping/kaping	number of times	ping:4
pira/pinten	how much	pinten:1,2,4
saiki/samenika	now	saniki:3,4
saka/saking	from, because of	seking:3,4 king:3,4
sapa/sinten	interrogative who	sinten:1,2,4
seméné; semono; semana/semanten	this much; that much; that much over there	(se)mènten; se)monten; (se)manten:1,2,3,4
sepréné/sepriki	up to now	sepriki:1,2,4
sing/ingkang	relative pronoun	sing:1,2,4
waé/kéwawon	only, just	mawon:1,2,3,4 mon,men:3,4
wis/sampun	already	mpun:1,2,3,4
yèn/menawi	if, when	nèk:4 yèn:4

Numbers after forms in the third column indicate other sources in which they are assigned to the madya category. 1=Walbeehm (1897) 2=Padmasusastra (1896), 3=Poedjosoedarmo (n.d.), 4=Wolff and Poedjosoedarmo (1982).

Semicolons separate members of deictic series in one style. Interlevel alternants (ngoko/krama) are separated by a slash.

Krama désa and madya vocabulary items are similar in that many priyayi consider both "substandard," albeit in unobviously different ways. Madya forms, which mark either informal or substandard non-ngoko speech styles (depending on one's perspective) are used by all speakers in at least some sorts of situations, and so are part of their working repertoires even if they classify such usage by outgroup. Although some conservative speakers identify madya as outgroup language by calling examples of madya speech *krama désa*, as we saw in chapter 3, all conservative speakers distinguish between vocabulary they will use—the madya forms in table 4.1—and vocabulary items which they say are used only by uneducated, typically rural speakers. Modern speakers similarly identify these latter kinds of expressions and forms as the dialect of uneducated villagers, what is usually called in the literature *krama désa*. In terms of social significance of use for educated urban speakers, then, *krama désa* vocabulary can be defined as the set of words which all such speakers classify as outgroup usage, and deny using themselves.

As a rule, madya and *krama désa* elements make complementary contributions to the referential meanings of sentences, and are parts of different types of paradigmatic sets. Obligatory madya forms are not found for the non-indexical referential vocabulary, and most (but not all) have distinct ngoko and krama equivalents in three-member paradigmatic sets. The bulk of the *krama désa* vocabulary, on the other hand, is comprised almost entirely of non-ngoko alternants which are lexically referential and have no distinct krama equivalents. *Krama désa* forms are in fact often coined by speakers in the false belief that a krama alternant to a ngoko word should or does exist.

Madya is a small vocabulary within a fairly clearly circumscribed range of categories, whereas *krama désa* is a relatively large and open-ended vocabulary set. At the same time, the types of resemblances which exist between sound shapes of many madya elements and their ngoko and/or krama equivalents generally contrast with those which exist between *krama désa* forms and their ngoko equivalents. As can be seen in table 4.1, many madya forms are contractions or elisions of their krama counterparts. But as has often been noted in the literature, *krama désa* forms result from extension of semi-productive correspondences already existing in patterned alternations between ngoko and krama forms. Through this hypercorrective process, which Uhlenbeck calls "kramafication" (1978:288), speakers push analogies between ngoko/krama pairs past the target established as standard usage by priyayi speakers. On the basis of the sound shape alternations between ngoko and krama words like *-ira/ -inten*—found, for instance between the words *pira* (ngoko) and *pinten* (krama) 'how much,' or *dina* (ngoko) and *dinten* (krama) 'day'—a new *krama désa* form for 'Chinese' has been coined from *Cina*, that is, *Cinten*.

No analogous relations can be found among madya equivalents of ngoko forms, many of which resemble their krama equivalents but are shortened, elided or otherwise colloquialized in ways discussed below. So there are good reasons for drawing a fairly sharp distinction between the vocabularies called madya and *krama désa*. These have not, however, always been kept in mind by scholars who doubtless recognized differences between the two vocabulary types, or by speakers with a subjective purview who do not. The forms *ndaweg* and *ndeg* ('go ahead,' 'take it,' and 'please') are not part of the repertoire of any of my informants, who use *ngga*—a short form of *mangga*—in madya. *Ndaweg* and *ndeg* are classifiable for them as *krama désa* forms which are virtually obsolete (at least in Surakarta).[9] The forms *negilo* . . . (also sometimes *negilé* . . .) are merely fast speech forms of *niki, lho* . . . and so are essentially identical to the members of that deictic series. (The orthographic device ". . ." is used here to indicate that the entire series of three deictics is being discussed; table 4-1 provides the members of each.)

For the series of deictics corresponding to ngoko *mangkono*, 'like this,' Walbeehm and Padmasusastra list two different types of equivalents in madya, kramafied "full" equivalents of the ngoko *ma(ng)kèten . . ./me(ng)kèten* . . . as well as the shorter form *ngèten* . . . The "full" form was classified by all my informants as *krama désa*, and none reported or were ever observed to use it.

---

[9]Padmasusastra uses *ndaweg* repeatedly in the *Serat Tatacara*. It should be noted that all of these forms can be used individually to perform certain types of independent acts of speaking such as thanking, inviting, urging, and so on. The commonly *ngga* used in fact alternates relatively freely in actual use with its krama counterpart *mangga*. But use of either counts as an individual speech act.

Table 4.2

DISCREPANCIES BETWEEN SOURCES

NGOKO/KRAMA	GLOSS	MADYA FORM(?)	PRESENT RESEARCH
*aja/sampun	negative imperative	mpun:4 ampun:1,4 aja:4	mpun (md) =wis (ng), ampun(md) =aja (ng)
akèh/kathah	many, much	akèh:1 okèh:1,2	optional
anggo/anggé	use (tr. verb)	nggé:3	optional
*ayo/mangga		ndaweg,deg:1,2	krama désa
arep/badhé	will (aux.)	ajeng:1,2,3,4	optional
bakal/badhé	will (aux.)	ajeng:1,2	optional
banget panrimaku/ matur nuwun	thank you	nedhanrima:1,2	krama désa, optional(?)
bésuk/benjing	future time	njing:3	optional
biyèn/rumiyin	long ago	siyèn:1 sengiyin:1,2 sengiyèn:1 riyin	krama désa krama désa krama désa optional
dhisik/rumiyin	right away, long ago	kriyin:1 riyin:3 siyèn:1,2	optional krama désa
*dudu/sanès	no, not (of nouns)	dédé:1,2,3,4 senès:2	krama désa
*durung/dèrèeng	not yet	durung:4	ngoko
généya/kados pundi	how is it that?	napaha:2	krama désa
jaréné/cariyosipun	it is said	turéné:1,2,3 criyosé:3 turé:1,3 tosé:3	krama désa optional krama désa
kabèh/sedaya	all, every	sedanten:2	krama, krama désa
kandhut	carry	kèndhat:1,2	krama désa
karebèn/kajengipun	forget it	jengèn:3	optional

Table 4.2 continued

kari/kantun	left behind	kèntun:1,2	krama désa
*kepriyé/kados pundi	how about it	prèhpun, prahpun, prihpun:1,2	krama désa(?) obsolete(?)
kliru/klintu	in error	klèntu:2	krama
*kowé/panjenengan	2nd person pronoun	kang salira:1,2 ndika:1,2,3	polite ngoko krama désa
lagi/saweg	continuative auxiliary	seg:3 saweg:3,4	krama désa optional
*manèh/malih	again	malih:1,2,4	krama
*mangkéné-mankono/mekaten	like this-like that	me(ng)kèten-me(ng)koten:1,2	krama désa
mbuh/mboten	I don't know	wikana:1,2 ikana:3	krama désa krama désa
*mung/namung	only (of nouns)	kur:1 gur:1,2	krama désa krama désa
ngerti/ngertos	understand	ngertos:3	optional
*nya/mangga	"please," "go ahead"	ndaweg,deg:1	krama désa
olèhé/anggènipun	nominalizer	(ang)salé:3	optional
rupané/rupinipun	apparently	rupiné:2	krama désa
*sepréné/sepriki	up to now	sepriki-sepriku:2	obsolete
siji/setunggal	one	senunggil:1,2 senunggal:1,2	krama désa krama désa
*sing/ingkang	which	kang:1,2 keng:1,2 dhing:1,2	formal ngoko formal ngoko krama désa
sumurup/sumerap	know, recognize	ninga:2	obsolete
teka(n)/dumugi	arrived, up to	dugi:3	optional
weruh/sumerap	see	ninga:1,2	krama désa

*See note to table 4.1, p. 139.

The single greatest number of differences in the vocabularies occur in the second person pronoun paradigm, which has been quite mutable over the last century. *Ndika* has fallen from use (at least in Surakarta) and counts now as part of out-group usage; to the extent it is still used, it can be classified now as *krama désa*. At the same time the form *sampeyan* has "fallen," as it were, from its formerly deferential usage into regular madya. A new colloquialized form *njenengan* (from *panjenengan* and *penjenengan*) has come into use, on which more below. *Kang salira*, discussed in chapter 2, is now used only in polite ngoko speech containing deferentials for reference to addressee. *Kur* and *gur*, ('only, just'), are listed by Walbeehm and Padmasusastra as alternants in madya for *mung*, but all my informants classified them as *kasar* forms which were used only by lower class speakers (i.e., their outgroup).

When the characteristics of madya forms are considered, then, it appears that this treatment of madya vocabulary actually diverges from Walbeehm's and Padmasusastra's in only three respects. Likewise, discrepancies between this description, and Poedjosoedarmo (n.d.) and Wolff and Poedjosoedarmo (1982) appears to result largely from different foci of research.

The present research shows *kalih* 'and, along with' to be the obligatory madya word for ngoko *karo*, and *(se)king* 'from, because, on account of' to be the obligatory madya equivalent of ngoko *saka* (with restrictions to be described below). *Ping* 'number of times' is obligatory in madya (as opposed to *kaping*, the krama equivalent). Walbeehm and Padmasusastra list none of these; Wolff and Poedjosoedarmo make no mention of *ping* as obligatory in madya. In modern Surakarta *ping* is used in both madya and ngoko, and appears in examples of madya in texts dating from the last century. The cases of *(se)king* and *kalih* appear to be more problematic, and may represent relatively recent innovations in madya vocabulary, or at least in written renditions of madya speech.

There is evidence for Padmasusastra's and Walbeehm's (indirect) claim that *saka* may be used in sentential madya in at least two sources. In Winter's well-known text *Javaansche Zamenspraken* (1848) we find one woman from the village saying to a friend:

> Malah mbeneri ing Septu Paing wau anak kula Si Clili
> mulih *saka ing* désa.
> As a matter of fact, it happens that this past Saturday
> Paing [a day of the Javanese calendar] my child Clili
> came home *from* the village.

Here a madya sentence—marked as such by use of the words *wau* and *kula* (which are also krama) together with ngoko words like *mulih* and *désa*—contains *saka ing*, meaning 'from.' Similarly, in a didactic set of small plays dealing with the dangers of smoking opium, the *Serat Erang-erang* (1916), Padmasusastra (under the name Wirapustaka) himself has one character say to another:

> Mang wau *saka* ing pundi?
> You just now (are coming) *from* where?

Here too, *saka* is is used in what is otherwise a sentence of madya.[10] Similarly in the *Serat Tatacara* one finds regular use in madya speech of *saka*, and neither *seking* or *king*. In two other texts which date from 1917, on the other hand, are examples of madya in which some word other than *saka* or the phrase *saka ing* meaning 'from' is used. In *Dora Sembada*, (Sutarja 1917), written for the education and edification of the peasants by a priyayi who taught in the Surakartan school system, one peasant says to another

> Mungguh lelara kolerah niku asalé nggih *saking* wong
> lara kolerah ugi.
> As for the disease cholera, that comes *from* people who
> are sick with cholera.

Although the form used here is (when transliterated into Roman orthography) *saking*, rather than *seking* or *king*, this is clearly a madya sentence (marked as such by *niku, nggih,* and the mixture

---

[10]As noted in chapter 1, the limitations and conventions of Javanese orthography may explain the failure of these authors to write the equivalent of *seking*, but then one would have to explain why other authors have been able and willing to provide more phonetically accurate representations of spoken language in their writings.

of ngoko and krama referential items) in which the author did not use *saka*.[11] In another work written by a priyayi and published in the same year, *Layang Neka Catur* (Samsirmiardja 1917) we find *king* in the madya sentence:

> *King* pundi anak wau?
> *From* where (are you) child (coming) just now?

in which the madya word *king* is used rather than *saka*.

Similar evidence that *kalih* may also have come to be introduced into madya in priyayi usage, or at least in the way priyayi writers represented madya usage around the turn of the century can be drawn from these texts. In *Javaansche Zamenspraken*, one of the characters says:

> Biyèn kula rak pinuju barengan mawon *karo* ndika teng omahé Nyai Labha.
> Before didn't I happen to go *along with* you to the house of Nyai Labha.

Here the word for 'along with' is *karo*, and in madya usage in this work *karo*, and never *kalih*, always appears. In other texts, however, *kalih* regularly appears in madya. So for example, from *Layang Neka Catur*:

> Lha nggih niku bedané Jawa *kalih* Cina . . . .
> Of course, that's the difference between the Javanese *and* the Chinese . . .

Kalih is consistently used in all madya conversation in this work and in *Dora Sembada*:

> Niku bener banget, rujuk *kalih* karep kula.
> That's very true, (it) fits *with* my intention.

---

[11]The spelling he used could well be an artifact of regular use of standard orthography; the symbol for shwa (the *pepet*) might have been omitted to avoid a non-standard spelling of a substandard word. Whether or not Javanese readers would have spontaneously reduced that vowel when reading aloud is a relevant but unanswerable question.

In the *Serat Tatacara*, written prior to the end of the century but well after the *Javaansche Zamenspraken*, *kalih* is consistently used in madya.

Despite these two cases, for which there appear to be consistent differences in usage and evidence of change in madya, the madya vocabulary appears to have been very stable as a whole.

Optional madya

In some sources there are forms classified as madya which are not structurally obligatory in or crucial delimiters of madya speech. Insofar as they have equivalents which can equally well be used in madya, these other forms can be counted for present purposes as *krama désa* if urban educated speakers reject them as outgroup usage. So for instance *nedhanrima* 'thank you' and *wikana* 'I don't know' are not obligatory in any style of madya used by the urban speakers I worked with. Even if these forms are used by some Javanese, they count for my informants as *krama désa* insofar as they are stigmatized forms stereotyped as village usage. Poedjosoedarmo (n.d.) lists *ikana* (from *wikana*) as dialectal (Indonesian: *dialek*), presumably alluding in a more technical way to the same social attributes adduced by native speakers with the term *krama désa*.

The form *sedanten*, originally *krama désa*, has evolved into optional krama, and in Surakarta is used by some (particularly young) speakers rather than the formerly unique standard krama equivalent (*sedaya*) of ngoko *kabèh*. All three may be used in some variety of madya or other. Padmasusastra may have classified *sedanten* as madya because for those of his social background and generation it was substandard usage. But unlike the madya vocabulary listed in table 4.1, it has gradually evolved into an alternate standard krama form.[12]

Poedjosoedarmo (n.d.) lists many forms treated here as "optional" in madya, as fits with his own particular descriptive

---

[12]This process, described by Walbeehm (1897), fits Labov's description of change from "above" and "below" the level of linguistic consciousness. In this respect his model of the mechanism of linguistic change (1972) applies to the Javanese case for this subclass of non-ngoko vocabulary.

ends. Similarly, other forms meaning 'it is said' listed by Walbeehm, Padmasusastra, as well as Poedjosoedarmo are optional in madya. Besides (composed of *atur-* plus *+-é*,)[13] and *wartosé* (from *wartos, krama désa*: news'), there appear *criyosé* (from *cariyos*, k:'story') and the ngoko equivalent *jaréné*, which itself has a short, informal alternant *jé*, also used in ngoko and madya. *Riyin* is also optional in, though typical of, madya speech, a short form of the standard krama *rumiyin* (which contains the petrified infix *-um-*). Just as *rumiyin* can be used in krama to mean 'right away' and 'long ago,' *riyin* may (but does not obligatorily) substitute for the ngoko words *dhisik* ('right away,' 'long ago') and *biyèn* ('long ago') in madya sentences. *Riyin* is not used in krama—at least in conservative dialects (see below)—but neither is it an obligatory constituent of madya.[14]

The interstitial structure of madya speech

Since forms like *sing, kula, mboten,* and *ping* and others must be counted on distributional grounds as belonging to two vocabularies—madya on one hand, either ngoko or krama on the other—some sentences which contain just such level markers are structurally ambiguous between two level classifications. It is true, as Geertz (1960:253) indicates, that "[I]n utterances of more than minimal length the chance that at least one krama/madya/ngoko style marker will occur is nearly unity." But if those "style markers" are identical in ngoko and madya, and happen to be combined in sentences with other ngoko elements, the result will

---

[13]*Atur* is a deferential which marks the status of person toward whom the action referred to is directed as being higher than that of the person asking. In the literature this subset of the deferential vocabulary is often called *krama andhap*.

[14]*Riyin* is not listed by Wolff and Poedjosoedarmo in their table of madya forms. They are concerned less with variation in the native Javanese community than with demonstrating the continuum-like nature of madya and distinguishing between high, middle, and low madya speech. But to do this they draw no distinction, as have I, between specifically madya forms, optional madya forms, or lexically referential ngoko/krama alternants typical in but not distinctive of madya speech.

be structurally classifiable as either ngoko and madya. A sentence like (6a), for example, has the elements *mung* and *sing* which count as both madya and ngoko, and except for the kin term and proper name (Mas Poino), all other elements are ngoko.

6a. Mung Mas Poino sing teka dhèk wingi.
6b. Mung Mas Poino sing dhateng kala wingi.
Mas Poino was the only one who arrived yesterday.

Sentence 6a counts structurally as both madya and ngoko, and further information concerning an occasion and context of use would be necessary to determine social significance.

Similarly, a question like (7a) contains two obligatory madya words which are identical with their krama counterparts, *kula* and *pinten*.

7a. Kula saged mendhet pinten?
7b. Kula isa tuku pinten?
How many can I take?

Since both other elements of (7a) are krama which may but need not be used in madya, the sentence could count structurally as either krama or madya.

But examples of these same sentence-types which contain both ngoko and krama such as (6b) and (7b) can only count as madya sentences, marked as such by the cooccurrence of elements of both ngoko and krama. In a sentence in which a ngoko word like *isa* appears, *kula* must be treated as madya (7b), as must *mung* or *sing* when they cooccur with the krama word *dhateng* (6b).

There are thus two senses in which madya refers to interstitial vocabulary and speech styles, "between" ngoko and krama. The fact that native speakers regularly classify structurally ambiguous examples such as (6a) and (7a) as ngoko and krama (respectively) reflects the structural and functional priority of each style over madya within the system as a whole.

KRAMA VS. MADYA, COLLOQUIAL AND OTHERWISE

We saw in chapter 3 that use of madya can be thought of as functionally ambiguous vis-a-vis social contexts of appropriate use. Conservative speakers identify it as socially interstitial, in the sense that it is appropriately spoken to members of an outgroup when neither ngoko nor krama styles are appropriate. For modern speakers it is also intermediate in that it is appropriate when one's relation with a speech partner peer is in flux and/or somewhat but not entirely familiar. The general difference in conceptions of use of madya which emerges from reports by these two sorts of speakers corresponds to contrasting structures of the ranges of examples of madya they find acceptable.

In many treatments of the levels these social-functional ambiguities of madya are downplayed or ignored, and its status for conservative speakers as substandard non-ngoko speech, appropriate for use with outgroup members, is disregarded. Generally, madya's structural intermediacy is linked to its use as language of intermediate formality. In this respect the following remarks are typical.

> In Javanese, level choice is a cline: one may speak on a purely low level or on a purely high level or on any of an infinite[15] number of levels in between, depending on how many and for which particular meanings one chooses the high as opposed to the low alternative forms. (Wolff 1976:221)

> Madya is not a set of fixed forms, but is rather a cline rising from a level very close to Ngoko up to a level very close to Krama. (Wolff and Poedjosoedarmo 1982:17)

> Madya can be viewed as a half-way house; it is a code of intimacy used to a person to whom one cannot use Ngoko; it is a code of nonintimacy to interlocutors to

---

[15]Strictly speaking the choice made by speakers finite since utterances are of finite length, and are made up of elements which have finite numbers of alternants.

whom Krama is too high. (Wolff and Poedjosoedarmo 1982:20)

In the Surakartan community this view is predominant among modern priyayi but not among conservative priyayi speakers, who judge speech level use with reference to an image of krama as standard register, and madya as substandard social dialect. They do not see madya as basically "informal *basa*," abbreviated non-ngoko speech with "the important function of putting the relation between addressee and addresser on a more intimate and confidential footing" (Uhlenbeck 1978:310).

To understand madya's place in the system of sentential speech levels is to understand its relations with all other types of level variants which make for socially distinct varieties of speech behavior. For this reason, yet another type of formal/informal variation has to be considered at least briefly here to deal with the question of the systematic status of madya as informal *basa* vis-a-vis informal krama, another kind of informal *basa*.

The stylistic variants studied thus far contrast as distinct sound-shapes which share linguistic "meaning," but there is another kind of variation in the realization of those distinct sound shapes in actual speech. These latter distinguish styles comparable to "colloquial" and "formal" speech in English and many other languages. It is as if such variation is superimposed on the lexical variants between which a speaker chooses to use a speech level. This second kind of variation creates a distinct yet related dimension of socially significant variation in language use. It is the interrelation of the two that is important for trying to find the "top line" of madya variation, what (if anything) distinguishes it from krama.

There are regular parallels between patterns of reduction and elision of words and morphemes in ngoko and krama speech, but they operate relatively more freely in ngoko than in krama speech. These can be described with "low-level" rules for abbreviation and elision of just the sort Labov (1972:70-110) argues can be isolated only in casual, colloquial speech. As he further suggests, they make for variation of which speakers are less aware, are less able to characterize, and/or spontaneously produce. Krama is normatively and inherently "formal" speech, opposed as such to the "colloquial" or "informal" ngoko. To an extent phonological reduction processes operate independently but also in conformance with systematic features of lexically distinguished levels.

Although the existence of intralevel variation has been recognized by most students of Javanese, the parallels between formal/informal krama and formal/informal ngoko on one hand, and between krama and madya on the other, have not been dealt with systematically.[16] Differences between conservative and modern speakers' acceptability judgments, to be discussed below, are best understood as reflecting two different ranges of application of these colloquializing processes, and further as correlating with two different views of speech styles, contexts of use, and speech partners.

Formal and informal ngoko

Before examining formal/formal variation in the "standard krama" used by priyayi who control "proper" non-ngoko language it is worth considering variation which makes for variant ngoko styles ranging from highly formal to colloquial, marked by variation analogous to that in krama.

The formal variety of ngoko is rarely used in modern Surakarta, and was presumably never appropriate outside of a few particular sorts of situations. Like formal/literary krama, such ngoko speech is marked by literary, often archaic (or archaicized) words, and by "full" or non-elided forms, unlike those common in colloquial speech. The latter sorts of intralevel alternations mark different degrees of formality or informality in ngoko speech. For example, the alternation between *piyé* and *kepriyé* (ngoko: 'how about it') by itself does not mark informal and formal ngoko as distinctly as does that between the highly formal or literary *menawa* ('when, if,' cf. krama *menawi*) and the more common *yèn* or still more colloquial *nèk*.

It is not difficult to devise pairs of ngoko sentences to illustrate the pronounced differences between the most formal and colloquial of ngoko styles, sentences 8 (formal) and 9 (informal):

---

[16]Wolff and Poedjosoedarmo (1982), for note that it exists, but do not extend their analysis to the place of such variation in relation to the particulars of krama/madya variation in the community.

8. Manawa ana kang kaya mangkono ana ing kéné, kepriyé?
9. Nèk ènèng sing kaya ngono nèng kéné, piyé?
   If there are any like that here, how about it?

Sentence 8 is very formal in feeling, and although all informants recognize such examples as formal ngoko, many younger priyayi informants (modern and conservative) reported they never speak that way, although (some further noted) their fathers might have occasion to. It exemplifies the style appropriate, for example, in the kind of speech called *wejangan*, words of wisdom and advice bestowed by a wise elder on a younger person; the medium lends dignity and importance to the message. Several older priyayi informants noted that prior to the war, it was not uncommon for the head of an office in the royal administration to address his assembled subordinates in this way when relaying messages from above, or giving general orders. I observed such usage only once, from an elderly gentleman to his nephew concerning the need and means for achieving domestic tranquility.

In ngoko speech, colloquialization processes operate over a very broad range of sound shapes and vocabulary. There are regular alternations, for instance, between "full" ngoko sound shapes containing two vowels with intervocalic glide, and monosyllabic alternants containing just the vowel of the second syllable. *Ga*, for example, is derived from *gawa* ('carry'), *dhé* from *dhuwé* ('have, own'), and *dhit* from *dhuwit* ('money'). Thus, one may say colloquially *ra dhé dit*, rather than *ora ndhuwé dhuwit* '(I) don't have money.' Similarly, *kaé* ('that over there') reduces regularly to *ké*, and *kuwi* to *ki*. Initial syllables of other polysyllabic sound shapes can be regularly elided; from *bocah* 'child,' for instance, is derived *cah*, and from *cilik* ('small') is derived *lik*.

The sublexical variation thus created in ngoko speech makes for another type of stylistic contrast—a sublevel or intralevel type of distinction—of a sort found in many if not all non-pidgin languages. It is important for an understanding of social variation in speech level use because the breadth of application of analogous processes in krama appears to vary in the speech community, and to correlate with views of madya containing krama lexemes as a variety of formal *basa*. Differences between uses of these ngoko and krama intralevel alternations exist insofar as conservative priyayi speakers appear to reduce and elide just those elements of krama speech which are trisyllabic and longer, and are grammatical/syntactic and deictic elements of the sort discussed above: words and phrases meaning 'how about,' 'this much,' 'if, when,' etc. Many of these have distinct madya equivalents. In conservative usage, reduction processes apparently do not extend in any general way to referential vocabulary, or to sound shapes composed of less than three syllables. This contrasts with the colloquialization processes which operate in all speakers' ngoko usage to derive reduced sound shapes for much broader ranges of vocabulary. Differences in the acceptability judgments on krama sentences, and madya speech containing krama lexemes discussed below, then, can be treated as indices of different ranges of applicability of these fast-speech processes in ngoko and krama.

This bears directly on the problem of determining if there is a "line" between krama and madya, because variation in acceptability judgments suggests that modern priyayi speakers and their non-priyayi peers colloquialize krama speech more regularly and broadly than do conservative speakers; if this is the case, madya sentences containing krama referential items used by modern priyayi speakers (and their non-priyayi peers who control full krama) can be treated as a krama style in which ngoko-type colloquial patterns apply relatively freely to reduce formality of otherwise formal speech.

The parallelism between "full" and colloquial ngoko forms and alternations "across" the line between krama and madya appears in a comparison between sets of reduced and elided madya/krama forms on one hand, and between colloquial ngoko and "full" ngoko forms on the other. In some instances, formal/informal alternants in a single paradigmatic set contribute either to intralevel variation, or to apparent cross-level variation. One example is the paradigmatic set which contains *saka/seka/ka* in ngoko, *seking/king* in madya, and *saking* in krama. The vowel reduction which makes for one informal alternant in ngoko (*seka*) is paralleled by a madya alternant to the full krama. Furthermore, the ngoko *saka* can be reduced to *seka* or *ka* only in particular syntactic environments,[17] which parallel those in which madya

---

[17]A convenient if imperfect analog in which illustrates this is the restriction on reduction of the sound shape of "to" from [tu] to [ta] (with reduced vowel) to environments in which it serves as part of an

154

forms *seking* and *king* alternate with krama *saking*. *Saka, saking,* and *seking* all have a general ablative meaning: 'from a place,' 'as a result of a condition,' 'according to,' etc., but the ngoko and madya forms cannot be shortened to *ka* and *king* respectively when used in the meaning translatable in English as 'according to.' So, (10) and (11) are both unacceptable:

10. Ka tuturé Pak dhokter, dhik Har lara banget.
11. King tuturé Pak dhokter, dhik Har sakit sanget.
    According to (the words of) the doctor, dhik Har is very sick.

The full or reduced ngoko forms—*saka/seka*, respectively—and the single bisyllabic form in madya, *seking*, may be used with this meaning, but the elided monosyllabic forms, *ka* and *king* respectively, cannot. This indicates the parallelism between processes within and across lexically defined speech styles, and suggests that a close examination of intralevel variation in krama, and interlevel variation between krama and madya, will provide clues for understanding variation in acceptability judgments.

Formal and informal krama

One insightful conservative priyayi observed to me one time after contrasting some formal and informal krama alternants that the kind of krama one speaks day-to-day is not always careful or polished; sometimes one speaks 'lazy krama' *(krama kesèd)*. Only in special situations and when on one's best behavior is it necessary to 'polish' (*mbesut*) one's speech. But if there is a "lazy" krama style, distinct from madya styles containing krama referential lexemes which are also informal ("sloppy") non-ngoko speech, we must decide what if anything distinguishes them, and how those distinctions are contextually salient and socially significant.

A few of the more ubiquitous formal and informal alternants in krama speech are listed in table 4.3, along with their madya and ngoko equivalents. They illustrate the kinds of parallels which exist among intralevel paradigmatic alternations. The relative formality

---

infinitive, and not, for instance, as a preposition. So one can say in English "He's got to go" or "He's gotta go," but one cannot say "He's gonna Chicago" as a colloquial form of "He's going to Chicago."

Table 4.3
SOME FORMAL/INFORMAL ALTERNANTS IN NGOKO AND KRAMA

NGOKO informal/formal	MADYA	KRAMA informal/formal
nèng, ènèng/ana	ènten, onten	wonten
---, nèng/ana ing	ènten, teng	wonten (ing)
nèh, menèh/maneh	melih	malih
(se)ka, sa(ng)ka	(se)king	saking
wé, waé/baé	mawon, men, mon	mawon/kémawon
yok/ayo	ngga	mangga/sumangga
lan	lan	lan/kaliyan
nyang/menyang	teng	dhateng
marang	teng	dhateng/ dhumateng
piyé/kepriyé	(ke)pripun, dos pundi	dos pundi/kados pundi
yèn, nèk/manawa	yèn, nèk	nawi/menawi
ki/iki, kiyi	niki	menika/punika
ki/kuwi/iku	niku	menika/punika
ké/kaé/ika	nika	menika/punika
pa/apa	napa	menapa/punapa
ngéné/mangkéné	ngèten	ngaten/mekaten
ngko, mengko	(me)ngké	mangké
ra/ora	mboten	mboten
di-	di-	pun-/dipun-

and informality of members of krama pairs varies, as do analogous alternations in ngoko. As mentioned above, *yèn* is an "everday" ngoko alternant to *menawa*, but it may also be used in krama as a less formal alternant to *menawi* (and its reduced form *nawi*). The contrast in formality between *kados pundi* and *dos pundi* ('how about it,' cf. ngoko *kepriyé* and *piyé*) both of which appear quite normally in krama, for example, is much less marked that the difference between *punapa* and *napa*.'[18] Although the form used in most situations is *menapa*, this is traditionally spelled *punapa*, a spelling pronunciation which may still be heard in the highly formulaic, flowery varieties of speech used on formal occasions called 'adorned language' (*basa rinengga*).[19]

This oversimplified summary suffices to show that the sound shapes of some madya forms can be related to their krama equivalents as short, elided alternants which resemble and in some cases are identical to informal krama alternants. Another example is *mawon*, which is both the obligatory madya equivalent for krama *kémawon*, and an informal krama alternant in the speech of all priyayi. Similarly, *ngaten* is not just the madya equivalent of *mekaten* for all priyayi speakers, but also the informal krama alternant to *mekaten* for these speakers, used in all three deictic meanings that are distinguished in the ngoko and krama series.[20]

---

[18]Wolff and Poedjosoedarmo indicate madya styles may be formal or informal (1982:6), but also speak of "lower" and "higher" madya. It is not clear whether they mean to refer with these adjectives to both types of variation. Clear differences do obviously exist, insofar as some variation involves use of ngoko/krama lexical alternants while other variation involves the forms being considered here.

[19]Because the concern here is day-to-day speech, this latter variety of krama will be ignored. A similar change in the relation of reduced form to "normal" form may have resulted in the present-day alternation between the forms *sumangga* and *mangga*. The former—now literary, formal, and sometimes deferential—stands historically as the "full" form (glossable as literally meaning 'hold over the head') from which *mangga* was derived by the same process of elision discussed above.

[20]Uhlenbeck (1978:244) has correctly noted that *ngaten* functions as informal krama; Poedjosoedarmo (n.d.) cites *ngaten* as krama without comment. Wolff and Poedjosoedarmo (1982:29) report that speakers

There are good distributional reasons for attributing double-level membership to this small number of very commonly used alternants. First, they appear in otherwise full or formal krama in the speech of all informants. Both *ngaten* and *mawon*, for instance, quite commonly cooccur with either the formal *dipun-* or informal *pun-*, and other full variants.[21] Secondly, they regularly appear in madya containing ngoko elements, unlike other krama elements. Conservative and modern priyayi speakers alike regularly switch back and forth between full, relatively formal krama and less formal styles which nonetheless count as krama. Other informal krama alternants do not count as madya since they are never used in sentences which contain any ngoko elements, and are universally rejected when they appear in such examples.

It is possible to argue that some examples of usage classified as madya in the literature are in fact informal krama. Uhlenbeck, for instance, has classified *ngaten* as madya (1978:313, but see footnote 72) and argued that an example of usage from a novel which he cites shows a switch from ngoko to madya (written in italics):[22]

Hlo kangmas ki kok ngono, penganten kok rikuh, *mangga, ta, [tindak] mrika mawon, mangke rak dipundukani.*

---

contrasted two madya sentences containing *ngaten* and *ngoten* as relatively "higher" and "lower" but are apparently at a loss as to why this should be. If one takes into account formal/informal krama variation, *ngaten* clearly "raises" the example because it is also informal krama, whereas *ngoten* is not.

[21]*Dipun-* is similarly reduced to *pun-* after being affixed to a root to create polysyllabic words.

[22]A possible interpretation of this switch from ngoko to non-ngoko speech not mentioned by Uhlenbeck is that this is a case of what Javanese call (among other things) *ngunandika*, what Wolff and Poedjosoedarmo (1982:70-79) describe as nondirected speech. Under this interpretation the ngoko segment is construed as "thinking out loud," or self-directed speech, which precedes the speaker's message to her elder brother: 'Why is my older brother acting like this, . . .'

Why do you behave like this dear older brother, you are a bridegroom so why should you feel embarrassed, *please [go]* (deferential|) there (to your bride), *otherwise they will of course rebuke you.*

Here are several krama forms with distinct madya alternants—*mangké* 'later' rather than madya *mengké* or *ngké*, and *dipun-* 'passive marker' rather than *di-* (or for that matter informal *pun-*)—together with *mawon*. They can be treated, therefore, as examples of informal krama rather than madya.

The same intralevel distinction between informal/formal krama helps to account also for another type of optional alternation in krama which (like that between *yèn* and *menawi*) does not mark a switch in level, but distinguishes relative formality of krama speech. Such alternants are krama *kaliyan* and ngoko/krama *lan*. (The more formal krama *akaliyan* may be ignored here.) *Kaliyan* is the obligatory krama equivalent of ngoko *karo* and madya *kalih* 'along with, in relation to' and always appears in formal priyayi krama usage. All three words can be translated for present purposes as 'along with,' 'in relation to.' At the same time, *kaliyan* may be used as a formal krama alternate for the word *lan* 'and,' which may itself be used in all levels; *kaliyan* then marks krama speech as being relatively more formal. So, *lan* in (12) and (13) (ngoko and krama respectively) refers to Rini's and Tuti's acts of going in a way which indicates nothing about whether they went together or not. In (14), *karo* is used (in a ngoko sentence) to refer to actions carried out together, and for this (15) is the obligatory krama equivalent. Between (13) and (15), then, there may be a difference either in referential meaning, or in formality.

12. Rini lan Tuti wis lunga menyang Jakarta.
13. Rini lan Tuti sampun késah dhateng Jakarta.
    Rini and Tuti already went to Jakarta.

14. Rini karo Tuti wis lunga menyang Jakarta.
15. Rini kaliyan Tuti sampun késah dhateng Jakarta.
    Rini and Tuti already went (together) to Jakarta.

When the syntax of a sentence is such that *karo* is the only possible ngoko form, then its krama equivalent *kaliyan* is obligatory in the krama version. Sentences 18 and 19 (ngoko and krama respectively) are both ungrammatical, and *kaliyan* in (17) can only be the krama equivalent of *karo*, as in (16).

  16. Rini wis teka karo Tuti.
  17. Rini sampun dhateng kaliyan Tuti.
      Rini already arrived along with Tuti.
*18. Rini wis teka lan Tuti.
*19. Rini sampun dhateng lan Tuti.
      Rini already arrived and Tuti.

The alternation between *lan* and *kaliyan* can thus serve in certain environments to distinguish referential meanings on one hand (contributing to different types of referential meaning of sentences) and pragmatic meanings on the other (marking different degrees of formality within krama).

Since *lan* is a colloquial alternant to a "formal" krama element and cannot be counted as only madya (and ngoko), there is good reason to call short forms like *mawon* and *ngaten*, which can appear in madya and krama, members of two vocabularies which are nonetheless distinct when taken as systematically related wholes.[23]

MADYA AS REGISTER AND DIALECT

Regular contrasts in acceptability judgments indicate that these colloquializing processes apply more widely and regularly in the non-ngoko speech of "modern" speakers than of "conservative" speakers. It appears, then, that for modern speakers what Uhlenbeck calls a "gradation which cannot be captured by postulating a set of distinct speech styles" and "freedom within clearly fixed limits" (1978:315) extends beyond the range of strictly madya speech styles to krama speech as well. Evidence of variation in acceptability of examples, in actual use of the speech levels, and

---

[23]Wolff and Poedjosoedarmo (1982: 25-38) call *ngaten* and *mawon* "krama" and "high madya," although in both cases there is no distributional reason for implying, as the latter designation does, that either has some "low madya" equivalent.

differences between combinations of madya and krama forms in particular, have a greater social significance vis-a-vis perceived links between language and social class.

There is a structural continuum of formality in modern speakers' repertoires ranging from "full" (formal) krama speech to "colloquial" krama speech to "high" madya speech containing krama lexemes. It is a continuum insofar as madya forms with distinct krama alternants may cooccur with krama elements which themselves have madya alternants. The flexibility with which modern speakers use their level repertoires is manifested in these intergraded syntagmatic patterns of combination, and fits moreover with the ways modern speakers characterize their own usage. It contrasts with conservative speakers, who see a clear distinction between informal krama on one hand, and madya with krama elements on the other. This fits with their view of the varieties of madya as instances of a social dialect and out-group code. Such roughly age-graded variation within the priyayi community manifests social change which has not affected the composition of paradigmatic sets so much as the encoded rules governing patterns of cooccurrence between them.

Speakers' acknowledgements of differences in patterns of use of non-ngoko usage emerge in comments only rarely, and then in partial, relative statements like those elicited with the classifications of examples discussed in chapter 3. Older priyayi sometimes complain that youngsters do not control good *basa*, that they mix it up with *basa kampungan* (i.e., madya). But in fact, those younger modern speakers are quite capable of speaking good krama and foregoing madya elements in favor of "good" krama alternants. Few speakers of any age or class recognize that the variation in priyayi speech patterns of which they are aware results less from differences in how they are able to speak (i.e., the styles in their repertoires) than in how they choose to speak (i.e., the ways they evaluate appropriateness of style to context).

Young conservative speakers who straddle this implicit sociolinguistic line between conservative and modern patterns of priyayi usage (discussed in chapter 3) are confronted most directly with this ambiguity and are able to articulate the situation most clearly. One expressed her ambivalence to madya speech with what might be the best summary of its ambiguous status one could wish for. We had been chatting one evening when her mother joined us.

As our chat continued, her elder brother dropped by for a moment, and I heard him use to his mother the sort of madya my informant rejected except as out-group usage. Later on, when I asked her about this, she said that two of her brothers spoke this way to their mother.[24] (Later, when I became acquainted with one of these brothers, he and I also exchanged madya with krama admixture.) Her father didn't like it (she went on) and no one in the family ever talked to him that way. At the same time, she did say (and I observed) that she would use speech like informal krama to her father. (He had tried teach his children to use the levels nonreciprocally in accordance with birth order, but had failed.) Then my informant provided something very close to a valid, pan-social characterization of the status of madya as she explained why she, unlike her brothers, never talked like this to her mother:

> If a person speaks to me in *basa kasar* [i.e., madya] there are three possibilities. They think that I'm *kasar*, and can't speak good *basa*, or they are *kasar* themselves. And sometimes there are people who use it to be intimate (*akrab*). This means they want to be familiar with me, but if that's the way it is, I'll always use ngoko or Indonesian.

She is in the middle of a situation which is difficult because it is transitional; she is of a generation of priyayi (in the traditional sense) of which many members use madya as a register. Like her parents, she generally associates it with her outgroup as their social dialect. The tensions generated as a result come out quite clearly in such statements. Variation and change in the structure and use of madya—the meeting point of the formerly elite and non-elite speakers—reveals the dynamics of sociolinguistic change going within and outside the priyayi class.

---

[24]Her mother and three siblings confirmed this statement; all these siblings save the eldest exchanged ngoko. The father of the household was of very high rank, the mother of relatively low descent status.

Acceptability judgments

Native speaker acceptability judgments relevant to the problem of delimiting madya and krama are the most copious for any of the problems dealt with in this chapter. In table 4.4 are presented slightly more than half of the sentences on the final short questionnaire discussed above. Each sentence contains at least one "full" or "informal" krama element which has a distinct madya alternant, and at least one madya element which itself has a differentiable krama equivalent. The groups of speakers labeled I and II here are made up of conservative and modern speakers, respectively; group I includes all speakers listed in groups A and B in table 3.1, while group II includes younger priyayi and non-priyayi speakers from group C in that same table. (No more than four respondents in group II for any given example were non-priyayi.)

Regular differences between speakers' evaluations can be attributed to differing social perspectives on speech level use, evaluational biases towards its users, and norms for use; all appeared in classifications of sentences discussed in chapter 3. Conservative speakers, we saw, identify madya speech primarily by class association as a social dialect; here it can be seen that they correspondingly reject examples in which krama elements with madya equivalents cooccur with madya elements which also have krama equivalents. Such examples "blur" the top line of madya, and "mix" what are for them functionally distinct styles; from the conservative point of view, they effectively conflate "good" non-ngoko language with "substandard" non-ngoko language, and are therefore largely unacceptable.

Modern speakers who identify examples of madya in terms of their "usualness," their intermediate degree of refinedness and formality, accept those same sentences as parts of the non-ngoko speech level continuum. Because no contrast in dialectal significance accrues to the use of madya as opposed to krama for these speakers, such "intermediate" examples are functionally homogeneous and structurally acceptable. The freer choice modern speakers seem to make between styles matches the greater heterogeneity of situations of use in which they speak, and the relative lack of a well defined set of situational norms.

By the usual structural criteria, examples in table 4.4 cannot really be treated either as "true" (albeit very informal) krama sentences, or as very formal madya. The former classification would effectively discount krama's status as standard *basa*, and so the status of priyayi as speakers of the standard. The latter imputes to such sentences structural characteristics of speech marked by distinctively madya elements which they lack. In madya sentences, ngoko or krama elements may appear when no madya equivalent exists, but in these sentences, which contain informal krama which is not also madya, ngoko is unacceptable. Consider, for example, two sentences taken from sentence type 2f. Although the majority of speakers in group II accepted the sentence listed as 20 below, none accepted (21) or (22), in which a ngoko conjugate is used either for *dados* (krama, no distinct madya alternant) or *tesih* (madya). In (21), the ngoko element *dadi* is acceptable in a madya sentence which does not contain "full" krama elements. But a sentence like (21), in which *dadi* (ngoko) cooccurs with *wonten* (krama) is unacceptable to all informants. Similarly, a sentence like (22), in which the ngoko word *isih* is used, is unacceptable because that word has an alternate madya conjugate.

20. Dados tesih wonten, ta.
*21. Dadi tesih wonten, ta.
*22. Dados isih ènten, ta.
 So there still are some.

Nawi is an informal krama alternant to *menawi*, and among modern speakers regularly occurs with *napa*, which can count both as obligatory madya and optional informal krama as in sentence 23. But *napa* can be used with ngoko referential elements as in sentence 25 whereas *nawi* as in sentence 24 cannot.

23. Nawi kalih, napa kénging?
*24. Nawi loro, napa kena?
25. Yèn loro, napa kena?
 If it's just two, how about it?

Table 4.4
VARIABLE ACCEPTABILITY OF KRAMA-MADYA MIXTURE

GROUP	Example Krama in [brackets] Madya *italicized*	Group I	%	Group II	%
1a	Criyosé Ari [badhé] ngampiri Rini [rumiyin]. [Criyosipun Ari badhé] ngampiri Rini *riyin*.	1/13 0/13	8 0	10/14 9/14	71 64
1b	[Nawi kula kémawon], *pripun*? [Nawi] kula mawon, *pripun*?	0/13 0/13	0 0	5/13 8/12	68 66
1e	Yèn *sing ngoten niku*, [dos pundi]?	6/13	46	13/13	100
1f	[Nawi sanès]*é*, [saking] Tuban. [Nawi sanèsipun], *seking* Tuban.	1/12 1/12	8 8	10/14 9/14	71 64
1g	[Seratipun sampun] *dugi*, dèrèng?	2/13	15	7/8	84
2a	[Menawi] kalih, *napa* kènging?	1/12	8	11/14	78
2f	Dados [taksih] *ènten*, ta. Dados [taksih wonten ingkang] saé kados *riyin*.	3/12 1/13	25 8	8/14 10/13	57 77
2g	[Ingkang] saé kados *riyin*.	0/12	0	10/13	77
2h	Lajeng *niki* [kados pundi]? Lajeng [menika] *pripun*?	1/12 0/12	8 0	8/14 8/14	57 57
3b	[Piyambakipun] mbèkta *napa*?	3/12	25	10/14	71
3c	Méja [menika] *napa* saé? Méja *niki* [menapa] saé?	2/12 3/12	16 25	10/14 7/14	71 50
3d	[Menawi] bidhal ngaten mawon, *pripun*?	0/12	0	10/13	77
3f	[Ingkang agengipun] semonten *niku*.	0/12	0	8/14	57
4a	Mboten [wonten] *melih*. [Sampun] mboten [wonten] *melih*. [Sampun] mboten *ènten melih*. *Mpun* mboten [wonten malih]. *Mpun* mboten [wonten] *melih*.	2/12 1/12 0/12 0/12 2/11	16 8 0 0 18	11/14 7/14 10/14 10/14 10/12	78 50 71 71 83
4g	Tuti *dugi*[nipun kaliyan] sinten?	3/13	23	7/13	54

165

Table 4.4 continued

5g	[Sampun] *teng* pundi mawon?	3/13	23	8/13	54
	[Sampun] *teng* pundi [kémawon]?	1/12	9	6/13	46
5k	Buku *niku teng* pundi [samenika]?	0/12	0	5/13	38
	Buku *niku* [wonten] pundi [samenika]?	0/12	8	12/13	92
	Buku *niku* [wonten] pundi *saniki*?	0/12	0	11/14	78
5l	[Namung] kula *niki* [ingkang] saged.	0/12	0	11/14	78
	[Namung] kula *niki sing* saged.	1/12	0	12/14	86
5m	[Menapa wonten] *melih*?	2/11	181	11/13	85
	Napa [wonten malih]?	3/16	9	12/13	92
6a	Ngantos *saniki* dèrèng [wonten].	0/12	0	8/11	73
6d	[Ingkang] bidhal *kalih* Tuti [namung] Pak Narso.	1/13	8	7/13	54
	[Ingkang] bidhal *kalih* Tuti *mung* Pak Narso.	1/13	8	1/13	8
6g	[Ingkang] saé piyambak *seking* Tuban.	0/11	0	9/9	100
6k	[Namung] kalih *niki sing* lumayan.	3/13	23	10/13	77
7a	[Sanès] *niku* [ingkang] kula [kajengaken].	1/11	9	4/14	29
	Senès [menika] kajeng kula.	2/11	18	7/14	50
7b	[Kopinipun] *napa* mawi gendhis?	1/11	9	13/13	100
7c	*Napa* dèrèng [wonten]?	1/10	10	9/13	69
	[Menapa] dèrèng *ènten*?	0/10	0	8/13	62
	Napa [sampun wonten]?	2/11	18	12/13	92
8d	[Ingkang] wingking kiyambak *niku*, gadhahan kula.	0/13	0	11/13	85
8m	[Namung] *niki* mawon.	0/11	0	9/12	75
9a	Cacah[ipun] mboten kirang *king* seket.	0/11	0	9/12	75
11g	*Nggèné* [wonten] pundi?	0/13	0	9/12	75
12g	[Menapa] *tesih ènten*?	2/6	33	10/12	83

An example from sentence type 4g is similarly unacceptable because it combines -*(n)é*—which is both the ngoko alternant and obligatory madya alternant to krama -*(n)ipun*—with *kaliyan*, which is only krama. The result is a universally unacceptable sentence, although -*é* is itself constitutive of madya:

*26. Tuti duginé kaliyan sinten?
      Who did Tuti arrive with?

So this special hybrid sort of language, a semi-krama distinguished by madya forms which are not identical with ngoko forms, cannot really be described as falling under a separate received category, nor thought of as a variety shared by all members of the speech community. One might then say that "krama" and "madya" are received native metalinguistic terms more useful from a strictly descriptive viewpoint for distinguishing paradigmatic alternants than these patterned combinations of those alternants which vary in acceptability for priyayi speakers.

Observed usage

Examples of use of this interstitial sort of speech style can be presented in support of the position that these judgments reflect facts of use, and not just semi-covert prejudices which speakers project onto decontextualized examples. It was difficult but not impossible to capture the spontaneous, casual type of speech so important for analyzing variation occurrences outside of a formal situation of use.

Time spent with informants was not devoted solely to interviews per se; the great fondness Javanese have for sitting around and chatting (*omong-omong, ngobrol*) afforded ample opportunity to observe spontaneous types of usage of both ngoko and krama among a wide variety of speakers. In table 4.5 are a few examples from diverse speakers and speech contexts.

Usage reported in sections I and II of table 4.5 represents semi-krama speech by non-priyayi speakers of relatively little education. The masseuse I had known for almost eight months when I recorded this utterance, and to her I habitually gave madya and recieved such language in return. The same is true of the bicycle repairman (*tukang sepéda*) quoted in part II, who had for

Table 4.5
OBSERVED OCCASIONS OF USE OF
KRAMA-MADYA MIXTURE

I. WITH A MASSEUSE.*

1. Tasih *ènten*, [menika panjenengan] tindak mrika, *mpun ènten* wong.
   There still *was* (someone there), [(and when) you] went there, *there already was someone* (there).
2. [Piyambakipun] *sing* pethek mrika, *teng* nggèn kula.
   [He]'s *the one who* gets massaged there, *at* my place.
3. Madosi kula [menika], sok *mpun* késah.
   (If you) look for me [topic marker], often (I've) *already* left.
4. [Mangké] jam tiga wungu *melih*.
   [Later] at three o'clock, (you) wake up *again*.
5. Mboten, *niki* radi sibuk, [kaliyan] ugi, *mengké ènten* tamu.
   No, *here* (I'm) kind of busy, [and] also, *later there'll be* a guest.

II. WITH A ROADSIDE BICYCLE REPAIRMAN

1. Dadi *mengké yèn mpun* wangsul, *niki* [dipun]sadé.
   So *later if* (you) have *already* returned, *this* is [to be] sold.
2. [Wonten], *mengké teng* kantor, *napa niku*? Yatra.
   [There is] *later at* the office, *what's that*? Money.

III. FROM DAGELAN BASIYO: BASIYO BECOMES A PEDICAB DRIVER

1. Lha *nggih* mboten [wonten] jamaké.
   Yeah, that's really something (lit. [there is] no *distance* to it).
2. Lha *wong nggih* antawis[ipun menika] tigang kilo *men* mboten [wonten], kok.
   Yeah, (as for) [the distance (topic marker)], it's not (lit. [there is] not) *even* three kilometers.

IV. FROM SANDIWARA BASA JAWA

1. *Nèk* ngaten, kula [badhé] pamit *riyin*, Pak.
   If it's like that, I [will] say goodbye *right now*, Pak.
2. Jenengé—mboten lali *niku*—janjané nggih [taksih sedhèrèkipun] piyambak.
   Her name—(I) haven't forgotten *that—actually* it [is] (lit. [still]) [her own sibling].
3. [Panjenengan sampun] ngurban[aken] kebahagiané kanggé tiyang [sanès].
   [You have sacrificed] (*your*) happiness for [other] people.
4. *Piyambaké niki* sawijining wanita *[ingkang]* mboten saged ngajeni [kaliyan] tiyang [sanès].
   She (topic marker) is a woman [who] can't be polite [with other] people.

V. FROM A MODERN PRIYAYI INFORMANT

1. Enjang [namung] ngantos jam sewelas, *ngoten*.
   (In the) morning [only] up to eleven o'clock *or so*.
2. *Nèk ngoten*, BéA[nipun] Mas Joko [bidanganipun] *napa*?
   In that case, [your] B.A. (is in) *what* [field]?
3. Ning rak *ènten*, Mas, [ingkang] sok mbèkta *napa-napa seking* dapur?
   But *aren't there* (some), Mas, [who]'ll sometimes bring *anything from* the kitchen?
4. [Janipun] *niki sing* leres.
   [Actually] *this is the one which is* right.
5. Biasa[nipun] mboten *ngoten*, lho, Mas.
   [Usually] it's not *'like that,'* y'know Mas.

VI. WITH AN OLDER NON-PRIYAYI*

Mrika[nipun] *napa nggih* laré-laré makem *teng* sekolahan?
[Over there], *is it also* (the case that) children eat *at school*?

---

*Krama segments and (insofar as possible) their translations are bracketed; madya segments and translations are italicized.

many months been repairing my ailing bicycle. By the time I observed these cases, we were in a relation of polite informality in which semi-krama or madya was regularly exchanged. Usage from *dagelan* and *Sandiwara Basa Jawa* (III and IV) exhibits similar shift or mixture between madya and krama.

The examples quoted under V are valuable because they come from conversation with a young, modern priyayi informant, one of three sisters with whom I exchanged madya for the greater part of the time we were acquainted. The intermediate formality of the situation is reflected in the style they used, and corresponds closely to that type of situation in which they themselves had told me it was appropriate. On one hand they felt that full krama was too stiff, and on the other ngoko was too familiar. The interspersal of distinctively krama elements in the speech of the informant recorded was not the result of attempts to speak "well," i.e., not of random and sporadic hypercorrection; she controlled full krama.

The final example is taken from a conversation with a wealthy non-priyayi—a *santri* ('devout Muslim')—with whom I had occasion to chat occasionally. He was about fifty years old, and so felt himself to be somewhat superior to and relatively familiar with me. This example is typical of the type of madya/krama style he used to me.

Cases of mixed language from conservative priyayi, young or old, are simply not forthcoming, and so cannot be presented. I believe that this is not a matter of chance, luck, or speakers' special attention to speech due to an observer's presence; such speakers choose krama, or choose madya, but will not mix the two as do their modern counterparts.

Deferentials in madya

Native speaker judgments on another type of example point to this same incipient change in priyayi conceptions of appropriateness of madya. It will be recalled that deferential terms of the krama inggil vocabulary are normatively used to superiors or equals for whose status one marks one's regard. Hence, conservative speakers never use krama inggil to refer to addressees to whom they speak madya.[25] This follows the logic that persons to whom they speak madya are of relatively low status, certainly lower than themselves, and therefore are not appropriately referred to that way. But among modern speakers, examples of such usage like (27) and (28), are perfectly acceptable, and very commonly used. (Deferentials and their glosses in the translations are italicized.)

27. Ajeng *tindak* pundi?
    Where are you *going?*
28. *Mundhut* sing niki mawon.
    Take this one.

Sentence 27 is marked as madya by *ajeng,* distinctive of but not obligatory in madya speech with this meaning. Modern speakers may use such language to speech partners they respect and with whom they are somewhat intimate, in a manner analogous to conservative usage of ngoko with deferentials to equals with whom they are in a relatively formal relation. In fact, three modern priyayi speakers said 27 and 28 exemplify the way they speak to their own fathers, to whom they use *basa* but with whom they nonetheless feel close. By using krama inggil they mark respect; by using madya rather than krama they mark familiarity. (Unfortunately I was not able to observe interaction between these speakers and their parents, or to check such reports with their parents.) In this sense, too, madya sentences containing krama inggil deferentials can be thought of as intermediately formal and respectful, standing

---

[25]This is an oversimplification which will stand for present purposes. Actually some krama inggil terms are more deferential than others; as Wolff and Poedjosoedarmo (1982:39-40) suggest, the more commonly used are less deferential. Some are now in such common use that it would be something of an insult not to use them to a person of even moderate status with whom one was not familiar. There is also evidence of a direct relation between relative deferential import of use of these words and the degree to which they are known within the community. See also Errington 1988:165-70.

midway between speech made up of ngoko with krama inggil, and that of krama with krama inggil.[26]

ONGOING COLLOQUIALIZATION AND SOCIAL CHANGE

To explicate the significances of variation in use of krama and madya speech styles as indexes of changing conceptions of social status, it worth considering briefly a theory of sociolinguistic change formulated in general terms but applicable to this specific case. Kroch has outlined a two part hypothesis:

> *First*, the public prestige dialect of the elite in a stratified community differs from the dialect(s) of the non-elite strata (working class and other) in at least one phonologically systematic way. In particular, it characteristically resists normal processes of phonetic conditioning (both articulatory and perceptual) that the speech of the non-elite strata regularly undergo.... *Second*, the cause of stratified phonological differentiation within a speech community is to be sought not in purely linguistic factors but in ideology. Dominant social groups tend to mark themselves off symbolically as distinct from the groups they dominate and to interpret their symbols of distinctiveness as evidence of superior moral and intellectual qualities.... They mark themselves off... by introducing elaborated styles and by borrowing from external prestige groups; but in the case of pronunciation they also mark their distinctiveness in a negative way—that is by inhibiting many of the low level, variable processes of phonetic conditioning that characterize spoken language and that underlie regular phonological variation. (1978:17-18)

---

[26]Wolff and Poedjosoedarmo (1982:6) indicate that deferentials may be used in madya, but give examples in which, outside of a context, they might well be taken to refer to a person other than speech partner.

Kroch is concerned here with prestige codes, what have been called here social dialects, and in fact he alludes to the ngoko/krama opposition as functioning in essentially this way (1978:30). This is only part of the social significance of linguistic etiquette, but his characterization of different types of usage does fit the Surakartan situation insofar as these colloquializing processes apply in conservative priyayi krama speech in ways which correlate with their conceptions of krama ("good non-ngoko language") as opposed to madya ("substandard non-ngoko language"). They reduce and elide just those krama forms made up of three or more syllables to create intralevel variation which does not extend to madya. The underlying socially based motivations discussed in chapter 3 can thus be rephrased with terms provided by Kroch: "full" krama distinguishes elite from non-elite and is maintained and distinguished from other non-ngoko styles among those who still sense the importance of the distinction.

We have seen that more modern priyayi speakers do not manifest the same degree of consciousness of their (traditional) elite status, and for them the social motivation for a rigid krama/madya dichotomy is missing. They allow low-level processes of phonetic conditioning to apply much more widely and regularly in their speech in ways which correspond to usage outside the formerly dominant social group. They do not set themselves off symbolically to the same extent, and adopt patterns of use of the speech levels which can be described along the continuum of formality.

This dynamic colloquialization process is going on outside of the conscious awareness of priyayi speakers, even though the variation appears clearly when presented systematically. This phenomenon is what Labov (1972) calls a type of "change from below the level of social consciousness," and is not affecting the paradigmatic structure of sets of leveled alternants so much as the rules for combining those alternants. Nonetheless some paradigmatic shifts can be attributed to the extension of such colloquializing processes, and deserve brief comment.[27]

---

[27] There is evidence which suggests that more consciously motivated types of change have affected other paradigmatic sets like the personal pronouns. This argument is sketched in Errington 1985, and developed in Errington 1988.

Colloquialized krama as madya

The relative freedom with which modern speakers colloquialize their speech is affecting the structure of a few paradigmatic sets, elevating formerly madya (or *krama désa*) elements to the status of informal krama. Two examples of this ongoing process are the paradigmatic sets containing *dugi* (from *dumugi*) 'arrive,' and *riyin* (from *rumiyin*) 'long ago, right away.' Both standard krama forms contain the petrified infix *-um-*. For conservative speakers these short forms are typical of substandard language and are therefore unacceptable in otherwise "standard" krama, but usable in and typical of madya. Modern speakers on the other hand treat each pair of alternants as relatively formal versus relatively informal element, rather than a standard versus substandard element. They will use both "full" and "short" forms in otherwise "full" krama or in madya (like examples from sentence groups 1g and 2g in table 4.4).

Colloquialized deferentials

Similar colloquializing processes which have operated in the past on relatively restricted ranges of forms in priyayi speech are now more widely applied to produce what might be called familiar deferentials in modern priyayi repertoires. Analogous reduction patterns in modern priyayi use of deferential forms results in striking contrasts for at least two paradigmatic sets.

The krama inggil verb *tindak* 'go' is commonly reduced in modern priyayi as well as non-priyayi usage to *ndak*. This form does not really count as typical madya by the criterion of linguistic meaning—it is a verb, referential of persons—or its distributional properties (it can appear in all varieties of krama and ngoko). Although for non-priyayi speakers this might be most typically used in the greeting "where are you going" in the form *ajeng ndak pundi (ajeng* is an optional madya conjugate of ngoko *arep* and krama *badhé*), younger modern priyayi use it also with the "standard" krama *badhé*. So, they might use a phrase like *badhé ndak pundi?* to an intimate superior such as one's father, as one informant told me: "My father is a high official, but he's my father, right? So I don't have to be too formal." This may be taken as another effect of changing evaluations of social relations discussed by Brown and Gilman, where the impetus to mark both familiarity and deference results in the colloquialization (and thus familiarization) of a deferential form.

Another form which has undergone colloquialization is the active form of the deferential verb meaning 'ask,' *nyuwun*, which is used to mark the higher status of the person who is referred to as the object of the act of asking, relative to some lower status person who is the asker.[28] At one time *nyuwun* had a distinct krama equivalent, *nedha*, which has become obsolete in this sense and now only means 'eat.' *Nyuwun*, which is now the non-ngoko alternant[29] to *njaluk* ('ask'), has itself been subject to colloquialization, yielding the form *nyun* (not to be confused with *nun* discussed below).

Virtually all conservative informants reported (so far as I was able to observe correctly) that they would use *nyun* only with lower-class speakers, and never with someone for whom they really felt any deference. The shortened colloquialized form offers a way to linguistically differentiate ingroup/outgroup social relations even when only one lexical item is available for both situations. This reduction process is not unique, but indicates in this case how nonelite usage is affecting the social use of the traditional elite.

It seems likely that these colloquializing processes are nothing new, but have had an increased range of application in non-ngoko usage among priyayi, a result of changing dynamics of social interaction in the community. So, it is possible that the form *menapa* ('what, question marker') discussed above came to replace its now-literary alternant *punapa* by a process of colloquialization which probably started among speakers in the elite community. Another relevant example is the phrase *kawula nuwun*, used traditionally as a highly deferential preface in an utterance to a highly deferred-to speech partner. Each of its component elements was colloquialized some time in the past, yielding the now standard *kula*—to which *kawula* is the markedly formal variant—

---

[28]This is the type of deferential largely ignored here, usually called in the literature *krama andhap*.

[29]Actually, there is a krama inggil deferential equivalent *mundhut* which means (among other things) 'ask', used to refer to an action of asking by high status person to low status person.

and *nun*, a fast-speech form of *nuwun* used in deferential formulae used in some context or other by all priyayi. This too is standard colloquial krama used by all priyayi, even (for instance) in formal prefaces to speech and so on. The extension of this process in the referential vocabulary, and the impact of regular application of shortening processes to non-ngoko language on the standard is, as Kroch suggests, an index of decreasing awareness among the Javanese elite of their traditional social primacy.

Changes in the paradigmatic and syntagmatic structures of madya and krama, and the increasing loss of a line between the two styles in use among younger modern priyayi, bespeaks fundamental changes in priyayi attitudes to other users and uses of the speech levels. If modern priyayi use their krama madya repertoires in different, more numerous types of combinations than do conservative priyayi, they have repertoires which are more flexible and readily adaptable to situations in which speech level use keys to formality/familiarity, rather than asymmetric status patterns. The components of their repertoires for ingroup usage resemble those of traditional priyayi, who also used madya for ingroup speech; but their uses of madya are radically different, and result from adaptation of priyayi into a new Surakartan social milieu.

5

CONCLUSION

"Change is a many splendored thing" wrote Benda of postcolonial Indonesia, "and it can move in various, often contradictory, directions" (1965:1062). His observation still holds almost two decades later. Some have sought to document the nature of such change through its effects on (among other things) the development of a modern, national language. Most notable among these, perhaps, have been Anderson's arguments (1966, 1978) that Indonesian is developing complementary modes of political discourse, which he very suggestively likens to ngoko and krama speech styles. Linguistic manifestations of such an apparent accommodation to traditionalism could be treated as consequences and indices of continuing relevance of the "great" Javanese priyayi cultural tradition in the formation of "modern" Indonesian society and political thinking.

Despite certain problems with Anderson's thesis, particularly the limited focus on "new" Indonesian vocabularies rather than language use, his observations do speak to language development processes which coexist with and complement the types of language change discussed here. He limits his analysis to "political discourse," but nonetheless presupposes a particular view of language, society, and cultural politics among Javanese speakers, whence the model for ostensibly speech level-like styles of Indonesian. His argument is based on the assumption that the system of Javanese linguistic etiquette, used in some form or other by all Javanese, embodies and is the vehicle for transmission of particular views of speakers, and that the speech levels' use conforms with traditional social organization and social ideology.[1]

---

[1] For further discussion see Errington 1986 and sources cited there.

For this reason, issues involving social/linguistic conduct and social/linguistic change among the Javanese, especially in the traditional elite community, are intriguing and highly relevant for understanding social change in Surakarta, in Java, and in Indonesia as a whole.

I have undertaken here to speak to these latter issues by focusing less on the membership of the Javanese vocabularies of respect and deference and more on patterned relations between combinations of those elements in speech, and the social significances they express in speech contexts. Some of these particulars might seem trivial and/or collectively imponderable, both unrewarding for and inaccessible to analysis (for anyone but a linguist). As we have seen, numerous complications are encountered in research on speech level use, even when it has as narrow a focus as that described here, on one urban subcommunity in one urban locale. Even within this restricted purview this study is hardly exhaustive. Although some aspects of the paradigmatic structure of the system (e.g., second person pronouns) have been touched on insofar as they proved essential for discussing syntagmatic patterning, many others have been ignored. Shifts in the structure and use of members of other types of paradigmatic sets (kin terms, deferentials, titles, etc.) could also be described as parts of changing social interaction in Surakarta. Members of these latter sorts of paradigmatic sets are in fact commonly alluded to by speakers in unelicited, spontaneous discussion as the most socially salient aspects of linguistic politesse.

I have drawn some general conclusions out of ubiquitous, unobvious changes in the niceties of speech level structure and function. Those details may seem ponderous to nonlinguists interested in sociocultural change in Java but they do fit the social whole, indirectly reflect larger changes in patterns of social interaction, and point to the changing place of priyayi in Surakarta and Indonesia. This study of some of the specifics of speech level use offers a special perspective on unobvious but basic changes in social relations, and gives evidence that traditional priyayi are assimilating into a different social milieu. The treatment owes whatever suggestiveness it may have to the quotidian nature of the phenomena on which it is focussed: less overt and easily overlooked aspects of the social meanings of language use.

I have argued that there have been changes in the forms of priyayi linguistic etiquette, manifested in variation in encoded syntagmatic structural rules of speech level repertoires. The changes dealt with here are occurring largely outside of the awareness of most speakers, and to a degree independently of their ideas (or ideologies) about how their language fits (or should fit) social contexts. These examples of "linguistic change from below the level of social awareness," to use Labov's phrase, are indicative of fundamental shifts in priyayi allegiances in different linguistic and social subcommunities.

Etiquette, the ethics of social interaction, is implemented in social conduct which is evaluated through tacitly shared understandings of social position, role relations, and persons' rights and obligations vis-a-vis others. Small or apparently trivial changes in forms of "proper" social conduct, and especially linguistic behavior, can be revealing correlates of broader, more general social changes that affect the ways members of a society deal with and evaluate their relations with each other. These are register functions of the speech levels. But insofar as components of the system of linguistic etiquette are associated with particular communities and subcommunities, their use may mark not just evaluations of social relations, but also speakers' social background and social identity. These are their functions as social dialects.

As unitary forms of social conduct, the speech levels were first dealt with as metonyms of social situations in traditional priyayi society. It was shown how delicately differentiated status relations, defined most generally by different types of "distance from a king," were marked in asymmetric patterns of speech. In chapter 2 was also discussed madya's functional ambiguity; it simultaneously served traditional priyayi to shade the marking of status differences, and non-priyayi as a non-ngoko (and therefore polite) speech style. The social changes discussed there—normative pressures brought to bear on priyayi etiquette, changing priyayi/non-priyayi and priyayi/priyayi relations, and the dissolution of the priyayi community—were shown to have affected priyayi speech level use. This background served also as preparation for the study of the particulars of speech level structure and function in the contemporary community in chapters three and four.

In chapter 3 the structures of priyayi speech level repertoires were first described with respect to patterns of combination of paradigmatic alternants to make up speech styles. This was undertaken with constant and crucial reference to informants' observations on language use, their answers to questions I posed to elicit statements bearing on particular structural and contextual features of examples of use, and observed use. If the methodological assumptions, analytic approach, and expository strategy are acceptable, then so too should be conclusions which follow about the structure of changing speech level use and their social significances in context.

It turned out first that repertoires of ngoko and krama speech were relatively homogeneous within the priyayi speech subcommunity, although some varieties of polite ngoko which are used by these speakers are unrecognized and largely unused among non-priyayi.

Comparisons of speakers' judgments on examples from the literature indicate that there has been at least one type of simplification of the repertoires which priyayi have used for ingroup speech exchange during the last century. There is evidence to suggest that madya styles have served different functions for different speakers in different subcommunities in colonial Surakarta: on one hand they functioned as surrogate ngoko or krama styles in asymmetric exchange patterns for priyayi, on the other as "regular" non-ngoko usage in symmetric or asymmetric exchange patterns. Madya appears to have fallen out of ingroup priyayi use at about the time that madya styles came to be normal for priyayi address of nonintimate non-priyayi, this a linguistic response to increasing pressures for social change. One consequence was a loss of delicacy in repertoires for marking status distinctions between priyayi speech partners, because the repertoires themselves became simpler.

It is likewise possible (if less likely) that some styles of ngoko and krama described in the older literature became obsolete as the types of status distinctions they were used to mark lost relevance for priyayi interaction. This would likewise fit with the apparent shift in patterns of speech level exchange used in familial contexts, which was treated in chapter 2 as a shift from what Brown and Gilman (1960) call the semantic of power (or status) to solidarity (or intimacy), and from asymmetric to symmetric patterns of exchange.

Given this picture of apparently homogeneous ngoko/krama priyayi repertoires, we turned to the functions of the system as a whole, considering the place of madya in contemporary priyayi repertoires and the community at large. This in turn served as background material and a source of insight into speakers' views on the nature of "proper" and actual madya usage, relevant to the study of the structure of madya repertoires in chapter 4.

Speakers' classifications of examples are not made arbitrarily, although they may be ambiguous. This because speakers classify examples from different presupposed social perspectives, and make tacit recourse to different structural and functional classificatory principles. It turned out that classifications covary with native speakers' perspectives on the users and uses of linguistic etiquette, and that these classificatory principles vary in relevance for different speakers when they classifying various types of examples.

Two basic conclusions were developed: one obvious (but important), the other less apparent. First, it became clear that all speakers classified some examples by outgroup, and in so doing, revealed their own allegiances to speech subcommunities. Insofar as younger "modern" priyayi count examples of specifically priyayi speech styles as outgroup usage, their classifications show that their allegiance to the traditional elite subcommunity is falling off. Their "conservative" elders and age-mates, on the other hand, tend to classify a complementary set of examples by outgroup, and so implicitly set themselves off from commoners and the madya speech style which they conceive to be typically used by commoners.

By treating classifications of examples of styles in the system as being themselves systematic related, general patterns and trends were drawn out and linked to contrasting pictures of speech level functions and of social relations. I suggested that general trends in classifications reflect two conceptual foci on linguistic etiquette and their fit with social contexts. Conservative speakers' classifications bespeak a normative focus on relative status, and fit the patterns of speech level exchange they report to have been commonly used among the traditional priyayi dealt with in chapter two. Presupposed in many of their classifications is an implicit comparison of speech partners' personal status, "high" and "low"; as the gentleman quoted in chapter 1 observed, the speech levels are used by comparing relative status of persons, weighing them, as it were, in the pans of a scale.

Modern priyayi and non-priyayi speakers on the other hand classified examples in ways which do not presuppose their use in asymmetric exchange (to mark status difference) so much as their places on a continuum of refinedness of speech. This is a classificatory schema which can be invoked independently of any possible pattern of exchange, symmetric or asymmetric. In this respect too it turned out that modern priyayi resemble non-priyayi speakers of their generation.

Such contrasting classificatory trends were then linked to speakers' explicit descriptions/prescriptions of appropriate use of examples, from which it became clear that modern and conservative priyayi differ at least in their views of how madya should be used. These statements were presented as evidence that correlative variation in the structure of the madya speech styles in their repertoires might be found. Contrasting features of madya repertoires which were discussed in chapter 4, then, were anticipated by and were explained with an eye to general social characteristics attributed to madya examples by modern and conservative speakers. It became clear that one reason the study of madya is fraught with difficulty is that the uses and structures of madya repertoires themselves vary within the Surakartan community.

It was argued in chapter 4 that there are contrasts between the non-ngoko speech level repertoires used by conservative and modern priyayi, and that both types of repertoires might differ also from those used in Surakartan court circles at the end of the last century. Conservative priyayi use formal and informal varieties of krama which are structurally distinct from the madya styles which are also parts of their speech level repertoires, but which they use to outgroup speech partners. Modern priyayi, like their non-priyayi contemporaries and peers, have no such functional or structural difference between krama and madya styles. This general conclusion about changing speech level repertoires was adduced from regular contrasts between the examples which were judged as acceptable and unacceptable by priyayi speakers.

With such general conclusions we can finally reconsider the general issue raised at the outset: how has social change in modern Surakarta affected the priyayi class as a whole, and priyayi speakers as individuals? Linguistic evidence indicates that the Surakartan priyayi community is losing its coherence as a distinct social subgroup, because traditional priyayi elite status is losing its social salience for younger priyayi. Descendants of the traditional priyayi are incorporating linguistically and socially into a less stratified, more heterogeneous, more Indonesian social milieu.

Zoetmulder has remarked on the possibility that Javanese might have been adopted as a national language that "Javanese could have become a language suited for all the new situations. However, it would have proved a much less adaptable instrument than Malay. The roots in the past would have proved an encumbrance" (1967:9). He alludes indirectly to the speech levels in this observation, which is relevant precisely because this resarch indicates that the Javanese speech levels, at least in priyayi usage, are in fact being adapted in response to fundamental changes in the Javanese social milieu. Javanese may be changing as an intrument for speaking of "new" or "modern" things (borrowing from and following Indonesian), but for priyayi, Javanese who are also Indonesians, the speech levels are developing into more flexible means for mediating social relations. As control of the speech levels has become less a mark of and prerequisite for elite membership, the most delicately differentiated repertoires of speech styles have become an obstacle to equitable, mutually acceptable linguistic interaction in Indonesian Surakarta. The forms of linguistic politesse are consequently coming to be used in new ways by the priyayi, and are being transformed in largely unconscious response to social and linguistic assimilation of priyayi into new milieux and interactional contexts. This is not to say that the speech levels are defunct or moribund; rather, they are losing structural/functional complexities for marking status differences among Surakartan priyayi. Though they remain conspicuous parts of a comparatively elaborate system of Javanese etiquette, they are changing along with the nature of the relations they are used to mediate.

If it is true that in Indonesia "the artificial dams, economic, political, but above all psychological of foreign overlordship are breaking down," and that "the Indonesian river is flowing more and more in an Indonesian bed," (Benda 1965:1073) this is due to the ascendance of ethnic cultural traditions in a panethnic national situation. This very specific study of the small but symbolically important subcommunity of Surakartan elite shows that the Indonesian river is more than the sum of its tributaries, and is changing priyayi social values—Indonesianizing them, as it were—at the same time that it may itself be undergoing some sort of Javanization on a priyayi model.

Perhaps the ideal role model of the traditional priyayi will be preserved insofar as it becomes Indonesianized, and the Javanese system of linguistic politesse will survive as it is transformed in a new Indonesian/Javanese society. The image of the traditional "feudalistic" priyayi is becoming an empty stereotype, devoid of living linguistic exemplars. Whether or not a viable image of priyayi gentility is sustained (or even sustainable) as an overt or covert model for an Indonesian elite, the last inheritors of a priyayi cultural tradition transmitted and transformed over the centuries are now coming to occupy different places in a fundamentally different sort of social and linguistic community.

Appendix

CORPUS OF SENTENCE TYPES

Sheet 1*

a) *(Ari) jaréné arep ngampiri Rini dhisik.*
   Ari said he will pick up Rini right away.
b) *Yèn aku waé, piyé?*
   If just I (do it), how about it?
c) *Rini wis teka.*
   Rini has already arrived.
   Rini sing durung teka.
   Rini's the one who hasn't arrived.
   Sing wis teka, Rini.
   The one who's already arrived is Rini.
d) *Yèn semono kuwi, isa.*
   As for as much as that, (it) can (be done).
e) *Yèn sing ngono kuwi, piyé?*
   As for one like that, how about it?
f) *Yèn liyané, saka Tuban.*
   As for the others, they're from Tuban.
g) *Layangé wis tekan, durung?*
   Did the letter get here yet, or not?

Sheet 2

a) *Yèn loro, apa kena?*
   As for two, may (it be done)?
b) *Rini karo Tuti lagi waé lunga.*

---

*Sheet numbers refer to individual questionnaires given to consultants consecutively.

185

Rini and Tuti just left.
c) *Kaya apa, ya?*
What (is it) like, huh?
d) *Sadurungé budhal.*
Before leaving.
e) *Arep nyang ndi?*
Where (are you) going?
f) *Dadi isih ana, ta.*
So there still are (some).
g) *Sing apik kaya dhisik.*
One that's good, like (the ones) before.
h) *Terus (iki) piyé?*
So, how about it (this)?
i) *Jariké Mas Har kèri nèng omah.*
Mas Har's batik cloth got left at home.
j) *Apa iki?*
What's this?

Sheet 3

a) *Isa apa ora?*
Can (it be done) or not?
b) *Pak Narso nggawa apa?*
What is Pak Narso carrying?
Dhèwèké nggawa apa?
What is he carrying?
d) *Méja iki apa apik?*
Is this table good?
e) *Yèn budhal ngono waé, piyé?*
If (I) just leave like that, how about it?
f) *Ana, sakulon omahku.*
There is, just south of my house.
g) *Sing gedhéné semono kuwi.*
One as big as that.
h) *Wis suwé Tuti ora èntuk layang.*
For a long time, Tuti hasnt gotten a letter.
i) *Mula arep kirim layang nyang Ibu.*
That's why she's going to send a letter to mother.

Sheet 4

a) *(Saiki) (wis) (ora) ana manèh, ta.*
   (Now) there's (already) (not) any more.
b) *(Isih) ping pira?*
   (Still) how many times?
c) *Wis ping pira?*
   Already how many times?
d) *Aku arep maca buku iki.*
   I am going to read this book.
e) *Wis apa durung?*
   (Is it) already (done) or not?
f) *Karo sapa?*
   With whom?
   Sing teka sapa?
   Who was the one who came?
g) *Tuti teka(né) karo sapa?*
   Who did Tuti come with?

Sheet 5

a) *Sangka ndi?*
   Where from?
b) *Sing iki piyé, ya?*
   How about this one, huh?
c) *Lagi apa, ya?*
   What are you doing, huh?
d) *Tekané dhèk apa?*
   When was the arrival?
e) *Dhèk mbèn ya (pancèn) ana.*
   Long ago there (certainly) were.
f) *Nèng ndi-ndi enèng.*
   They're everywhere.
g) *Wis nyang ndi waé?*
   Where all (have you) gone?
h) *Piyé manèh, ta?*
   What else do you expect?
i) *Suk apa (budhalé)?*
   When (is the departure)?

j) *Gampang sing ndi?*
Which one is easy?
Gampang sing iki.
This one is easy.
k) *Buku kuwi nèng ndi saiki?*
Where's that book now?
l) *Mung aku iki sing isa.*
I'm the only one who can do it.
m) *Apa ana manèh?*
Are there anymore?
n) *Aku kena nyilih buku iki.*
I may borrow this book.
Dhèwèké kena nyilih buku iki.
He may borrow this book.

Sheet 6

a) *Nganti saiki (durung ana).*
Up to now (there haven't been any).
b) *Sing dingonoké dhèk mau dudu iki.*
The one done like that just now isn't this one.
c) *Saya suwé, saya larang.*
The longer (the time), the more expensive (it gets).
d) *Sing budhal karo Tuti mung Mas Naryo.*
The one who left with Tuti was only Mas Naryo.
e) *Sing apik dhéwé saka Tuban.*
The best ones are from Tuban.
f) *Mung loro iki sing lumayan.*
Only these two are any good.
g) *Kudu latihan nganti isa.*
(You) have to practice until (you) can (do it).
h) *Aja nganti kliru.*
Don't go wrong.
i) *Nganti saiki durung ana.*
Up to now, there haven't been any.
j) *Dhèwèké turu nganti soré.*
He slept until evening.

Sheet 7

    a) *Dudu kuwi sing dakkarepké.*
        That's not what I meant.
        Dudu kuwi karepku.
        That's not my intention.
    b) *Kopiné apa nganggo gula?*
        Does the coffee have sugar in it?
    c) *Apa durung ana?*
        Aren't there any yet?
        Apa wis ana?
        Are there already some?
    d) *Béda karo jaman saiki.*
        (It's) different from the present era.
    e) *Aku ora tau nyang Bali.*
        I've never been to Bali.
    f) *Isih durung sida.*
        It still hasn't come about yet.
    g) *Durung suwé, tamaté.*
        The ending won't be much longer.
    h) *Sing iki kok apik banget.*
        Why, this one is very good.
    i) *Isané mung rèwèl waé.*
        All he can do is make trouble.
    j) *Larang ngono, emoh aku.*
        As expensive as that, I don't want it.

Sheet 8

    a) *Mengko mundhak kesel.*
        Later (you'll) get sore.
    b) *Aku lagi maca buku iki.*
        I'm reading this book.
    c) *Kabèh kuwi apik banget.*
        All of that is very good.
    d) *Sing mburi dhéwé (kuwi) dhèkku.*
        The one furthest in the back is mine.
    e) *Luwih sangka pitu.*
        More than seven.

f) *Sing iki luwih apik.*
   This one is better.
g) *Semarang kuwi adoh tenan.*
   Semarang is really far away.
h) *Saka wediné, ora isa apa-apa.*
   He was so scared, he couldn't do anything.
i) *Wong kuwi dhuwur tenan.*
   That person is really tall.
j) *Regané pancèn larang.*
   It's really expensive.
   Larané rada banget.
   He's pretty sick.
k) *Ora pati apik.*
   It's not that good.
l) *Mung waé . . .*
   But . . .
m) *Mung iki waé.*
   Just this one.
n) *Mengko waé.*
   Later!
o) *Sing iki mengko daktuku.*
   This one I'll buy later.

Sheet 9

a) *Cacahé ora kurang saka sèket.*
   The total is not less than fifty.
b) *Sing teka sepuluh luwih sethithik.*
   The ones that came numbered slightly more than ten.
c) *Isih kurang pira?*
   How many are still lacking?
d) *Piyé, isa mbédakaké, ora?*
   How about it, can (you) tell them apart, or not?
e) *Wong kaya ngono kuwi brangasan.*
   A person like that is short-tempered.
f) *Yèn iki karo sing kuwi mau, piyé?*
   If it's this with that one just now, how about it?
g) *Wis tau mrana, ya?*
   (You've) already been there, right?

 h) *Omahé wis kliwatan.*
   The house is already passed by.
 i) *Soal iki mengko gampang.*
   This problem will be easy (to deal with) later.
 j) *Aku ora ngerti regané.*
   I don't know the price.
 k) *Sedéla manèh, budhalé.*
   The leaving will be in just a minute.

Sheet 10

 a) *Iki wis rada rusak.*
   This is already rather broken.
 b) *Udané deres banget.*
   The rain is very hard.
 c) *Kuduné ya ngono, ning ora.*
   It should be that way, but it's not.
 d) *Wong kuwi dhuwur banget.*
   That person is very tall.
 e) *Regané larang tenan.*
   The price is really high.
 f) *Sanajan udan, dhèwèké nékad waé.*
   Although it was raining, he did it anyway.
 g) *Iki wis rusak banget.*
   This is already quite ruined.
 h) *Gedhung kuwi dhuwur banget.*
   That building is very tall.
 i) *Basané wis apik tenan.*
   His language is already very good.
   Basané durung apik tenan.
   His language is not yet really good.
 j) *Wit kuwi rada gedhé.*
   That tree is rather large.
 k) *Jakarta kuwi rada adoh.*
   Jakarta is rather far.
 l) *Aku kudu budhal saiki.*
   I must leave now.
 m) *Kowe kuwi kok durung budhal.*
   Why haven't you left yet?

n) *Sing wis bayar kena mlebu.*
Those who have already paid may go in.
o) *Bukuné wis entèk kabèh.*
The books are all gone.
p) *Dhuwité wis entèk kabèh.*
All the money is gone.

Sheet 11

a) *Karangané pancèn apik.*
The composition is certainly good.
b) *Buku iki sing apik dhéwé.*
This book is the best one.
c) *Omah iki pancèn apik.*
This house is certainly good.
d) *Omahé saiki luwih gedhé.*
His house is larger now.
e) *Apa isa kurang regané?*
Can the price be less?
f) *Mengko ngliwati alun-alun, ya?*
Later (you) pass by the square, right?
g) *Nggoné nèng ndi?*
Where is the place?
h) *Pancèn ora pati apik.*
(It's) certainly not very good.
i) *Méjané amba banget.*
The table is very wide.
j) *Kabaré luwih apik.*
The news is better.
k) *Wongé pinter tenan.*
He's really smart.
l) *Regané pancèn lumayan.*
The price is certainly good.
m) *Kayuné rada kandel.*
The wood is rather thick.
n) *Rasané luwih alus.*
The feel of it is smoother.
o) *Jarik niku luwih alus.*
That cloth is smoother.

Sheet 12

a) *Omah-omahé lumayan kabèh.*
   All the houses are good.
   Bocah-bocahé dhuwur kabèh.
   All the boys are tall.
b) *Swarané Ari sing kasar dhéwé.*
   Ari's voice is the roughest one.
   Jariké Ari sing apik dhéwé.
   Ari's cloth is the best one.
   Bambang sing pinter dhéwé.
   Bambang's the smartest.
c) *Yèn omah sing pancèn apik, larang.*
   As for a house which is good, (it's) expensive.
d) *Bukuné luwih kandel.*
   The book is thicker.
   Sing ireng kuwi luwih alus.
   That black one is smoother.
e) *Sing larang kuwi rada alus.*
   That expensive one is rather smooth.
   Sing rada rusak kuwi pitu.
   (There are) seven which are rather broken.
   Sing dhuwur rada apik.
   The tall one is rather good.
f) *Aku iki ora isa.*
   I can't.
g) *Apa isih ana?*
   Are there still some?
h) *Soalé angèl banget.*
   The problem is very difficult.
   Wong sing dhuwur banget pira?
   How many people are very tall?
   Sing dhuwur banget (kuwi) pitu.
   There are seven who are very tall.
   Sing apik banget (kuwi) larang.
   The ones which are very good are expensive.
   Sing abang (kuwi) alus banget.
   The red ones are very smooth.

i) *Wité kurang gedhé.*
 The tree isn't big enough.
 Sing abang kuwi kurang alus.
 That red one isn't fine enough.
j) *Ari (kuwi) kalah pinter.*
 (That) Ari isn't as smart.
 Bocahé kalah dhuwur.
 The child isn't as tall.
 Bocah kuwi kalah dhuwur.
 That child isn't as tall.
k) *Sing larang kalah alus.*
 The expensive one is not as smooth.
 Bambang (niku) kalah dhuwur.
 Bambang is not as tall.
l) *Luwih sangka sepuluh.*
 More than ten.
m) *Muridé kurang sregep.*
 The pupils don't work hard enough.

REFERENCES CITED

Abercrombie, David
1967   *Elements of General Phonetics.* New York: Aldine.

Alisjahbana, S. T.
1971   Indonesian and Malay. In *Current Trends in Linguistics*, vol. 8. ed. T. Sebeok. The Hague: Mouton. pp. 1088-1109.

Anderson, Benedict R. O'G.
1978   Cartoons and Monuments: The Evolution of Political Communication Under the New Order. In *Political Power and Communications in Indonesia.* ed. Karl Jackson and Lucian Pye. Berkeley: University of California Press. pp. 282-321.

1972   The Idea of Power in Javanese Culture. In *Culture and politics in Indonesia.* ed. Claire Holt. Ithaca: Cornell University Press. pp. 1-69.

1966   The Languages of Indonesian Politics. *Indonesia* 1:89-116.

Bachtiar, Harsja
1973   *The Religion of Java*: a commentary. *Majalah ilmu-ilmu sastra Indonesia* 5 (1):85-115.

Bax, Gerald W.
1974   *Language and Social Structure in a Javanese Village.* Unpublished Ph.D. dissertation, Tulane University.

1975 Urban-rural Differences in Speech Level Usage in Java. *Anthropological Linguistics* 17 (1):24-32.

Benda, Harry
1965 Decolonization in Indonesia: The Problems of Continuity and Change. *American Historical Review* 70 (4):1058-1073.

Benveniste, Emile
1971 *Problems in General Linguistics.* Miami Linguistics Series. tr. by Mary E. Meek. Coral Gables: University of Miami Press.

Bonneff, Marcel
1981 Un apercu de l'influence des aspirations démocratiques sur la conception et l'usage des 'niveaux de langue' en Javanais: le mouvement Djowo-Dipo et ses prolongements. In *Papers on Indonesian Languages and Literatures.* ed. Nigel Phillips and Khaidir Anwar. Cahiers d'Archipel 13. Paris: Ecole des hautes études en sciences sociales.

Brown, Roger and Albert Gilman
1960 The Pronouns of Power and Solidarity. In *Style in Language.* ed. Thomas Sebeok. Cambridge: MIT Press. pp. 253-76.

Dirdjosiswojo
1957 *Krama inggil.* Yogyakarta: Kalimosodo.

Djojoadikusumo
1970 *Herinneringen uit 3 tijdperken: t'en geschreven familie overleving.* Amsterdam: Ge Nabrink.

Dwidjosusana, R.I.W., et. al.
n.d. *Paramasastra Jawi enggal.* Sala, Indonesia: Fadjar.

Emmerson, Donald K.
1976 *Indonesia's Elite: Political Culture and Cultural Politics.* Ithaca: Cornell University Press.

Errington, J. Joseph
1988 *Structure and Style in Javanese: A Semiotic View of Linguistic Etiquette.* Conduct and Communication Series. Philadelphia: University of Pennsylvania Press.

1986 Continuity and Discontinuity in Indonesian Language Development. *Journal of Asian Studies* 45 (2):329-53.

1985 On the Nature of the Sociolinguistic Sign: Describing the Javanese Speech Levels. In *Semiotic Mediation in Psychosocial Perspective.* ed. Elizabeth Mertz and Richard J. Parmentier. San Diego: Academic Press.

1984 Self and Self-conduct Among the Traditional Javanese Priyayi Elite. *American Ethnologist* 11(2):275-90.

1982 Speech in the Royal Presence: Javanese Palace Language. *Indonesia* 34:89-101.

Fox, James J.
1974 Our Ancestors Spoke in Pairs: Rotinese View of Language, Dialect, and Code. In *Explorations in the Ethnography of Speaking.* ed. Richard Baumann and Joel Scherzer. Cambridge: Cambridge University Press. pp. 65-85.

Frake, Charles
1980 Plying Frames Can Be Dangerous: Some Reflections on Methodology in Cognitive Anthropology. In *Language and Cultural Description.* ed. Anwar S. Dil. Stanford: Stanford University Press. pp. 45-60.

Friedrich, Paul
1966 The Linguistic Reflex of Social Change: From Tsarist to Soviet Russian Kinship. In *Explorations in Sociolinguistics.* ed. Stanley Lieberson. Bloomington: Indiana University Press. pp. 31-57.

Geertz, Clifford
1960 *The Religion of Java*. Chicago: University of Chicago Press.

1980 *Negara*. Princeton: Princeton University Press.

Gumperz, John J.
1968 The Speech Community. In *Encyclopedia of the Social Sciences*. New York: Macmillan. pp. 381-86.

Haas, Mary
1951 The Declining Descent Rule for Rank in Thailand. *American Anthropologist* 53:585-87.

Hadidjojo, Sri Rm. Ngabehi
1952 *Djodho kang pinasthi*. Jakarta: Balai Pustaka.

Halliday, M.A.K., Angus McIntosh, and Peter Strevens
1972 The Users and Uses of Language. In *Readings in the Sociology of Language*. ed. Joshua Fishman. The Hague: Mouton. pp. 139-69.

Haugen, Einar
1966 Dialect, Language, Nation. *American Anthropologist* 68:922-35.

Head, Brian
1978 Respect Degrees in Pronominal Reference. In *Word Structure*, vol. 3 of *Universals of Human Language*. ed. Joseph H. Greenberg. Stanford: Stanford University Press. pp. 151-211.

Hjelmslev, Louis
1944 Editorial. *Acta linguistica* 4:i-iv.

Hockett, Charles F.
1950 Age-grading and Linguistic Continuity. *Language* 26:449-57.

Hymes, Dell
1972 Models of Interaction of Language and Social Life. In *Directions in Sociolinguistics: the Ethnography of Communication.* ed. John J. Gumperz and Dell Hymes. New York: Holt, Rinehart, and Winston. pp. 35-71.

Irvine, Judith T.
1979 Formality and Informality in Communicative Events. *American Anthropologist* 81:773-90.

Jackson, Karl D.
1978 Urbanization and Patron-client Relations: the Changing Quality of Interpersonal Communication in the Neighborhoods of Bandung and the Villages of West Java. In *Political Power and Communications in Indonesia.* ed. Karl D. Jackson and Lucian W. Pye. Berkeley: Stanford University Press. pp. 343-92.

Jakarta, Arsip Nasional
1918 *Memorie van overgave opgemaakt door den Resident van Soerakarta, F. P. Sollewijn Gelpke.*

Jakobson, Roman
1971 Quest for the Essence of Language. In *Selected Writings*, volume 2. The Hague: Mouton. pp. 345-59.

Jasawidagda
1957 Wawasan bab mekaripun basa Jawi. In *Medan bahasa, basa Jawi.* pp. 34-43.

Kroch, Anthony
1978 Toward a Theory of Social Dialect Variation. *Language in Society* 7:17-36.

Labov, William
1972 *Sociolinguistic Patterns.* Philadelphia: University of Pennsylvania Press.

1971   The Notion of 'System' in Creole Languages. In *Pidginization and Creolization of Languages*. ed. Dell Hymes. Cambridge: Cambridge University Press. pp. 447-72.

1969   The Logic of Nonstandard English. *Georgetown Monographs on Language and Linguistics*, volume 22. pp. 1-31.

Lyons, John
1977   *Semantics*, volume 2. Cambridge: Cambridge University Press.

Malinowski, Bronislaw
1961   *Argonauts of the Western Pacific*. New York: Dutton.

Padmasusastra (see also Ng. Wirapustaka)
1896   *Serat Urapsari*. Betawi: G. Kolff.

1907   *Serat Tatacara: ngadat sarta kalakuwanipun tetiyang Jawi ingkang taksih lumengket dhateng gugon-tuhon*. Photocopy of a transliteration by S. Siswosuharto from the 1907 edition. Betawi: Kanjeng Gupermen.

1911   *Layang basa Solo (Javaansche Samenspraken)* met eene inleiding door Dr. D. A. Rinkes. Betawi: Pirmah Papirus.

Poedjosoedarmo, Soepomo
1968   Javanese speech levels. *Indonesia* 7:165-90.

n.d.   Perkembangan madya. Photocopy.

Poedjosoedarmo, Soepomo, and Th. Koendjono
1976-77   *Undak-usuk bahasa Jawa*. Yogyakarta: Laporan FKSS, IKIP Sanata Dharma, Proyek Pengembangan Bahasa dan Sastra Indonesia dan Daerah.

Prawirohardja, Dalil.
1958 Mingsad-mingseding basa. *Medan bahasa, basa Jawi* 8:21-26.

Quinn, George
1983 The Case of the Invisible Literature: Power, Scholarship, and Contemporary Javanese Writing. *Indonesia* 35:1-36.

Ras, J. J.
1979 *Javanese Literature Since Independence*, edited with an introduction. The Hague: Martinus Nijhoff.

Ricklefs, M. C.
1974 *Jogjakarta under Mangkubumi, 1742-1792: a History of the Division of Java*. London Oriental Series, no. 30. Oxford: Oxford University Press.

1983 The Crisis of 1740-41 in Java: the Javanese, Chinese, Madurese, and Dutch, and the Fall of the Court of Kartasura. *Bijdragen tot de Taal-, Land-, en Volkenkunde* 139 (2):268-90.

Romaine, Suzanne
1982 *Socio-historical Linguistics: Its Status and Methodology*. Cambridge: Cambridge University Press.

Samsirmiardja
1917 *Layang neka tjatoer Djawa*. Batavia: Drukkerij Ruygrok.

Sastraatmadja
1930 *Dwikarsa*. Weltevreden: Balai Pustaka.

Sastrawirya, M.
1931-32 Tata-krama Jawi. *Pustaka Jawi*. December 1931-July 1932. Surakarta.

Saussure, Ferdinand de
1966 *Course in General Linguistics*. tr. Wade Baskin. New York: McGraw-Hill.

Scherer, Savitri
1975   Harmony and Dissonance: Early Nationalist Thought in Java. Unpublished M.A. thesis, Cornell University.

Schrieke, B. J. O.
1957   *Indonesian Sociological Studies,* volume 2. The Hague: W. van Hoeve.

Scott, James, C.
1972   Patron/client Politics and Political Change in Southeast Asia. *American Political Science Review* 66(1):91-113.

Seto, B. M.
1958   Urun rembag: bab mekaring basa Djawi. *Medan bahasa, basa Jawi* 8:33-42.

Silverstein, Michael
1977   The limits of awareness. Transcript of a lecture given to the Harvard Anthropology Seminar, Cambridge, and the Penn Anthropology Colloquium, Philadelphia.

Soebroto, St.
n.d.   *Unggah-ungguh ing basa.* Surakarta: Empat Serangkai

Subalidinata, R.S. and Nartoatmojo, Marsono
1975   *Sejarah ejaan bahasa Jawa dengan huruf Latin—dan ejaan bahasa Indonesia yang disesusaikan dengan ejaan bahasa Indonesia yang disempurnakan.* Widyaparwa no. 12. Yogyakarta: Balai Penelitian Bahasa.

Sutarja.
1917   *Dora Sembada.* Weltevreden: Indonesische Drukkerij.

Sutherland, Heather
1975   The Priyayi. *Indonesia* 19:57-80.

1979   *The Making of a Bureaucratic Elite.* ASAA Southeast Asia publications series. Singapore: Heinemann.

Tambiah, Stanley, J.
1976   *World Conqueror and World Renouncer.* Cambridge: Cambridge University Press.

Tanner, Nancy
1967   Speech and Society Among the Indonesian Elite: a Case Study of a Multilingual Community. *Anthropological Linguistics* 9:15-39.

Trudgill, Peter
1974   *Sociolinguistics: an Introduction to Language and Society.* Hammondsworth: Penguin.

Uhlenbeck, E. M.
1978   *Studies in Javanese Morphology.* Translation series no. 19. The Hague: Koninklijk Instituut voor Taal-, Land-, en Volkenkunde.

Walbeehm, A. H. J. G.
1897   *De taalsoorten in het Javaansch.* Batavia: Albrecht and Co.

Willner, Ann Ruth
1966   *The Neotraditional Accommodation to Political Independence: the Case of Indonesia.* Center for International Studies, Research Monograph no. 26. Princeton: Woodrow Wilson School for Public and International Studies.

Winter, C.F., Sr.
1848   *Javaansche zamenspraken, uitgegeven met een bijvoegsel bij het Javaansche woordenboek door T. Roorda.* Amsterdam: Johannes Muller.

Wirapustaka (see also Padmasusastra)
1916   *Serat Erang-erang.* Batavia: Papyrus.

Wolff, John U.
1976　　　The Functions of Indonesian in Central Java. In *Pacific Linguistics* Series C, no. 42. South-east Asian linguistic studies. ed. Nguyen Dang Liem. Canberra: School of Pacific Studies, Australia National University. pp. 219-35.

Wolff, John U. and Poedjosoedarmo, Soepomo
1982　　　*Communicative Codes in Central Java.* Linguistics series VIII, data paper no. 116. Southeast Asia program, Department of Asian Studies, Cornell University.

Zoetmulder, P. J.
1967　　　*The Cultural Background of Indonesian Politics.* Essay series no. 1. Columbia: Institute of International Studies, University of South Carolina.

AUTHOR INDEX

Abercrombie, D. 27
Alisjahbana, S. T. 66
Anderson, B. 2, 34, 36, 177

Bachtiar, H. 2
Bax, G. 21, 25, 71, 77, 82, 116
Benda, H. 3, 177, 183
Benveniste, E. 9
Bonneff, M. 54
Brown, R. 16, 21, 59, 175, 180

Dirdjosiswojo 45
Djojohadikusumo 56, 57
Dwidjosusana 45

Emmerson, D. 2
Errington, J. 36, 74, 80, 87, 101, 126, 171, 173, 177

Fox, J. 86
Friedrich, P. 4

Geertz, C. 2, 8, 36, 38, 44, 53, 73, 74, 149
Gilman, A. 16, 21, 59, 175, 180
Gumperz, J. 6

Haas, M. 38
Halliday, M. 14, 15

Haugen, E. 18
Hjelmslev, L. 9
Hockett, C. 23
Hymes, D. 6

Irvine, J. 15

Jackson, K. 35
Jakobson, R. 22
Jasawidagda 53-54

Kroch, A. 173-74, 177

Labov, W. 18, 23, 26, 125, 126, 129, 131, 147, 151, 173, 179
Lyons, J. 15

Malinowski, B. 6
McIntosh, A. 14

Padmasusastra 42, 45-51, 54, 76-77, 81, 84, 97, 128-29, 137, 139, 141, 144-45, 148
Poedjosoedarmo, S. 20, 24, 29, 42, 44, 67, 76-77, 79, 81-82, 85, 125, 137, 139, 144-45, 147-48, 151-52, 157-58, 160, 171-72
Prawirohardja 66

Quinn, G. 53, 54

Ras, J. J. 45
Ricklefs, M. C. 34
Rinkes, D. A. 54
Romaine, S. 27

Samsirmiardja 146
Sastraatmaja 49
Sastrawirya 65, 106
Saussure, F. de 7, 9, 22
Scherer, S. 53
Schrieke, B. 34
Scott, J. 35
Seto, B. M. 67-68
Silverstein, M. 126
Soebroto 45
Strevens, P. 14
Subalidinoto xiii
Sutarja 145
Sutherland, H. 2, 53

Tambiah, S. 35
Tanner, N. 65
Trudgill, P. 15

Uhlenbeck, E. M. 10, 12, 25, 29, 74, 82-83, 110, 129, 141, 151, 157-58, 160

Walbeehm, A. H. 25, 50, 72, 137, 139, 141, 144-45, 147
Willner, A. R. 2
Winter, C. F. 48, 54, 145
Wirapustaka 145
Wolff, J. 20, 24, 29, 42, 44, 67, 76, 79, 82, 85, 125, 131, 137, 139, 144-45, 148, 151-52, 157-58, 160, 171-72

Zoetmulder, P. J. 2, 183

INDEX OF JAVANESE WORDS

-é 81-82, 136, 148, 167, 168
-aké 81, 87, 136
-aken 81, 87
-ipun 82, 167
-mu see "kowé"
-um- 148, 174

abang 10-12
abdidalem 97
abrit 10-12
adipati 46
ajeng 142, 171, 174
akaliyan see "kaliyan"
akrab 114, 162
alus 88, 93, 102, 104, 105, 108, 109, 113, 124, 136
anak 35, 76, 82, 145-46
andhap 100, 101, 105, 148, 175
arep 75, 78, 93, 142, 174
atur 148
awu 38-39, 68

badhé 174
bagongan 101
bakul 45, 112
bakulan 100, 115, see "bakul"
banget 136, 142, 146, 155
bapak 35, 75
basa 5, 10, 87, 88, 93, 94, 97, 100-4, 111-13, 115, 124, 127, 128, 130, 134, 151, 153, 157, 161-62, 164, 170, 171
basan see "basa"
biasa 75, 88, 95, 98, 102
biyèn 148
bocah 153
bupati 46

c(a)riyos 148
cah see "bocah"
campuran 93, 102
cendhèk 92, 100
cilik 43, 97, 101, 111, 153
Cina 141
Cinten 141

dadi 77, 164, 169
dados 164, 165
dagelan 130, 168
dalem 37, 87
désa 100, 129, 137, 140-41, 144-45, 147, 174
d(um)ugi 174
dhahar 74
dhateng 48, 81, 138-39, 149, 156, 160
dhé see "dhuwé"
dhisik 142, 148
dhit see "dhuwit"
dhusun 48, 100
dhuwé 153

dhuwit 153
dhuwur 105, 109, 112
di- 81, 156-59
digsura 78, 124
dina 141
dinten- 141
dipun- 81, 156-59
dugi 174
dos pundi 123, 156-57
dumugi 174

ènten 82, 156
èstri 48

ga *see* "gawa"
gawa 153
griya 87
gur *see* "mung"

ibu 39
ikana *see* "wikana"
iki 122
inggil 13, 87, 89, 93-95, 97-99, 103-9, 175
ingkang 11-12, 48, 81, 139, 143
ipé 41
isa 149
isih 164

jé *see* "jaréné"
jaler 48
jangkep 81, 104
jaréné 148
jé *see* "jaréné"

ka *see* "saka"
ké *see* "kaé"
kaé 153
kabèh 147

kacèk 112
kados pundi 122, 138, 142-43, 156-57
kaku 135
kalih 81, 138, 144-47, 159, 164
kaliyan 138, 156, 159-60, 167-68
kalusen *see* "alus"
kampung 60, 101, 111
kampungan 100, 161
kang salira 46, 73, 143-44
kang sarira 46
kaping 139, 144
kaprah 67
karo 94, 138, 144, 146, 159-60
kasar 100, 102, 105, 109, 113, 144, 162
kaya 112
kawula *see* "kula"
kedhaton 94, 101
kémawon 11, 112, 122, 156-58
kena 112
kepatihan 53
kepénak 136
kepripun 122-23
kepriyé 122-23, 143, 152-53
kesèd 155
ki *see* "kuwi"
king 2-3, 17, 21, 30, 34-42, 51-52, 61-62, 80, 96-97, 139, 145- 46, 154-56, 166, 179
ko- *see* "kowé"
kok- *see* "kowé"
kowé 72-74, 76, 87, 92, 112
kraton 35, 94, 97

kula 76, 82, 127-29, 138, 144-46, 148-49, 165- 66, 168-69, 175
kur *see* "mung"
kuwi 138, 153, 156

lan 77, 156, 159-60
langkung 104
lik *see* "cilik"
lugu 93, 98
lurah 56
luwes 66, 135

mangga 138-39, 141-43, 156-57, 158
mangké 158
mangkono 141
mangkèten *see* "ngèten"
Mas 64, 68, 112, 149, 169
mawon 11-12, 112, 122, 127, 139, 146, 157- 60, 165- 66, 171
mbesut 155
mbok 39
mboten 82, 112, 139, 143, 148, 156, 165-66, 168-69
mekaten 138, 143, 156-57
menapa 81-82, 138, 156-57, 175
menawa 77, 153, 156
menawi 122, 139, 152, 156-57, 159
mengké 156, 159
mengkèten *see* "ngèten"
menika 112, 122
menyang 93
ming *see* "mung"
mirah 112
mlebet 94
mriyayèni 63

mulih 145
mundhut 171, 175
mung 122, 129, 139, 143, 144, 149, 166

naming *see* "namung"
namung 112, 122-23, 128, 139, 143
nandalem 80, 94-96, 98-99, 103, 107
napa 82, 112, 127, 138, 156-57, 164-66, 168-69
nawi *see* "menawi"
ndak *see* "tindak"
ndaweg 141-43
ndeg *see* "ndaweg"
ndika 45, 47, 143-44, 146
nedha 176
nedhanrima 142, 147
negila *see* "niki"
nèk 122, 152
ngajèni 93, 96
ngaten 138, 157-58, 160, 169
ngerti 77, 143
ngèten 141
ngga *see* "mangga"
nggih 145-46, 168-69
ngké *see* "mengké"
ngobrol 167
ngoten 138, 165, 169
ngunandika 158
niki 112, 122, 127, 129, 138, 141, 156, 165-66, 168-69
niku 112, 138, 145-46, 156, 165-66, 168-69
njaga 75
njagi 75, 78
njaluk 175

njenengan *see* "panjenengan"
nun *see* "nuwun"
nuwun, nun 175
nyang *see* menyang
nyun *see* "nyuwun"
nyuwun, nyun 175-76

omah 87, 146
omong-omong 167
ora 76, 114, 139, 156

padinan 98, 102
padmi 37, 39
pancer 38
pangéran 48, 56
panjenengan 73-75, 78-80, 93-94, 96, 98-99, 103, 107, 138, 143-44
panjenengandalem 79-80, 94
pantes 96
pasar 100, 101
peken 100, 127
pepet 146
ping 139, 144-45, 148
pinten 112, 139, 141, 149
pira 77, 139, 141
pirsa 77
piyé *see* "kepriyé"
piyambak 104, 166, 169
pripun *see* "kepripun"
pun *see* "dipun-"
punapa 156-57, 176
pundi 174
putra 37

r(um)iyin 148, 174
ra *see* "ora"
Radèn 68, 73
rasa 106, 135

ratu 46

saé 88
saka 127, 139, 144-46, 154-55
saka ing *see* "saka"
saking 81, 98, 139, 146, 154, 156
salah 67
sampéyan 46, 74, 79, 144
sampéyandalem 80, 87, 94, 97
sandiwara 130
santri 170
sedanten 142, 147-48
sedaya 142, 147
seka *see* "saka"
seking 127, 139, 144-46, 154-55, 165, 169
selir 37, 39
sentana 37
sepéda 167
sing 11-12, 75-76, 78, 81-82, 114, 127, 139, 143, 149, 165-66, 168-69
sliramu 73-74
sreg 135
sumanak 66
sumangga 156-57
sumerep 77

tesih 138, 164, 167
tiga(ng) 112
tindak 93, 98-99, 171, 174
tiyang 48, 64, 100, 169
tukang 167

umur 112
unggah-ungguh 5, 10
urmat 93

waé 11, 122, 127
wau 145
wartos 148
wayah 37
wayang 101
wejangan 153
weruh 77, 144
wikana 143, 147
wong 43, 64, 100, 111, 114, 145, 168
wonten 82, 138, 156, 164-66

yèn 122, 152, 156, 159
yu 112

MONOGRAPHS IN INTERNATIONAL STUDIES

Africa Series

ISBN Prefix 0-89680-

36. Fadiman, Jeffrey A. *The Moment of Conquest: Meru, Kenya, 1907.* 1979. 70pp.
    081-4 $ 5.50*

37. Wright, Donald R. *Oral Traditions From The Gambia: Volume I, Mandinka Griots.* 1979. 176pp.
    083-0 $15.00*

38. Wright, Donald R. *Oral Traditions From The Gambia: Volume II, Family Elders.* 1980. 200pp.
    084-9 $15.00*

41. Lindfors, Bernth. *Mazungumzo: Interviews with East African Writers, Publishers, Editors, and Scholars.* 1981. 179pp.
    108-X $13.00*

43. Harik, Elsa M. and Donald G. Schilling. *The Politics of Education in Colonial Algeria and Kenya.* 1984. 102pp.
    117-9 $12.50*

44. Smith, Daniel R. *The Influence of the Fabian Colonial Bureau on the Independence Movement in Tanganyika.* 1985. x, 98pp.
    125-X $11.00*

45. Keto, C. Tsehloane. *American-South African Relations 1784-1980: Review and Select Bibliography.* 1985. 159pp.
    128-4 $11.00*

46. Burness, Don, and Mary-Lou Burness, ed. *Wanasema: Conversations with African Writers.* 1985. 95pp.
    129-2 $11.00*

47. Switzer, Les. *Media and Dependency in South Africa: A Case Study of the Press and the Ciskei "Homeland".* 1985. 80pp.
    130-6 $10.00*

48. Heggoy, Alf Andrew. *The French Conquest of Algiers, 1830: An Algerian Oral Tradition.* 1986. 101pp.
    131-4 $11.00*

49. Hart, Ursula Kingsmill. *Two Ladies of Colonial Algeria: The Lives and Times of Aurelie Picard and Isabelle Eberhardt.* 1987. 156pp.
    143-8 $11.00*

50. Voeltz, Richard A. *German Colonialism and the South West Africa Company, 1894-1914.* 1988. 143pp.
    146-2 $12.00*

51. Clayton, Anthony, and David Killingray. *Khaki and Blue: Military and Police in British Colonial Africa.* 1989. 235pp.
    147-0 $18.00*

52. Northrup, David. *Beyond the Bend in the River: African Labor in Eastern Zaire, 1865-1940.* 1988. 195pp.
    151-9 $15.00*

53. Makinde, M. Akin. *African Philosophy, Culture, and Traditional Medicine.* 1988. 175pp.
    152-7 $13.00*

54. Parson, Jack, ed. *Succession to High Office in Botswana. Three Case Studies.* 1990. 443pp.
    157-8 $20.00*

55. Burness, Don. *A Horse of White Clouds.* 1989. 193pp.
    158-6 $12.00*

56. Staudinger, Paul. *In the Heart of the Hausa States.* Tr. by Johanna Moody. 1990. 2 vols. 653pp.
160-8 $35.00*

57. Sikainga, Ahmad Alawad. *The Western Bahr Al-Ghazal Under British Rule: 1898-1956.* 1991. 183pp.
161-6 $15.00*

58. Wilson, Louis E. *The Krobo People of Ghana to 1892: A Political and Social History.* 1991. 254pp.
164-0 $20.00*

59. du Toit, Brian M. *Cannabis, Alcohol, and the South African Student: Adolescent Drug Use 1974-1985.* 1991. 166pp.
166-7 $17.00*

Latin America Series

8. Clayton, Lawrence A. *Caulkers and Carpenters in a New World: The Shipyards of Colonial Guayaquil.* 1980. 189pp, illus.
103-9 $15.00*

9. Tata, Robert J. *Structural Changes in Puerto Rico's Economy: 1947-1976.* 1981. xiv, 104pp.
107-1 $12.00*

11. O'Shaughnessy, Laura N., and Louis H. Serra. *Church and Revolution in Nicaragua.* 1986. 118pp.
126-8 $12.00*

12. Wallace, Brian. *Ownership and Development: A Comparison of Domestic and Foreign Investment in Colombian Manufacturing.* 1987. 186pp.
145-4 $10.00*

13. Henderson, James D. *Conservative Thought in Latin America: The Ideas of Laureano Gomez.* 1988. 150pp.
148-9 $13.00*

14. Summ, G. Harvey, and Tom Kelly. *The Good Neighbors: America, Panama, and the 1977 Canal Treaties.* 1988. 135pp.
    149-7 $13.00*

15. Peritore, Patrick. *Socialism, Communism, and Liberation Theology in Brazil: An Opinion Survey Using Q-Methodology.* 1990. 245pp.
    156-X $15.00*

16. Alexander, Robert J. *Juscelino Kubitschek and the Development of Brazil.* 1991. 429pp.
    163-2 $25.00*

17. Mijeski, Kenneth J., ed. *The Nicaraguan Constitution of 1987: English Translation and Commentary.* 1990. 355pp.
    165-9 $25.00*

Southeast Asia Series

31. Nash, Manning. *Peasant Citizens: Politics, Religion, and Modernization in Kelantan, Malaysia.* 1974. 181pp.
    018-0 $12.00*

38. Bailey, Conner. *Broker, Mediator, Patron, and Kinsman: An Historical Analysis of Key Leadership Roles in a Rural Malaysian District.* 1976. 79pp.
    024-5 $ 8.00*

44. Collier, William L., et al. *Income, Employment and Food Systems in Javanese Coastal Villages.* 1977. 160pp.
    031-8 $10.00*

45. Chew, Sock Foon and MacDougall, John A. *Forever Plural: The Perception and Practice of Inter-Communal Marriage in Singapore.* 1977. 61pp.
    030-X $ 8.00*

47. Wessing, Robert. *Cosmology and Social Behavior in a West Javanese Settlement.* 1978. 200pp.
    072-5 $12.00*

48. Willer, Thomas F., ed. *Southeast Asian References in the British Parliamentary Papers, 1801-1972/73: An Index.* 1978. 110pp.
033-4 $ 8.50*

49. Durrenberger, E. Paul. *Agricultural Production and Household Budgets in a Shan Peasant Village in Northwestern Thailand: A Quantitative Description.* 1978. 142pp.
071-7 $10.00*

50. Echauz, Robustiano. *Sketches of the Island of Negros.* 1978. 174pp.
070-9 $12.00*

51. Krannich, Ronald L. *Mayors and Managers in Thailand: The Struggle for Political Life in Administrative Settings.* 1978. 139pp.
073-3 $11.00*

56A. Duiker, William J. *Vietnam Since the Fall of Saigon.* Updated edition. 1989. 383pp.
162-4 $17.00*

59. Foster, Brian L. *Commerce and Ethnic Differences: The Case of the Mons in Thailand.* 1982. x, 93pp.
112-8 $10.00*

60. Frederick, William H., and John H. McGlynn. *Reflections on Rebellion: Stories from the Indonesian Upheavals of 1948 and 1965.* 1983. vi, 168pp.
111-X $ 9.00*

61. Cady, John F. *Contacts With Burma, 1935-1949: A Personal Account.* 1983. x, 117pp.
114-4 $ 9.00*

63. Carstens, Sharon, ed. *Cultural Identity in Northern Peninsular Malaysia.* 1986. 91pp.
116-0 $ 9.00*

64. Dardjowidjojo, Soenjono. *Vocabulary Building in Indonesian: An Advanced Reader.* 1984. xviii, 256pp.
118-7 $26.00*

65. Errington, J. Joseph. *Language and Social Change in Java: Linguistic Reflexes of Modernization in a Traditional Royal Polity.* 1985. xiv, 211pp.
120-9 $20.00*

66. Binh, Tran Tu. *The Red Earth: A Vietnamese Memoir of Life on a Colonial Rubber Plantation.* Tr. by John Spragens. Ed. by David Marr. 1985. xii, 98pp.
119-5 $11.00*

68. Syukri, Ibrahim. *History of the Malay Kingdom of Patani.* Tr. by Conner Bailey and John N. Miksic. 1985. xix, 113pp.
123-3 $12.00*

69. Keeler, Ward. *Javanese: A Cultural Approach.* 1984. xxxvi, 523pp.
121-7 $18.00*

70. Wilson, Constance M., and Lucien M. Hanks. *Burma-Thailand Frontier Over Sixteen Decades: Three Descriptive Documents.* 1985. x, 128pp.
124-1 $11.00*

71. Thomas, Lynn L., and Franz von Benda-Beckmann, eds. *Change and Continuity in Minangkabau: Local, Regional, and Historical Perspectives on West Sumatra.* 1986. 363pp.
127-6 $16.00*

72. Reid, Anthony, and Oki Akira, eds. *The Japanese Experience in Indonesia: Selected Memoirs of 1942-1945.* 1986. 411pp., 20 illus.
132-2 $20.00*

73. Smirenskaia, Zhanna D. *Peasants in Asia: Social Consciousness and Social Struggle.* Tr. by Michael J. Buckley. 1987. 248pp.
134-9 $14.00

74. McArthur, M.S.H. *Report on Brunei in 1904*. Ed. by A.V.M. Horton. 1987. 304pp.
    135-7 $15.00

75. Lockard, Craig Alan. *From Kampung to City. A Social History of Kuching Malaysia 1820-1970*. 1987. 311pp.
    136-5 $16.00*

76. McGinn, Richard. *Studies in Austronesian Linguistics*. 1988. 492pp.
    137-3 $20.00*

77. Muego, Benjamin N. *Spectator Society: The Philippines Under Martial Rule*. 1988. 232pp.
    138-1 $15.00*

78. Chew, Sock Foon. *Ethnicity and Nationality in Singapore*. 1987. 229pp.
    139-X $12.50*

79. Walton, Susan Pratt. *Mode in Javanese Music*. 1987. 279pp.
    144-6 $15.00*

80. Nguyen Anh Tuan. *South Vietnam Trial and Experience: A Challenge for Development*. 1987. 482pp.
    141-1 $18.00*

81. Van der Veur, Paul W., ed. *Toward a Glorious Indonesia: Reminiscences and Observations of Dr. Soetomo*. 1987. 367pp.
    142-X $16.00*

82. Spores, John C. *Running Amok: An Historical Inquiry*. 1988. 190pp.
    140-3 $14.00*

83. Tan Malaka. *From Jail to Jail*. Tr. and ed. by Helen Jarvis. 1990. 3 vols. 1,226pp.
    150-0 $55.00*

84. Devas, Nick. *Financing Local Government in Indonesia.* 1989. 344pp.
    153-5 $16.00*

85. Suryadinata, Leo. *Military Ascendancy and Political Culture: A Study of Indonesia's Golkar.* 1989. 222pp.
    179-9 $15.00*

86. Williams, Michael. *Communism, Religion, and Revolt in Banten.* 1990. 356pp.
    155-1 $16.00*

87. Hudak, Thomas John. *The Indigenization of Pali Meters in Thai Poetry.* 1990. 237pp.
    159-4 $15.00*

88. Lay, Ma Ma. *Not Out of Hate: A Novel of Burma.* Tr. by Margaret Aung-Thwin. Ed. by William Frederick. 1991. 222pp.
    167-5 $20.00*

ORDERING INFORMATION

Orders for titles in the Monographs in International Studies series may be placed through the Ohio University Press, Scott Quadrangle, Athens, Ohio 45701-2979 or through any local bookstore. Individuals should remit payment by check, VISA, MasterCard, or American Express. People ordering from the United Kingdom, Continental Europe, the Middle East, and Africa should order through Academic and University Publishers Group, 1 Gower Street, London WC1E, England. Orders from the Pacific Region, Asia, Australia, and New Zealand should be sent to East-West Export Books, c/o the University of Hawaii Press, 2840 Kolowalu Street, Honolulu, Hawaii 96822, USA.

Other individuals ordering from outside of the U.S. should remit in U.S. funds to the Ohio University Press either by International Money Order or by a check drawn on a U.S. bank. Most out-of-print titles may be ordered from University Microfilms, Inc., 300 North Zeeb Road, Ann Arbor, Michigan 48106, USA.

Prices do not include shipping charges and are subject to change without notice.